The TUC

D

Also by Robert Taylor

THE FIFTH ESTATE

WORKERS AND THE NEW DEPRESSION

THE TRADE UNION QUESTION IN BRITISH POLITICS SINCE 19.

THE FUTURE OF THE TRADE UNIONS

The TUC

From the General Strike to New Unionism

Robert Taylor

palgrave TUC

First published 2000 by
PALGRAVE
Houndmills, Basingstoke, Hampshire RG21 6XS and
175 Fifth Avenue, New York, N.Y. 10010
Companies and representatives throughout the world

PALGRAVE is the new global academic imprint of
St. Martin's Press LLC Scholarly and Reference Division and
Palgrave Publishers Ltd (formerly Macmillan Press Ltd).

ISBN 0–333–93065–7 hardback
ISBN 0–333–93066–5 paperback

This book is printed on paper suitable for recycling and
made from fully managed and sustained forest sources.

A catalogue record for this book is available
from the British Library.

Library of Congress Cataloging-in-Publication Data
Taylor, Robert, 1943–
    The TUC : from the general strike to new unionism / by Robert Taylor.
      p. cm.
    Includes bibliographical references and index.
    ISBN 0–333–93065–7
    1. Trades Union Congress—History. 2. Labour unions—Great Britain–
–History. I. Title.

    HD8383.T74 T39 2000
    331.88'06'041—dc21

                                                    00-041485

Transferred to digital printing 2001
Printed and bound by Antony Rowe Ltd, Eastbourne

To Aft

Contents

Preface

The British Trades Union Congress is the oldest national institution representing organised workers to be found anywhere in the world. It lacks a comprehensive history. This volume is an interim study which seeks to focus on some of the more important leaders and events that shaped the TUC during the twentieth century. Over that hundred-year period the TUC often played a highly effective and influential role in the history of Britain in peace as well as war. In many ways the TUC's achievements remain an unwritten and too often unknown story. Through the words and actions of some of the TUC's greatest figures this book seeks to narrate and assess its development in the last century. David Low, the *Manchester Guardian's* finest cartoonist, used to draw the TUC as an affectionate, amiable, lovable but rather shambolic and frisky carthorse, hardly a symbol of modernity. But like his figure of Colonel Blimp it became a kind of icon. Decent, slow, circumspect, insular, sometimes arrogant, but also loyal, emotional and often grateful for very little, the TUC grew, prospered and then endured. It is often forgotten that it was the TUC who took the leading role in the creation of the Labour Representation Committee in 1900 that became the Labour Party six years later. Without the TUC and its affiliate unions there would never have been a Labour Party or a Labour government at all.[1] The Socialists, at least in Labour's early years, were very much a minority, usually in ideological conflict with one another. It was the TUC who stood for unity, common sense and practicality. Moreover, the TUC was also very much a self-standing institution, which developed an industrial as well as a political perspective. Its best general secretaries sought to develop a distinctive and separate purpose for the TUC, apart from its umbilical connection of sentiment and mutual self-interest with the Labour Party. Trade unions through affiliation to the TUC had to deal with governments of all political persuasions. They were bargainers first and foremost, seeking deals, negotiating agreements and settlements for their members at work and not simply obedient servants of a party or ideology. Walter Citrine, the TUC's greatest general secretary, put it well in 1926 when he wrote:

> The British trade union movement has its roots very deeply in economic soil, and, unlike some of the Continental movements, it is

not so susceptible to revolutionary change that at the wave of a wand it can become suddenly transformed. It has been built up to redress immediate economic injustices, not to change violently and fundamentally the social system in accordance with an abstract theory.

Citrine – he became Sir Walter in 1935 and was made a Labour peer in 1946 – can rightly be described as the founder of the modern TUC. For the 20 years from September 1926 to September 1946 he was to be its most impressive general secretary. Nearly 40 years ago he wrote an excellent two-volume autobiography. There has been no other full-length study of Citrine since then. This is a pity. He was a formidable figure – a brilliant administrator, a profound philosopher of modern trade unionism, a far-sighted architect of a new kind of TUC with a sustained interest in public policy and in transforming its relations with the state, a principled pragmatist who transformed the organisation into a highly respected, sensible and responsible body, which became an Estate of the Realm during the Second World War.

Ernest Bevin, the extraordinary founder and general secretary of the Transport and General Workers Union, was – as he once remarked immodestly of himself – one in a million. In this book I assess his role in alliance with Citrine during the Second World War. As Minister of Labour and National Service, Bevin became the key figure in Winston Churchill's coalition government, perhaps its most important member after the Prime Minister himself. He came to symbolise the indomitable will and spirit of the British working class in what was to be its finest hour. Alan Bullock's trilogy of Bevin's life is not going to be replaced in the near future. But I hope my chapter on the Bevin–Citrine alliance in the war, however, goes some way to refocus his achievement in relation to the TUC.

Arthur Deakin and Frank Cousins, successive general secretaries of Bevin's union, stamped their own autocratic personalities on the TUC's development during the years of the so-called post-war settlement of full employment, the planned economy and the welfare state. My chapter on those two men seeks to examine their importance in forging a close relationship between the TUC and successive governments as well as the Labour Party after 1945. Deakin's reputation – in my opinion – has suffered at the hands of posterity, in some ways unfairly. He was certainly no Bevin but by any other standards he proved to be a strong and articulate defender of Labourism during its golden age, even if he was hated by the left and found himself increasingly out of touch with the times as full employment fuelled wage-push inflation and unofficial strikes. Cousins has received better treatment, although he was disliked and even feared by many of his colleagues on the TUC general council. Geoffrey Goodman's biography remains indispensable. But it is by no means the last word on a man even he describes as the 'awkward warrior'. The chapter is taken from one I contributed to a centenary volume on the Labour Party, published in April 2000 by Macmillan.

George Woodcock, TUC general secretary from September 1960 to February 1969, was a fascinating figure, a genuine working-class intellectual recluse, who tried to modernise the TUC at a time when popular feelings towards trade unionism were turning sour. Woodcock never wrote his memoirs. Nor is there a biography of him. There should be. The chapter on Woodcock in this book is derived from an essay I wrote on him in a volume on post-war industrial politics published in April 2000 by Ashgate.

Vic Feather was TUC general secretary for only four years but they turned out to be some of the most turbulent in the organisation's modern history. There is only a brief biography of him by Eric Silver. He deserves much more of our attention. In his dealings with Harold Wilson's government and with that of Edward Heath he proved to be a canny and indefatigable defender of the TUC and responsible trade unionism.

Jack Jones, general secretary of the Transport and General Workers Union from 1969 until 1978, was the colossus of the Labour Movement. He was the inspiration behind the Social Contract between the TUC and the Labour party and then the Labour government during the still controversial 1970s. His own memoirs are worth reading. But more is needed. With the help of his union's own archives, I devote a chapter of this book to his enormously constructive contribution to the history of the TUC.

Both Len Murray and then Norman Willis had to preside over a TUC that was pushed by Conservative governments from the epicentre of British politics to its margins in only a brief period of time. The rise and fall of the TUC as an Estate of the Realm is too big a subject for this book to discuss sensibly. But my chapter seeks to describe and assess the role Murray and Willis played in those years of remorseless contraction and decline after 1979.

John Monks is the new moderniser of the TUC. Since he was elected its general secretary in September 1993, he has restored respect and authority to the organisation after its long, troubled retreat into the wilderness. The TUC is once more listened to and heeded by Whitehall departments and among employer associations. From the issue of

Britain's position in Europe to the concept of social partnership in the workplace, from the need to reform Britain's inadequate education and training system to new forms of company law to encourage employee participation, Monks is setting a new, positive TUC agenda after years of protest and defeat. It is far too early to assess his contribution but a brief account of his first years as TUC general secretary completes this millennium volume.

Of course, the modern history of the TUC is much more than the lives of the handful of white men who dominated many of its proceedings in the twentieth century. I am well aware of the enormous contributions many others – both men and women – made to build the TUC into not only Britain's largest voluntary pressure group but a key national institution in the public life of the country. But this volume has one specific purpose: to highlight, through the public lives of some of its key leaders who were at the centre of the TUC's activities since the early 1920s, the enormous importance of the trade union movement in making Britain the country it is today. An introductory chapter seeks to place the TUC's overall role into that wider political economy.

I should like to thank John Monks, the TUC's general secretary, for his assistance in the preparation of this volume. David – now Lord – Lea was also supportive throughout. Mike Power in the TUC's media department helped to bring this book to fruition. Christine Coates was helpful at the TUC Library, now based at the University of North London. I am also grateful to Christine Woodland and Richard Storey for their assistance at the Modern Record Centre in the University of Warwick where the TUC archive is stored.

This book is dedicated to A. F. Thompson of Wadham College, Oxford, who was an inspiring teacher of modern history when I was an undergraduate at the college in the early 1960s. Throughout my 30 years as a journalist he remained an important influence on my thought on labour and trade union matters as well as being a friend.

London
June 2000

Introduction: The TUC –
An Overall Assessment

'The Trades Union Congress is now universally recognised as a force which radiates its influence, not only in our country but in many other lands.' Queen Elizabeth II spoke in warm tribute at the dinner in the Guildhall in the City of London held in honour of the TUC's centenary on 5 June 1968. Beside her at the resplendent top table sat the Labour Prime Minister Harold Wilson and George Woodcock, the TUC's general secretary. Her Majesty went on:

> Just as the British legislature is rightly regarded as the Mother of Parliaments, so the British trade union movement, as the oldest in the world, has furnished the principles upon which the workers of many other countries, and especially the developing nations, have built their own unions and the links which have long been established between them owe much to the sustained support given by the TUC. Despite the handicaps of the early days, British workers were the first to gain freedom to combine for the furtherance of their objectives and to take an essential part in the evolution of industrial democracy. Perhaps in Britain we can regard ourselves – without too much conceit – as having an art for give and take. This finds expression, both in our political institutions and in industrial relations and in trade union branches and committees, and in their negotiations with employers, trade unionists have distinguished themselves in this art, and, in doing so, have gained the necessary experience to fill the highest positions of responsibility in the land. And today the Trades Union Congress represents nearly nine million workers by hand and brain and has become their unchallengeable representative in the national and industrial sphere. It is my pride to wish you well on your 100th birthday and as you cross the threshold of your second century, to pray that you may flourish and that you will continue to provide wise leadership on which the future of our country so much depends.[1]

The Queen's lavish praise for the TUC was a sign of the times. It went much further than 10 Downing Street believed was necessary. Some of the Prime Minister's aides were troubled by the Queen's reference to 'workers'. In 1968 Harold Wilson could proclaim: 'The TUC has arrived. It is an estate of the realm, as real, as potent, as essentially part of the fabric of our national life as any of the historic estates.'[2]

The TUC is the oldest national, independent trade union organisation in the world. Its inaugural congress, which began on Tuesday 2 June 1868 at the Mechanics' Institution, David Street in Manchester, was attended by a mere 34 delegates claiming to represent 118,367 trade union members. The TUC's birth took place almost without notice at the time, even among the existing trade unions and trades councils. Its origins stemmed from the initiative taken by the Manchester and Salford Trades Council whose members wanted to establish an annual national meeting of trade unionists on the lines of the British Association for the Advancement of Science and the Social Science Association from which manual workers had been excluded. Their intention seemed more to establish a debating society than an organisation to represent the interests of labour. A number of papers were presented to the inaugural conference on a wide range of topics. They included: 'trade unions – an absolute necessity'; trade unions and the political economy; the effect of trade unions on foreign competition; the regulation of hours of work; the limitation of apprentices; 'the present inequality of the law in regard to conspiracy'; intimidation, picketing, coercion, and so on; the necessity of compulsory inspection of workplaces where women and children were employed; the legalisation of trade societies; and the 'necessity of an annual conference of trade representatives from various centres of industry'.[3] A resolution was passed at the Manchester gathering declaring it was 'highly desirable' that trade unions should not only meet annually but also 'take action in all parliamentary matters pertaining to the general interests of the working classes'.

During its early decades of existence the TUC was concerned mainly with lobbying parliament as well as seeking greater legal security for trade unions from the ravages of the courts and the threat of litigiously minded employers. It expressed no intention to interfere in any way with the internal affairs of affiliate trade unions or indeed the processes of voluntary collective bargaining where it existed. In the words of George Howell, the first effective secretary of the TUC's parliamentary committee, the TUC's promoters and founders did not propose to 'interfere in the legitimate work of trade unions, their organisation, mode of management, constitution, rules, or other matters of internal economy'. The TUC's purpose was instead 'to promote cooperation in respect of general questions affecting labour and to watch over its interests in Parliament'.[4] Its activities concentrated on those specific functions with some notable success. With no political party in existence to represent the working class, the TUC became the voice of labour in a political system which, after parliamentary reform legislation in 1868 and 1884, ensured an estimated 60 per cent of the male working class were enfranchised. Deputations from the TUC pressing the policy demands of the labour interest on government departments became a regular feature of public life in late Victorian Britain. A sprinkling of senior union leaders in the TUC were even appointed by governments to sit on royal commissions and public inquiries. In 1886 the TUC's then secretary, Henry Broadhurst, was made parliamentary under-secretary at the Home Office in Gladstone's third ministry, the first working-class man to occupy government office.

The TUC was deferential in its attitude to the state and it remained focused on a lobbying and petitioning role in parliament. There was no real threat from the TUC to the existing economic and social order. Moves to achieve direct representation through the trade unions for the working class in the House of Commons were limited in their success. Twenty years after the TUC's formation there were still only eight trade-union-sponsored Members of Parliament. The TUC was, in fact, very much a loyal part of the broad progressive alliance that constituted Gladstonian Liberalism. But trade union high regard for the Grand Old Man did not mean any toning down of their sense of working-class identity when it came to the promotion of the labour interest. However the TUC was provided by its affiliate unions with limited resources – only a part-time general secretary and a parliamentary committee that did not meet on a regular basis. Indeed, the TUC under Howell and Broadhurst was neither an inclusive nor really persistent common voice for trade unionism. In the words of Ross Martin, the TUC's function was 'largely marginal to the principal concerns' of both governments and trade unions up to 1890.[5] The Webbs were scathing about what they saw as the TUC's inadequate performance in their influential book, *Industrial Democracy*, published in 1897. 'Whatever outward resemblances to an effective political machine it may possess, it lacks all the essential conditions of efficiency and success', they wrote. In their opinion the TUC parliamentary committee lacked intellectual leadership and suffered from a 'combination of sturdy independence, naive self-complacency and an extremely narrow outlook'. With no full-time staff or outside expert advisers available on a regular basis, the TUC was not in a position to establish itself at that time as an informed and effective organisation to represent organised labour's common interests. As a result, the annual congress had become 'an unorganised public meeting utterly unable to formulate any consistent or practical policy'.[6] The local trade councils were equally the object of sweeping criticism from the Webbs. They regarded them as useless bodies equipped with limited power and viewed with deep suspicion by affiliate unions who saw those councils as potentially competitive rivals to their own independence. The Webbs in 1897 blamed the TUC's frailties on the narrow opinion shared by most unions of what its role ought to be. They were content to restrict the TUC as a lobby limited to handling only a small range of specific trade union issues but not able to speak out and press for a wider agenda of social and political reform. 'The trade unions join the congress for the promotion of a parliamentary policy desired, not merely by a majority but by all of them', argued the Webbs. 'It is a violation of the implied contract between them to use the political force, towards the creation of which all are contributing, for the purposes of any particular political party.' In their view the TUC would only become effective if it was able to achieve 'concerted federal action between the trades'. But they believed the leaders of the larger unions were 'with all their capacity and force, usually quite unfit' to bring about such a development. As the Webbs argued:

> Each man knows his own trade and the desires of his own union but is both ignorant and indifferent as to the needs or desires of every other trade. Before they can form anything like a cabinet with a definite and consistent policy, they must learn how to frame a precise and detailed programme which shall include the particular legislative regulations desired by each trade, whilst avoiding the shibboleths of any political party.

They did not believe this was an impossible dream, pointing out that the TUC Junta which dominated the organisation in its first few years had been able to create 'an extremely efficient cabinet' that paved the way for the achievement of the 1871 and 1875 legal settlement which appeared to have given the trade unions the legitimacy and security under the rule of law that they wanted.

In fact, during the 1890s a detectable change was evident in the TUC's position. The spread of unionisation among the country's unskilled manual workers, highlighted by the drama of the 1889 London dock strike, was undoubtedly a factor, as was the emergence of new general unions who brought a much more militant and often Socialist voice into TUC debates. So was the increasing concern being displayed by the state on how it ought to respond to what was becoming known in official circles as the 'labour question'. The creation of the Board of Trade's Labour Department in 1893 and the increase in ministerial concern with the passage of the 1896 Conciliation Act and its voluntary provisions to resolve industrial disputes, as well as legislation to safeguard workplace conditions, also strengthened the TUC's potential role as a lobbying interest group.

Inside the annual congress, Socialists began to appear in greater number with enough self-confidence to challenge the Lib–Lab TUC establishment. In 1895 an attempt was made by the old guard to turn back the Socialist advance inside the TUC. It was decided to ban trades councils from claiming representation at the annual conference. Only paid union officials or members of an affiliate union who were employed could attend in future as accredited delegates. Even more importantly, the TUC introduced what became the infamous union block vote, ending the system whereby delegates had been allowed to vote on resolutions as individuals. The Webbs criticised that particular reform, pointing out prophetically that this would lead in future congresses to the spectacle of 'the big officials holding the pack of voting cards allotted to their own unions, listening contemptuously to the debating of the smaller trades and silently voting down any proposition which displeases them'.[7]

The TUC itself was also beginning to acquire a greater institutional presence during the 1890s. A full-time clerk was appointed to administer its affairs in 1896, followed by the arrival of a part-time legal adviser four years later. In 1903 the TUC purchased its first typewriter and installed a telephone when it moved into new premises. With the retirement of Sam Woods in 1904, the post of TUC general secretary was made into a more intensive one, although this did not mean it could not be taken on by a Member of Parliament.

But the permanency of the TUC's position was still by no means secure and unchallenged. The General Federation of Trade Unions was formed by the TUC in 1899 and for some years appeared to pose a competitive threat. Originally established solely as a means for channelling financial support to trade unions involved in industrial disputes, the GFTU also acquired an international role for organised labour. Some union leaders even assumed the new body would eventually supersede the TUC. Indeed, by the outbreak of the Great War in August 1914 it still remained unclear whether the TUC as a national institution would become the sole representative body for organised workers. The Labour Party – formed after a resolution from the Amalgamated Society of Railway Servants before the 1899 congress proposed successfully the creation of a Labour Representation Committee – appeared to have usurped much of the TUC's influence as a parliamentary lobbyist while more militant union leaders were looking to different structures – the Transport Workers' Federation and the Triple Industrial Alliance – to pursue more radical strategies of industrial confrontation. By 1913 the Socialists G. D. H. Cole and William Mellor could claim: 'The TUC is a highly academic body – a debating society rather than a legislative assembly ... The existence of such an ill-defined body is a source of weakness to the Labour Movement and the Parliamentary Committee must hand over its works and powers to other bodies more fitted to the task.'[8]

The Webbs were equally dismissive of the TUC's position in 1913, describing the annual congress as remaining as it had been in its earlier years, 'a parade of the trade union forces than a genuine Parliament of Labour'.[9] As they wrote:

All the incidental circumstances tend to accentuate the parade features of Congress at the expense of its legislative capacity. The Mayor and Corporation of the city in which it is held give a public welcome to the delegates and usually hold a sumptuous reception in their honour. The strangers' gallery is full of interested observers. Distinguished foreigners, representatives of government departments, deputations from the Co-operative Union and other far-reaching organisations, inquisitive politicians, and popularity-hunting ministers sit through every day's proceedings. The press table is crowded with reporters from all the principal newspapers of the kingdom, whilst the local organs vie with each other in bringing out special editions containing verbatim reports of each day's discussions. But what more than anything else makes the Congress a holiday demonstration, instead of a responsible deliberative assembly, is its total lack of legislative power. The delegates are well aware that Congress resolutions have no binding effect on their constituents and therefore do not take the trouble to put them in practicable form or even to make them consistent one with another.

The Webbs deplored the absence of order, the inadequate discussion of issues and the tiresome procedural wrangles that often dominated congress and TUC proceedings. Above all, they lamented the shortage of responsible trade union leadership on display. They were equally scathing of the work of the TUC's Parliamentary Committee. Its potentially massive workload was contrasted with its extremely limited resources. The Webbs explained:

> The members of the Parliamentary Commitee leave their provincial headquarters fifteen to twenty times a year to spend a few hours in the little TUC offices at 19 Buckingham Street, Strand, in deliberating upon such business as their secretary brings before them. Preoccupied with the affairs of their societies and unversed in general politics, they either confine their attention to the interests of their own trades or look upon the fortnightly trip to London as a pleasant recreation from hard official duties. In the intervals between the meetings the secretary struggles with the business as best he can, with such clerical help as he can afford to pay for out of his meagre allowance. Absorbed in his own parliamentary duties, for the performance of which his constituents pay him a salary, he can devote to the general interests of the trade union world only the leavings of his time and attention.

As a result the TUC's activities were confined to sending a few deputations annually to government departments, carrying out limited consultation with friendly politicians and drafting a report to congress about parliamentary business for which they were not directly responsible. 'The TUC expects the parliamentary affairs of a million and a half members to be transacted by a staff inferior to that of a third-rate trade union', they concluded.

The experience of the Great War of 1914–18 did not immediately enhance the TUC's status and authority much either, even if it strengthened the overall influence of trade unions in their relations with the state. The key institution in organised labour's war effort was not the TUC but the War Emergency Workers' National Committee, made up of representatives from the TUC, the GFTU and the Labour Party. As Ross Martin concluded:

> In the case of union-government dealings on larger and more urgent matters, the TUC almost invariably either acted alongside other labour bodies or was excluded altogether. Moreover, its representative function at this level was not only shared with others but was usually shared to a degree that reduced its role to something less than primus inter pares.[10]

Indeed, given the prominence of the parliamentary committee's formal position in the labour movement, it had remarkably little to do officially with the mainstream of wartime negotiations between unions and government. Both the 1915 Treasury Agreement covering war labour mobilisation and the suspension of restrictive labour practices and the 1919 National Industrial Conference seeking a new relationship between capital and labour, revealed the limited role the TUC continued to play in public policy-making or the functioning of the wider political economy.

It was not until the early 1920s that the TUC really began to emerge as a credible, inclusive and unrivalled national representative body for organised workers, mainly as a result of its own structural reforms and the setbacks suffered by a resort by some unions to industrial militancy. In 1921 the parliamentary committee was replaced by the general council. At the same time the TUC established four joint policy departments with the Labour Party. In addition, a National Joint Council was created, made up of equal numbers of Labour MPs, members of the party's national executive committee and representatives from the TUC. But it was not until 1926 that the general council formed its own administration. The headquarters of the two wings of the Labour Movement, however, were to remain in the same premises sharing library facilities, first in Ecclestone Square, in London's Belgravia, and from May 1928 at Transport House, Smith Square, with the Transport and General Workers Union which owned the building. Only in 1958 did the TUC finally move to separate headquarters of its own in Great Russell Street in London's Bloomsbury district, where it remains to this day, complete with a conservation order and an Epstein statue of mother and child.

The growth in the TUC's importance in the early 1920s was well reflected in the emergence of a permanent administrative staff to service its burgeoning committee system. When Fred Bramley was appointed TUC general secretary in 1922 it was stipulated that he should devote his whole time to the work of the general council. No longer could the post be held by a Member of Parliament. After 52 years of existence, the TUC had finally become a fully-fledged national institution, authorised by its affiliate unions to establish itself as a more effective and recognised voice for the common interests of organised labour. But even the TUC's 1920–21 modernisation was only partial, uneven and heavily circumscribed. The tenacious strength of trade union autonomy ensured that the TUC was not about to be transformed into an unquestioning and centralised body, a general staff for an obedient army of labour. By comparison with its early decades, the TUC had certainly come of age. However, its twentieth-century aspirations to be an indispensable Estate of the Realm had only just begun.

At the beginning of a new century we need to assess the TUC's relative achievement since the early 1920s. Today, despite almost 20 years of remorseless decline in strength and influence from its high-water mark of 1980 when the TUC's affiliate trade union membership totalled over 11 million workers and nearly 60 per cent of the entire labour force were in a trade union, the TUC remains the largest voluntary association in Britain. During its long life, the TUC grew from humble and uncertain beginnings into a highly influential, respected and respectable organisation – part labour interest pressure group in the wider political economy and part parliamentary lobbying organisation seeking to influence the political system in the labour interest. The TUC not only claimed to articulate the collective demands of trade union members over the whole spectrum of public policy-making but also sought to express the wider aspirations of workers by hand or brain, whether they were members of a trade union or not. It was also keen – as far as was possible – to guide or jolly along affiliate unions behind united policy positions. The TUC's role as a mediator and conciliator of inter-union relations was always to be a constant preoccupation for its general secretaries from Walter Citrine to John Monks. It also sought, with more limited success, to act as a facilitator in the spread of best practice, common strategies and professional expertise to its member unions.

The TUC, for most of its history after 1921, faced no serious direct challenge to its assertion that it should be treated by governments and employer associations as the sole representative voice and national organisational centre for both manual and non-manual trade unions. It has always been the TUC's comprehensive and inclusive character, not divided organisationally by ideology, religion or class interest, unlike most other national trade union centres in the world, that made it so distinctive. Such an impressive unity of representation and purpose provided the TUC with an understandable credibility as well as legitimacy in the eyes of most governments of all parties during the twentieth century, whenever they wanted to assess organised labour's demands or call on the trade unions to shoulder burdens such as pay restraint or rearmament in a perceived national interest.

The TUC can look back with a genuine sense of pride to its many achievements in the twentieth century. It became a formidable organisation whose influence was of immense importance in the development of public policy, particularly during the 40 years between the outbreak of the Second World War in September 1939 and the arrival of Margaret Thatcher in 10 Downing Street in May 1979. The TUC's constructive impact on events was crucial during the Second World War when its officials gained as of right daily access to Whitehall departments. Out in the regions and in local communities and workplaces the TUC proved highly successful in ensuring the interests of organised labour were neither overlooked nor taken for granted in the mobilisation for total victory. The achievement of 'full' employment in the immediate post-war years and the creation of a welfare state based on principles of social citizenship, redistributive taxation and universal provision after 1945 owed much to TUC pressure on successive Labour and Conservative governments. The TUC turned into a powerful guarantor of the so-called post-war social settlement. It pressed consistently for economic growth and higher productivity and efficiency.

The TUC also played an important if understated role in the development of the country's education and training system, particularly in the creation of comprehensive schools, the promotion of lifelong learning and the encouragement of vocational and adult education.[11] It took a keen direct interest in the nationalisation of the commanding heights of British industry – coal, iron and steel, the railways, gas, water and electricity. In the early 1930s the TUC debated whether the public ownership of industry and the introduction of industrial planning should require forms of worker participation or public accountability. Its own approach was important for the emergence of the structure of the public corporations that were established after 1945. The TUC was also an effective advocate for the principle of compulsory social insurance and the use of the income tax system as a means of creating greater equality in a class-divided society through substantial measures of redistribution.

In the 1960s and 1970s the TUC helped to secure legal rights for workers in the provision of statutory redundancy payments, the introduction of maternity pay and compensation for unfair dismissal, the right to equal pay for men and women as well as the outlawing of forms of workplace discrimination on grounds of gender and race. The TUC always adopted a strong and positive attitude towards the development of comprehensive health and safety at work legislation with a key role to be played by trade union representatives in organised workplaces.

During most of the twentieth century the TUC established an intricate network of informal as well as formal influence that criss-crossed the interstices of the British state. The TUC general council's annual reports, especially over the years from 1940 to 1979, reveal a wealth of impressively detailed evidence of the organisation's close and diverse involvement in public policy-making which stretched far beyond the immediate demands of the workplace or the needs of collective bargaining. No royal commission or public inquiry ever seemed to be complete without a representative from the TUC sitting on it. From the problem of football hooliganism to Christmas bonuses for old age pensioners, the TUC pressed a collective view on to governments and it was one that was invariably not only listened to, but acted upon. The TUC explained its consultative role with governments in its evidence to the 1968 Donovan Commission:

Whilst there can be no obligation on the government to consult the TUC or individual unions on questions which closely affect the interest of their members, over the last fifty years there has grown up a pattern of consultation the scope of which is very wide ranging. All governments recognise that it is not possible to run a country purely through a Parliament. It might be said that Governments treat the TUC as a sort of industrial Parliament; in the first place to obtain the benefit of the views of the views and experience of the trade union movement in framing legislation or developing policies in general, and second, to secure the approval and endorsement of the TUC for the broad terms of legislation which will have a day to day influence on the work of trade unions.[12]

To its political critics on the left as well as the right, the TUC by the 1970s seemed to have grown much too powerful for its own good. It was said to be over-burdened by national responsibilities as the vital pillar of an increasingly corporatist state. Over successive national incomes policies from 1948 to 1977 the TUC – often against its own better instincts – was persuaded to come to the rescue of Labour governments in economic trouble by agreeing to accept forms of pay restraint or even a wage standstill on behalf of the rank and file of affiliate unions. Such a restrictive strategy in a parliamentary democracy and open market economy led inevitably to widespread discontent among trade union activists and workplace disaffection that provoked the eventual rejection of incomes policies by many rank and file workers.

But the TUC never – at any stage – sought to further a view of trade unionism, which was designed to turn itself into an obedient servant of an over-centralised state. For most of the twentieth century, the TUC tried to defend the freedom of trade unions and workers from attempts at control or direction by any external body, not least governments. As it explained in its evidence to the Donovan Commission:

No state, however benevolent, can perform the function of trade unions in enabling workpeople themselves to decide how their interests can best be safeguarded. It is where trade unions are not competent, and recognise they are not competent, to perform a function, that they welcome the state playing a role in at least enforcing minimum standards but in Britain this role is recognised as the second best alternative to the development by workpeople themselves of the organisation, the competence, the representative capacity, to bargain and to achieve for themselves satisfactory terms and conditions of employment. In general, therefore, because this competence exists, the state stands aside, its attitude being one of abstention, of formal indifference.[13]

It is true such an apparently arm's-length attitude was by no means always a consistent feature of TUC behaviour. As we shall see, during the 1970s in particular and again after 1997, the TUC looked to government and not to the voluntary bargaining of affiliate trade unions for the acquisition of individual as well as collective rights for working people. However, this did not involve any explicit or clear-cut break with the so-called voluntarist tradition of industrial relations that helped to shape British trade union structure and behaviour from the middle of the nineteenth century in their feelings towards the role they believed the state should play in their affairs. But over time it brought a transformation in the TUC's purposes as it struggled to develop a new modernising role in a globalising economy. By the end of the twentieth century the TUC saw its role as that of a vital social partner in the development of an enterprise culture and industrial consensus aimed at improving productivity and competitiveness. Echoes of such a cooperative approach with industry could be found as long ago as TUC general secretary Walter Citrine's modernisation agenda after the 1926 General Strike and again in the making of the TUC's bold post-war reconstruction programmes between 1942 and 1945. But it was not really fully articulated and acted upon until John Monks's New Unionism of the 1990s. Critics on the left would argue that such a conciliatory strategy was symptomatic of the TUC's diminished national authority after the lost opportunities of the Social Contract period during the misunderstood 1970s. They believe the TUC capitulated in the face of aggressive, resurgent capital and a New Labour government, hostile and suspicious that trade unions might try to restore the supposed irresponsible power it was claimed they wielded over state and society 20 years earlier.

Such strictures were, however, misplaced. In truth, today's TUC remains in practice what it always has been – a voluntary and weakly organised federation of disparate sectional and producer interests shaped by external events over most of which it was able to exercise little or only limited control. But the TUC has also – for the most part – retained an acute appreciation of what was ever possible. It has usually stood for and sought to achieve a principled pragmatism. As it explained in a 1970 report on structure and development:

> The TUC is primarily concerned with developing policy rather than acting as an executive body. It produces a means through which unions can collectively achieve objectives which they cannot achieve or which it could be difficult for them to achieve separately. It identifies things which unions should be doing but which for one reason or another they are not doing and stimulates them to take the necessary action. It reminds individual unions or groups of unions of their duty to take into account the interests of other unions and the broader interests of trade unions as a whole. It thus establishes standards of good union practice.[14]

The TUC was well aware of the limitations such a constraint placed on its ability to take any public policy initiative. As the same 1970 structure document argued:

> The TUC has the perennial problem of reconciling the special interests of particular unions or groups of members with the general interests of the trade union movement and of deciding when which set of interests should prevail. This has on occasion led the TUC to make general statements which, because they are capable of different interpretations, offend none and are minimally acceptable to all. A propensity not to offend and not to appear to be interfering with union autonomy has historically often led the TUC to eschew taking initiatives.

Unlike other nationally based trade union federations in the western world the TUC was not able to acquire an unquestioned authority or power over the actions of its affiliate members. It was never to be given the role of collective bargainer with specific employers or industries. Nor was it even allowed to compile information on wage data or advise individual unions on their pay claims, let alone train and keep in contact with shop stewards and local officials of affiliate unions. What powers and influence the TUC ever enjoyed have only come from the willingness of affiliate trade unions to delegate to it.

Inevitably, the TUC's resulting weakness has often exasperated governments, impatient for the trade unions to act in concert together in the resolution of problems of national concern. It is arguable, however, whether TUC general secretaries have not on occasion exaggerated their own inability to exercise authority over affiliate unions. But as a 1975 TUC report on its powers acknowledged:

> It would be meaningless for the general council to be given powers to direct and instruct unions unless unions in their turn have the same powers over their members. What a union can do would and must ultimately be determined by its members. The only real sanction the TUC has is suspension or expulsion: the use of other sanctions such as the imposition of fines on unions is neither desirable nor practicable and in any case it would run directly counter to the way in which the TUC has been developing in recent years which is to win the support of unions for agreed policies by argument and persuasion.[15]

Indeed, when expulsion from the TUC was used as a punishment – as it was against the Electricians' Union in 1961 and 1988 and against 32 unions in 1972 when they refused to comply with the TUC's policy of resistance to the Industrial Relations Act – it weakened the organisation and proved to be highly divisive and ultimately counter-productive.

It was very much the internal structures of both the TUC itself and affiliate unions that impeded innumerable attempts at reform or modernisation after 1921. Citrine noted in his memoirs that the TUC's perennial problem over reforming itself in response to changing times came down to one of the power 'to act on policy issues in a cohesive manner'. As he recalled:

> This could be done only by a central body representing all the unions. People who thought like myself had for years been talking about a general staff of labour. 'All power to the general council', they declared. Such slogans seemed not only eminently desirable but just plain common sense. We did not realise how conservative a force the trade union movement could be in relation to its own affairs.[16]

The intellectual, working-class George Woodcock was confronted by those same forces of conservatism inside the trade unions during the 1960s when he made sporadic efforts to modernise both the TUC and trade unionism in general to meet the difficult conditions imposed on industrial relations by the coming of full employment, wage-push inflation and unofficial strikes.

It would be wrong to restrict any overall portrait of the TUC to its domestic activities during the past century. We should never forget the TUC's important influence in the wider world beyond Britain. It was partly instrumental, for example, in the creation of the tripartite Geneva-based International Labour Organisation in 1919 with its mission to establish worker rights everywhere. The TUC was often to take the lead in seeking the mobilisation of the international Labour Movement against state oppression and employer exploitation of workers. It was a formidable force for common sense and solidarity in international trade union organisations, starting with the International Federation of Trade Unions between the wars when Citrine was president after 1928. In the 1930s the TUC adopted a robust and realistic view of what needed to be done to confront the European dictators with its sound conviction that military force would be needed to defeat Fascism. In the Cold War after 1949, the TUC pursued a pragmatic and flexible approach without compromising its fundamental opposition to the real and subversive threat of Soviet Communism. Although less dogmatic in its anti-Communist attitudes than the American trade union movement, the TUC was nevertheless resistant to the attractions of the Soviet Union. It was the key organisation in the break away from the Communist-dominated World Federation of Trade Unions in 1949 and the subsequent formation of the International Confederation of Free Trade Unions in London's County Hall.[17] Inevitably, the American Federation of Labor was unimpressed by the TUC's anti-Communism, believing it was never rigorous enough. Perhaps its president George Meany never forgot the angry reception he received from rank and file delegates when, as AFL fraternal delegate at the 1945 Congress in Blackpool, he denounced Stalin's Soviet Union for its widespread use of labour camps. More controversially, it is arguable that the TUC, for much of the post-war period, made too sure its own foreign policy kept too closely in line with the views of the mandarins of the Foreign Office.

Just as important and too often overlooked was the TUC's practical and influential role in helping to bring about the transformation of the British Empire into British Commonwealth through its pioneering work in the colonies. Technical and educational assistance provided through the TUC encouraged the development of individual trade union movements, especially in Africa, the West Indies and the Indian sub-continent. The TUC helped to train a cadre of able trade union officials who emerged during the period of decolonisation after 1945. Much of this work was done through a close cooperation between the Colonial Office and especially the TUC's Colonial Labour Advisory Committee which was established in 1940.[18] Both the TUC and successive governments agreed on the need for the encouragement of responsible trade unionism in the colonies. By the war years the government was recruiting qualified British trade unionists – through the TUC – to serve as labour officers attached to local colonial labour departments.

The sheer diverse range of the TUC's activities after 1921 looks impressive, especially when the organisation has always been much less powerful than many outside the trade union movement might have believed or recognised. Contrary to a widespread popular belief, the TUC has never been – nor has it ever claimed to be – a highly centralised institution that was in a position of authority to issue directives from on high to be accepted unquestioningly by obedient and loyal member unions. It has always remained – to the ill-concealed exasperation of many politicians and even union officials – a loose confederation of often disparate affiliate unions with often divided interests, keen to protect their own precious autonomy from intrusion by the TUC itself. In other western European market economies – notably in Scandinavia, but also in Germany, the Low Countries and Austria – national trade union centres acquired substantial collective authority over their affiliate members during the twentieth century backed up by the threat and even use of sanctions against errant unions. This enabled them to establish a dominance at the national centre vis-a-vis the state and employer associations and guaranteed them a continuous and legitimate role in economic policy coordination, something that was never really possible in Britain outside wartime conditions. At moments of national crisis, however, the TUC always responded impressively to the challenges imposed upon the trade unions by unpredictable outside events. But its pace of change was normally slow and circumspect. The need for internal unity in the TUC was paramount, even if it could arouse impatience among those who wanted to see a more dynamic role being played by the organisation. However, on certain occasions the TUC was also able to display an impressive decisiveness as a representative organisation, surprising its enemies and delighting its friends. It is also true the TUC often proved to be at its most effective in resisting external pressures rather than in seizing the initiative in an innovatory way. As the TUC told the House of Commons select committee in 1994:

> No individual union acting alone can exercise the same influence as all unions acting together through the TUC. It is through our lobbying

and campaigning activities at national level that the TUC adds value to the work of individual unions. There is still a clear imperative demanding a single trade union voice on a wide range of economic and social issues. Equally there is a need for one organisation at national level advocating the benefits of trade unionism and campaigning for proper protections for people at work.[19]

But the TUC has almost always tried to punch well above its weight. To the outside world Congress House may have seemed like a substantial and imposing organisation. But at all times the TUC has been very much a shoestring operation, dependent on the willingness of its affiliate unions to provide it with limited authority and financial resources to promote the wider influence of organised labour in the political economy beyond the workplace. The powers of the TUC general council were always of crucial importance. How much autonomy should affiliate unions give to it? The rules, drawn up in 1921, with important revisions in 1928 and 1939, provided the general council with a diversity of specific functions. It was to resolve inter-union disputes; establish close relations with trade union and labour movements overseas and have the duty of keeping a 'watch on all industrial movements and attempt where possible to coordinate industrial action'.[20] As the TUC's draft constitution declared: 'It shall promote common action by the trade union movement on general questions such as wages and hours of labour and any matter of general concern that may arise between employers and trade unions or between the trade union movement and the government, and shall have power to assist any union which is attacked on any vital question of trade union principle.' In addition, 'where disputes arise, or threaten to rise between trade unions, it shall use its influence to promote a settlement'. But some unions feared such wording might encourage the TUC to overdo its intrusive powers. Under pressure from the Miners' Federation, it was agreed that the general council's new powers of intervention could only be exercised 'subject to the necessary safeguards to secure the complete autonomy of the unions and federations affiliated to Congress'. Efforts to ensure the TUC general council could intervene powerfully in industrial disputes were met with stiff resistance. In Alan Bullock's words, the general council 'could plead, persuade, invite, cajole, but never give orders. It was to act as a general staff to an army which had no chain of command or commander in chief and whose divisions would decide for themselves whether to fight or not.'[21]

Most of the powers provided for the TUC general council were in fact almost the same as those which had been exercised by the TUC parliamentary committee it had replaced in 1921. But initial caution was backed by a willingness to accept that the newly modernised TUC might be reshaped in the future by the pressure of time and events. 'There is no finality in our conception of organisation', the young Ernest Bevin told the 1920 Congress. 'But we realise there is greater danger in trying, before we are allowed to create confidence by the existence of a body, to ride roughshod over the natural conservatism of our movement.'[22] Wisely, Bevin believed it was best not to enforce too rigid and precise a definition of what the TUC stood for but to allow the organisation to develop at its own pace. Nonetheless, the TUC's ability to act in a collective way on behalf of all its affiliate unions was always limited by circumstances. The internal difficulties in achieving cohesion often set a severe limit on the TUC's capacity to become a strong Estate of the Realm. When we assess the overall achievements of the TUC during the last century this point should never be forgotten. All the TUC general secretaries had to wrestle with that fundamental problem to varying degrees.

However, a less noticed limitation on the role of the TUC in the political economy stemmed from the British state's ambivalent attitude to trade unionism. In other European countries national trade union federations were drawn not only into public policy decision-making but also into shouldering some of the administrative burdens required in a modern state. In Sweden, for example, the trade union movement organised the unemployment insurance system and underpinned the practical administration of welfare benefit provision. In policy areas like the provision of old age pensions and payment of sickness benefits, trade unions in many European countries played a pivotal role. This did not happen in Britain during the twentieth century, although in their formative years most trade unions had been staunch enthusiasts of mutuality and self-help, of localised action in the development of civil societies. The unions had not campaigned for the creation of a large centralised collectivist state, fearing such a development would threaten their own autonomy and workplace voluntarism. In many western European societies trade union confederations built up robust and permanent organisational linkages with the state and employer bodies over a wide range of public policy issues. This was most apparent in the administration of industrial and vocational training and publicly funded active labour market programmes as well as in the development of more ambitious social dialogues or social pacts and macro-economic national policy coordination. It is true that during the Second World War and again in the 1960s, but more noticeably in the 1970s, the TUC came into tripartite structures of governance it advocated but it always seemed to be a tentative, contested and half-hearted process that never reached any satisfactory conclusion.

The British state was as culpable as the TUC in not wanting to embrace wholeheartedly a European-style social partnership model, complete with rights and obligations for employers, unions and workers. But then neither governments nor trade unions really wanted to encourage an over-concentration of power and influence in centralised institutions. Both remained – at least until the end of the 1990s – keen to reinforce and widen but not dismantle or undermine forms of tripartite voluntarism that had grown up during wartime. In their attitude they were responding to the nature of the industrial relations system where unions traditionally defended their autonomy, their customs and practices from any outside threats posed by an intrusive state, hostile employers or a capricious legal system. As Professor Colin Crouch has argued, the shift that took place in the locus of collective bargaining from industry and sector-wide arrangements to enterprise or plant level which really began in the 1960s in the private sector had 'fewer implications for British than for many other unions, since they were rarely able to transcend this level during the period when most advantages seemed to lie with centralised unions capable of national coordination'.[23]

All of this may help to explain the genuine limitations on what the TUC could achieve as a potential Estate of the Realm. The reality always fell short of the aspirations. But it would be wrong as a result to adopt a cynical or world-weary attitude to the outcome. Within its self-imposed as well as substantial external restrictions the TUC was able to play a positive and distinguished role in the evolution of modern Britain. The Queen's sympathetic words about the TUC in London's Guildhall that June evening in 1968 are proof enough of this. In its principled pragmatism, the TUC in the twentieth century reflected all the strengths and weaknesses of the British Labour Movement, which was rarely able to set or accomplish its own public policy agenda without serious difficulties.

1

Walter Citrine and TUC Modernisation, 1926–1939

We have passed from the era of propaganda to one of responsibility and the things that are said in this Congress cannot be said lightly and ought not to be said without mature thought.[1]

The primary function of the trade union movement is to get better conditions here and now ... Trade unionism should concentrate more upon trying to secure changes in capitalism which will elevate working-class standards.[2]

The modern TUC is very much the personal achievement of Walter McClennan Citrine. He was its general secretary from the aftermath of the General Strike in September 1926 to September 1946, just over a year after the end of the Second World War and the election of the first majority Labour government. Citrine was only 39 years of age when elected to head the TUC after the sudden death of Fred Bramley in October 1925. He was the youngest man ever to have held the post in its history. Citrine became one of the most important figures in the formation of the mid-twentieth-century Labour Movement but his contribution has not received the acknowledgement it deserves. If he is remembered at all today, Citrine is seen as primarily an efficient administrator, who brought a badly needed order and coherence to the TUC's often disorganised activities. His filing system, introduced to organise TUC head office business in the 1920s, was to last for nearly 70 years. 'Poor fellow, he suffers from files', the young Aneurin Bevan once sneered about Citrine.[3] His practical book on the ABC of chairmanship, published in 1939, still remains a useful, sensible guide on how to run a public meeting. 'It is Citrine on Chairmanship not *Das Kapital*, which is the standard text book for the lad anxious to better himself in the Labour party', opined veteran political journalist Alan Watkins on the cover of its more recent edition.[4] The voluminous annual TUC general council reports, often full of intimate details of meetings between TUC leaders and prime ministers that make a mockery of the 30-year rule on the prohibition of official documents to the public gaze, were very much due to Citrine's determination to ensure all affiliate unions were kept fully informed about the TUC's many activities. At a time when the managing of institutions, especially those inside the Labour Movement, was seen as a thankless and boring task best left to under-valued backroom clerical staff, Citrine demonstrated the importance of effective administration for the achievement of trade union success. Under his shrewd direction the TUC began to recruit and retain a highly intelligent and loyal cadre of committed enthusiasts – many university graduates – to serve in its growing full-time secretariat. They were dedicated to the promotion of the labour interest through the creation of often informal networks of influence that grew up with many Whitehall departments beyond the confines of the Ministry of Labour. The impressive *esprit de corps* among staff, still to be found inside Congress House, derives from that tradition of high-minded excellence and dedication to public service which really first began with Citrine. It was his ambition to build up the TUC as a professional institution that could hold its own against senior civil servants and captains of industry in furthering the cause of trade unionism.

Citrine was certainly regarded as a different type of trade union leader in the 1920s compared to his predecessors at the TUC, perhaps above all because of his dedicated and ethical commitment to public service professionalism. With his expertise in shorthand, he filled his notebooks with detail as a meticulous accumulator of facts. He 'has character, industry and intellect', admitted Beatrice Webb in her diary after Citrine paid her and Sidney Webb a visit at their Hampshire home in Liphook in July 1927. 'He is the first intellectual to be at the centre of the trade union movement.' She described him as having the manners, clothes and way of speaking of a 'superior bank clerk', adding he was 'a non-smoker, non-drinker, small slow eater, takes a daily cold bath, sleeps with his windows open – altogether a hygienic puritan in his daily life'. 'He has the integrity and loyalty of the better type of British mechanic', she noted. Although Mrs Webb did not believe Citrine would 'become a hanger-on of the directors of capitalist industry', she feared he suffered from the weakness of 'personal vanity and the sort of conceit which arises from continuous association with uneducated and unself-controlled superiors'.[5]

But it would be quite wrong – on the basis of such middle-class condescension – to conclude that Citrine was merely a cold-blooded, tidy-minded and methodical bureaucrat, slavishly dedicated to the protection of TUC rules and procedures. He was far more than just the Mr Polly of the TUC. Indeed, he turned out to be an insightful and idealistic philosopher of industrial relations, laying down with great clarity a strategic vision of what the TUC's role ought to be in a modern political economy that has stood the test of time. Even before he became TUC general secretary, Citrine had demonstrated he was capable not only of managing a large organisation but also of possessing a realistic grasp of complex industrial and political issues. This had been evident during his time as the elected full-time district secretary of the Electrical Trades Union on Merseyside in October 1914 and more especially after he became the ETU's assistant general secretary in the summer of 1920, when he saved the union from the prospect of financial ruin, until his appointment as Fred Bramley's deputy in January 1924.[6] It was during those formative years that Citrine developed his fundamental views about trade unionism that were modified but not substantially changed during his lengthy period as TUC general secretary.

Citrine always remained, despite accusations of being an elitist, first and foremost a firm believer in the primacy of collective bargaining. 'I infinitely preferred voluntary agreements to state regulations in the relations between employers and workpeople', he explained in his memoirs. 'I found that the men serving employers' associations were chaps much like myself and they knew that continuous strife was of no ultimate benefit to either side.'[7] The way to avoid endless conflict was to establish mutual trust and respect between trade unions and employers. 'We knew that ours was a continuing relationship and that if one snatched a temporary advantage by sharp practice the other would be sure to get his own back some time or other. We fought each other in negotiations but we never broke faith.'

Attending annual meetings of the Trades Union Congress immediately after the Great War of 1914–18 as one of the ETU's delegates, Citrine also gave some initial thought to what he envisaged should be the TUC's future. 'I felt it lacked authority and that the movement needed a central executive body which could act decisively on behalf of trade unionism as a whole', he suggested. 'I had not the slightest thought of superseding the TUC by any new creation but solely of widening its powers.' Citrine believed this meant its evolution into becoming 'a general staff for labour and by labour I mean the trade unions'.[8] Bramley held the same view. The need to balance or reconcile the voluntary traditions of industrial relations with the call for giving greater delegated centralising power to the TUC was a problem that was to trouble Citrine during all his years as its general secretary.

But he was left in little doubt during the early 1920s about the difficulties that stood in the way of strengthening the TUC's power and authority in relation to its affiliate member unions. The wave of union mergers which led to the formation of the Transport and General Workers Union in 1922 and the General and Municipal Workers Union two years later was a factor in holding back the TUC's own growth as an effective representative voice of trade unionism as a whole. The existence of such large general manual unions with boundless ambitions to expand in a highly competitive labour market tended to restrict some of the hopes held inside the TUC that it would be able expand its own role in the wider trade union interest. When Citrine first started work as Bramley's assistant on 20 January 1924 the TUC had recently gone through its most radical period of reconstruction since its foundation in 1868.[9] The position of TUC general secretary had been transformed from a part-time to a permanent, full-time job with the retirement of Charles Bowerman, who had been the TUC's secretary from 1911 to 1923 while remaining a Labour Member of Parliament throughout his years in office. The TUC also replaced its Parliamentary Committee with a general council. The new body was provided with the task of resolving inter-union disputes, promoting 'common action by the trade union movement on general questions such as wages and hours of labour' and 'any matter of general concern that may arise between employers and trade unions or between the trade union movement and the government'. The general council was also empowered 'to keep a watch on all industrial movements, and where possible, to co-ordinate industrial action', as well as 'assist any union which was attacked on any vital question of trade union principle'. But some unions feared such an unequivocal commitment might threaten their own freedom of action. A clause was added to the description of the general council's authority, making it quite clear that its new powers were 'subject to the necessary safeguards to secure the complete autonomy of the unions and federations affiliated to Congress'.[10] A system of functional committees was also established along with a number of specialist departments. In addition, the TUC and the Labour Party agreed to coordinate their activities through the creation of a number of committees and departments covering research, international affairs, legal matters and publicity which were administered under their joint control. A National Joint Council of Labour was founded covering the two bodies, but it proved to be less of a success. While the two organisations occupied the same premises in London's Eccleston Square and moved in with the TGWU when Transport House was opened in May 1928, joint arrangements were often subject to mutual strain and criticism and led to occasional outbursts of mutual ill-feeling during the period of the first minority Labour government in 1924 when the TUC complained it not been consulted at all on anything of importance by Prime Minister Ramsay MacDonald.

In fact, from the moment of his arrival at TUC headquarters Citrine was keen to establish some distance for the organisation he worked for from the internal affairs of the Labour Party. At a dinner of the parliamentary Labour Party when still assistant secretary, he insisted that 'the necessity for a closer collaboration between the Labour party and the TUC' needed to be 'compatible with the different functions of each and our different memberships'.[11] He told his audience of senior party leaders including MacDonald and Philip Snowden that the trade unions needed to work for all workers, irrespective of what their political opinions might be, and as a result they 'must have a different view on some questions from the Labour party and this applied to economic and social subjects well as politics'. It meant that the TUC, 'while affording every possible support to the party generally must occasionally express a different view. It must retain the right of independent political opinion and expression. I hoped it would never surrender that right.'

Citrine's outspoken comments at that Commons dinner were an early sign of his determination to strengthen the industrial wing of the Labour Movement and ensure it would never be subordinate to the demands of politicians, not even if they were supposed to be the TUC's allies in the same noble cause. Citrine was soon to realise that severe limits stood in the way of his ambitious objective of transforming the TUC into a national representative organisation for affiliate trade unions with power and authority over them to enforce collective decisions they made among themselves. In 1924 Bramley gave him the sensitive and thankless task of examining the possibility of a reform of trade union structures on industrial lines in response to a congress resolution that had called for this. The result was a highly detailed report written by Citrine himself for presentation to the 1925 Congress. It might have displeased some senior union leaders but it demonstrated his realism as he spelt out the formidable obstacles to the grandiose vision of British trade unionism then held by some on the left. Citrine did so through highlighting what he described as the 'defects' of existing trade union structures. He believed 'sectionalism' between the unions was one of the most serious obstacles to the creation of TUC unity and he saw no evidence it would be easily eradicated. 'It will continue vigorously as long as the small unions seem to fulfil more effectively the most immediate interests of their members', he explained. 'Its removal is only possible by a clearer recognition of the mass interests of the working class. It is no use fulminating against sectionalism. It exists and may continue to exist for a long time.' Citrine also highlighted the weakness caused by the ceaseless competitive struggle being fought between the unions in the search for more members with its 'waste of effort, material and money'. Further weaknesses, perceived by Citrine, included the varied rates of union contributions and benefits and the job demarcation lines running through industries that provoked bitter, self-destructive and protracted inter-union disputes. But it was the lack of any policy coordination between the unions which Citrine believed was the greatest weakness of all. 'It is seldom that even a group of closely related unions can act decisively and promptly in time of necessity', he explained. 'Looked at from a critical standpoint the efforts of the trade union movement have been concentrated almost entirely upon its limited object of betterment of conditions.' If the unions were to establish a united front for the achievement of their more ambitious common objectives such as the control of industry or closer relations with the state, he believed they would have to eradicate the weaknesses highlighted in his memorandum.[12]

In his incisive analysis of the bewildering diversity of class, industrial and occupational, federal, confederal and craft unionism, Citrine was conscious of the problems raised by such a complex structure that made the hope of establishing a more cohesive and centralised TUC look quite unrealistic. But his sobering memorandum also revealed what Citrine would really have ideally liked to have seen happen to make the TUC a much more dynamic and effective organisation. To a perhaps surprising degree, he revealed himself as something of an enthusiast for the romantic idea of one big union. Although never a revolutionary syndicalist in the tradition of the American Industrial Workers of the World (the Wobblies), he wrote positively of how such an approach would strengthen the forces of organised labour against employers and the state. As he explained of what he called class or general unionism:

All workers, irrespective of grade, craft or occupation, would be in one all-embracing union. They would sink their craft and sectional prejudices and would aim at a single standard of conditions for all who toil. If we look at the mission of trade unionism as being that of functioning on behalf of the working class as a whole, it is certain that this is the most theoretically perfect type of organisation. The one big union would be by far the most comprehensive type of industrial organisation which could be devised. Such a union would have its central executive endowed with executive power corresponding to that of our national centralised trade unions. The executive would be representative of the various industrial groups in which the members were engaged. The work of the union would be departmentalised to conform to those industries and would be staffed by specialists with a knowledge of the work of their members. In its local or geographical relations, the one big union would have its branches in the various areas, each of which would be departmentalised in a similar manner to the national executive. Reaching down from the branches there would be a system of shop stewards representing each of the different types of workers and these would in turn be organised together into workshop committees.

In Citrine's opinion, it was the concept of 'class unionism' which would meet the demands for a new trade union structure that had been made by left-wing union leaders at the 1924 Hull Congress. 'It would reduce the number of unions to the lowest possible minimum', he explained.

It would be a power to secure control of industry and as an instrument against capitalism would function with a mighty force which no other type of organisation could exert. Sectionalism would be done away with. Competition for members would no longer exist. Demarcation conflicts would be at an end and coordination of policy would be realised in its most complete form.

But ever the realist, Citrine also went on to question whether such an idea of one big union, for all its superficial attractions, was really practical politics in the industrial world of the 1920s.

The very magnitude of the idea makes its realisation difficult and it seems so far removed that one runs the risk of being called a visionary in seriously contemplating it. The task of its achievement would be enormous. It would mean nothing more or less than the complete amalgamation of all existing unions into one huge aggregation.

He pointed out that the TUC was itself 'the nucleus of one big union', structured in 17 separate trade groups and supervised by the general council. 'It could be developed until it became capable of functioning on behalf of the whole trade union movement', he suggested. Citrine visualised the existing trades councils being transformed under the TUC's authority into 'actively functioning bodies' in a relationship with the general council that was similar to that between district or management committees and affiliate unions. They in turn would be connected to shop stewards and workshop committees, which would have restricted functions 'to the consideration and settlement of domestic matters strictly limited to the factory, workshop or undertaking to which they are attached'. However, Citrine acknowledged that the trade union movement was still far removed from such a possibility, although he argued the one big union concept 'might usefully be borne in mind as the direction in which future efforts towards developing trade union organisation should be made'.

In the remorseless logic, clarity and maturity of his arguments, the 37-year-old assistant secretary laid bare the underlying weaknesses of the British trade union movement at that time, strong in its use of bellicose rhetoric but reluctant to recognise the industrial realities of its weak and uncoordinated structures that held it back from any decisive shift to greater forms of centralisation which would threaten union autonomy. 'I knew then in 1925 that there would have to be a revolution in thinking before the executives of the trade unions would follow the course I outlined. They were intensely jealous of their autonomy and afraid of their authority being usurped', he recalled.[13] The final report on trade union structure was not actually published by the TUC until 1927, but by then Citrine had accepted that little could be done in the way of fundamental modernisation on the lines he wanted in the face of a trade union structure shaped not by reason or common sense but by history, tradition, custom and competition.

The industrial crisis

In fact, Citrine was anxious about the immediate prospects for the trade unions in the summer of 1925. His pessimism was not shared by most union leaders in the aftermath of Red Friday on 31 July 1925. Many of them exulted over what they believed to be the proven strength of organised labour and the way the TUC's threat of collective action in support of miners had forced Conservative Prime Minister Stanley Baldwin and his cabinet to climb down in the coal crisis. Baldwin had announced the government would provide a nine-month-long subsidy for the industry and appointed former Liberal Home Secretary Sir Herbert Samuel to chair an independent commission with the thankless task of finding solutions to the problems of the coal industry. Citrine took a more sober view than many of his colleagues of what all this might portend. 'We must not become inflated with any sense of victory', he warned in July 1925. 'Nothing would be more fatal than a false sense of security and reliance on the silent might of the trade union movement.' As ever, Citrine was thinking ahead strategically. 'We must regard this struggle as nothing more than a skirmish of outposts. We were not tested. We have won a moral victory without bringing our guns into action.'[14] Citrine sensed this was not going to be the end of the matter, that the government would feel compelled at some point to confront the TUC and the unions and call their bluff. The open way the cabinet prepared its contingency plans for the prospect of a general strike, with the formation of the Organisation for the Maintenance of Supplies, suggested ministers were not going to bow the knee to the TUC in the future. Citrine also doubted whether rank and file trade unionists would really be willing to respond to a general strike call if doing so meant challenging the authority of a democratically elected government. As he explained in his July 1925 memorandum:

> In time of strike on the narrow issue of resisting a reduction in wages or an extension of hours, there would not be much trouble in securing the loyalty of the men. But if the issue was raised in a constitutional sense it might easily be that the law-abiding British trade unionists would desert the organisation and rally to the standards of constitutional authority. Against that there is always the feeling that working class people throughout history have tended to stick together in times of crisis, certainly until the position had become hopeless. But even with the greatest loyalty what authority is there to serve an orderly and national general strike? The general council has not that power today. In apportioning the transport unions – who incidentally cannot always be expected to be the storm troops of the movement – the council were wise in limiting the scope of the struggle.[15]

As Citrine noted, it might be easy to win pledges of promised financial support from affiliate unions in solidarity with strikers in another union, but ensuring the money was actually handed over for that purpose was another matter. The executives of affiliate unions would simply not be prepared to shoulder the responsibility for calling general strikes.

What we ought to do is surely to seek the greater concentration of power in the hands of somebody able to logically, intelligently and promptly use it. What is that body? The general council? Is it possible at one stride to get power vested in the general council to call a strike of the whole movement on a national issue? I am afraid not.

In a signed article published in *Labour* – the TUC's own magazine – in September 1925, Citrine wrote: 'Nothing could be more harmful and perhaps fatal than to engender a false sense of security and reliance on the latent might of the trade union movement.'[16] He called on the unions to display a 'calm consideration' on how to develop an 'industrial strategy based on the principles of centralised power and united leadership'. Citrine was gloomily prophetic about the outcome of any further industrial conflict that dragged in the state. He suggested it was 'almost inevitable that in any future dispute of considerable magnitude the government will at some point become involved. It may be that a capitalist government next time will show no inclination to evade the issue but will be prepared to force matters to a conclusion on grounds of their own choosing.' Citrine argued that the trade unions had forced the government to back down from a confrontation with them on Red Friday, mainly because of their own disciplined unity, public sympathy for the miners, as well as the TUC's determination not to allow the crisis to degenerate into a direct conflict with the powers of the state. But he added:

Our objective was a purely trade union one, legally and morally justifiable. We took every precaution to avoid being stampeded into a policy of violence. If the challenge of the movement could have been given the appearance of a denial of the government's right to govern and as the beginning of open war between society as at present constituted and the whole organised working class movement, a very serious situation might have arisen.

Citrine was convinced the trade unions would not be able to adopt similar tactics in the future with rank and file support unless the issues affected their daily lives and were 'a matter of vital interest to the whole working class'. 'We cannot be sure of their loyalty and unity in support of aims which it may be possible to attain by other paths – by the ballot box and political action, instead of by direct industrial methods.'

Citrine was also concerned about the question of where ultimate authority should lie in the trade union movement for the calling of 'general combined action'. 'The TUC general council does not possess it', he wrote. 'No single body or organ of the trade union movement possesses it.' By limiting the threat of industrial action on Red Friday to the transport unions, the general council had acted wisely, he maintained. 'Had it been necessary to call a general stoppage we should have realised where our weakness lies. Mainly in the fact that the general council, though it has been invested with extended powers, is not yet in a position to carry out of itself even the expressed will and determination of the unions.' The raising of financial and other support as well as the responsibility for calling a strike was not concentrated in the TUC general council but diffused through union organisations, Citrine pointed out. 'Many – perhaps a majority – even of the union executives could not constitutionally act without the sanction of a ballot vote of their members.' Such a cumbersome, slow-moving procedure would make it hard for all the unions to coordinate their strategies when speed of decision-making was the paramount consideration. But the alternative was for the unions to delegate authority to call such strikes to another body like the TUC general council. However, if this was to happen the general council would have to be entrusted with effective means to determine tactics and strategy.

In late 1925 Citrine believed that 'from the welter of conflicting opinions and ideas' a desire for such centralisation was 'steadily emerging', so that 'in time of necessity' the TUC would be able to 'organise the unions to fight as a single army'. 'The march of events is forcing a greater realisation of the mutual interdependence of all unions', declared Citrine as 'the large scale industrial dispute' replaced smaller, localised, sporadic strikes and lock-outs. He believed the mining crisis would merely be the 'forerunner of other attacks to come'. 'It is logical, legitimate and morally justifiable to prepare for such eventualties', argued Citrine. But 'any attempt to abuse the power of the movement or to fight upon anything other than a simple and easily understandable and strictly industrial issue would be fraught with grave dangers of disaster'.[17]

The acting general secretary made no attempt to hide his anxiety about the industrial outlook facing the trade union movement in the winter of 1925–26. In an interview with Herbert Tracey, the TUC's chief press officer, in December 1925, he may have seemed 'calm and dispassionate', 'methodical with an orderly mind and a tidy work table', but Citrine was pessimistic about the consequences of a growing trend by workers towards 'centralised mass action' with solidarity 'no longer a sentiment but a basis of policy'.[18] The extension of strikes to cover workers not directly involved with the issue in dispute would, he believed, lead to a nation-wide industrial conflict and the state would not be able to abstain from intervention because of its responsibilities to the well-being of society as a whole. Citrine believed that in such circumstances the government would be unable to avoid allying with the employers as it sought to maintain essential food supplies and meet other community needs. 'The government is forced to engage in strike-breaking or abdicate its functions as a government', Citrine admitted as he predicted the country was 'moving to a total crisis in its economic affairs'. So what could the unions do about this? To that vital question he was unable to provide any satisfactory answer. But his mood at the time suggests he was reluctant and apprehensive about leading the TUC into a conflict with the government which he did not believe the trade unions could possibly win.

The candour of Citrine's arguments indicates that he was trying to alert his general council colleagues to the realities of what was a highly volatile and unpredictable situation. The time for rhetorical posturing was coming to an end. Unions would have to face the consequences of their own words. He believed no government would tolerate any disruption of essential food supplies. 'A general strike is a literal impossibility', he concluded. Citrine revealed his gloomy thoughts in more detail in a memorandum he presented to a joint meeting of the TUC's special industrial committee and Miners' Federation leaders on 19 February 1926. In public, he agonised over the 'problem of trade union leadership'. Citrine believed industry was moving into a new era of large-scale national strikes that would replace small isolated stoppages. In an often inchoate way the unions were broadening their bargaining horizons beyond limited sectional interests and recognising that on working hours, wages and essential labour conditions it was better to fight together than individually. But Citrine was unconvinced that the trade unions were really prepared to abandon their traditions and practices and display the necessary practical collective solidarity to ensure success. The British trade union movement had 'been built up to redress immediate economic injustices not to change violently and fundamentally the social system in accordance with any abstract theory'.[19] He insisted it would be through the 'hard school of experience' that trade union members would be 'brought to a full realisation of the necessity for establishing that form of organisation which will best enable the movement to function as a single effective unit'.

Moreover, Citrine insisted that all his trade union life he had 'steadfastly adhered to the conviction that the control of policy must be vested absolutely and completely in the hands of the rank and file', and not by implication to a body like the TUC. The growth of national collective agreements since the end of the Great War was making such a commitment to worker participation over vital decisions more difficult to achieve and the need for centralised trade union authority ever more necessary. Citrine cast doubt on the sense of talking about a disciplined army of labour when trade unions first had to be accountable to their own members. The trade unions in times of crisis had not been endowed with the authority to make decisions on their own responsibility without recourse to securing rank and file approval. Citrine believed there was 'no workable alternative to the concentration of power in the hands of comparatively few people if decisive and effective action was to be taken on a large scale in cases of urgent necessity'. But this also meant that effective mass action could only be sought when the trade union movement was 'fighting for the maintenance of essential principles'. As he explained:

> Nothing would more surely lead to the disintegration of the movement than a reckless abuse of power and the responsibility which its possession must bring, is of itself a guarantee against precipitate or improper use of the might which the trade union movement is steadily building up. The traditions, temperament and the inherent commonsense of our movement will prevent anything like a dictatorship of officials. We need not fear the phantom of a bureaucracy. The need at the moment is for a movement to inculcate a thorough recognition by the workers of the class consciousness and confidence which the new strategy will entail and the sweeping away of the suspicion, jealousies, misunderstanding and resentments which the mischievous doctrine of 'don't trust your leaders' was calculated to foster.[20]

Such a realistic analysis from Citrine on the eve of the 1926 General Strike highlighted his conviction that the TUC would have to move forward carefully if it was to avoid a confrontation with the state which it could not possibly hope to win and which might lead to its humiliating defeat. The acting general secretary did not relish the prospect of having to lead the trade unions in such a perilous, high-risk direction. But Citrine was also aware that a national showdown between the forces of capital and labour was becoming inevitable. He wanted therefore to see the TUC at least make some contingency planning so it would not find itself out-manoeuvred by the government. Late in 1925 he suggested that the executives of affiliate unions should make changes in their rulebooks so that they could at least, after consultation with the TUC general council, call on their own members to participate in sympathy stoppages. 'I was out, by this process, to take the first step towards getting authority more centralised', he explained. 'I felt to take the power vested in the general council would be too great a step to take at one stride. It appeared to me, therefore, that if the executives themselves could be endowed with authority and trusting to the enthuasism of the moment in time of crisis, there would not be much doubt that they would cede in accordance with the general council's realities.'[21] But Citrine's senior colleagues on the TUC's industrial committee 'refused point blank to entertain the suggestion'. Ben Tillett, veteran union leader and then chairman of the Transport and General Workers Union, even warned him that if he persisted with such an idea he would split the trade union movement from top to bottom.

It would be wrong, however, to suggest that Citrine was seeking to avoid a confrontation by advocating a strategic retreat. As he argued in a speech he made in Tottenham on 8 March 1926, the full text of which is contained inside his fascinating mining crisis diaries:

> No matter how we may blank our eyes or try to conceal the facts from ourselves we are always up against the fact that at some point the forces of capital and labour must be arranged in opposite camps. As a consequence there must be the same phenomenon of a test of the relative strength of each side – capital on the basis of production for profit, labour about to get as much as possible for the worker out of the capitalist system and by improving its own capacity for assistance, organising strongly to wrest from capital that surplus now known as profit.[22]

Citrine sketched what he saw as the evolution of trade unionism since its mid-nineteenth-century position of 'defence not defiance' through to 1889 New Unionism and the emergence of solidarity strikes after 1911. 'In my opinion our trade union movement has never given sufficient attention in recent years to finding its own direction', explained Citrine. 'There have been ideas partially articulated by people who did not understand what they would imply. As a consequence of that, coupled with the switching over of the industrial movement into political channels from 1900, there has scarcely been an industrial psychology at all.' He wanted the trade union movement to recognise that economic liberty must always condition political power. Unless you have an active, virile movement at the point of production, all your political power is valueless. I do not want to be interpreted as trying to preach the doctrine of anti-politics. I am not a fool, I hope, and as long as people are endowed with two hands they should use both and I am perfectly confident that without a strong political weapon, it would be impossible for Labour and the working class to fulfil its destiny and mission so easily as it could by the addition of political power. I am trying to preach the fundamental lesson that the trade union movement as such has become overshadowed by the importance of the political movement and the working class with a remarkable frailty has swung from side to side. I don't want the working class movement to swing away from political power to industrial power as it has done in the last few months. I prefer there should be a clearer recognition of the two different spheres.

The tangled story of the 1926 General Strike has been told many times.[23] What needs emphasising is Citrine's own personal role in the industrial crisis and how it strengthened his existing views about what the role of the TUC should be. In the heated and protracted discussions among members of the TUC general council he often appeared to play a subordinate role to that of the senior figures on the TUC general council like Jimmy Thomas, general secretary of the National Union of Railwaymen, Arthur Pugh from the Iron and Steel Trades Confederation, and above all Ernest Bevin, the powerful general secretary of the new giant Transport and General Workers Union. But Citrine was to provide a calm, rational, sensible and sobering influence in the course of what were highly emotional events. The unpublished extracts of his diaries suggest that the General Strike – lasting eight days from midnight of 3 May until 12.20 p.m. on 12 May 1926 – was never really the congenial or stoical affair symbolised by football matches between strikers and the police. There was an underlying tension, a genuine fear of the possibility of the eruption of bloody conflict between trade unionists and the armed forces running through many of its pages. Citrine's earlier pessimistic realism was strengthened during the early days of the stoppage. As he wrote on 5 May:

I sit in the committee and wonder how it is all going to end. We are constantly reiterating our determination not to allow the strike to be directed into an attack on the constitution but while there is any suspicion of this it seems impossible for the government to capitulate.

Probably the usual British compromise will be arranged at the finish and whatever we may see in the form of temporary organisation to run services, we must remember that the loss the strike is causing can be measured in millions.[24]

After five days of the strike he noted: 'We can hold out for three or four weeks at the longest. I do not think it possible to continue longer than that. Even the most ardent advocates of the general strike have usually reasoned in terms of a few hours or a days' stoppage at the most.' 'Can we afford to risk complete defeat?', he wondered.

I do not mean defeat in the sense of our movement never being able to recover but to risk the disintegration that may follow rapidly from a return to work in certain sections. The logical thing is to make the best conditions while our members are solid. We must retreat, if we have to retreat under compulsion, as an army and not as a rabble. At the same time we must not get too badly rattled merely because the government is talking big.

Perhaps, however, much to Citrine's surprise and that of his general council colleagues, little evidence was reported from around the country, at least up until 11 May, that those who had been called out on strike in the first wave by their unions were anxious for an early return to work if this meant deserting the miners. 'The men are as firm as a rock', he admitted. So why was the TUC leadership growing increasingly apprehensive about the course of the dispute? 'I think it is because most of us know that no matter how determined our men are now, once the strike has reached its highest point and the maximum of members have been called out, a gradual decline in economic power must ensue', he wrote in his diary. 'Then we shall have dribblings back to work here and there and possibly large desertions.' On 11 May he noted: 'We have kept the destructive elements strongly under control so far but I am afraid that if there is any feeling of the miners being let down there will be strong passions afterwards.'[25] By then, however, pressures for a settlement were growing more intense inside the TUC general council. Citrine quoted Thomas as saying: 'I have given you of my best. I feel there is no more service I can render. I feel it in my bones because I know much more than others know. But having felt that my only effort has failed, I repeat to you that I can make no further contribution.'[26] The calling off of the national strike required an inevitable but unsatisfactory climbdown by the TUC general council. In return for abandoning its action the TUC won no assurances at all from the government that it would respond in a positive way to Samuel's report recommending an immediate pay cut for the miners coupled with talks to restructure the coal industry. Citrine reflected bitterly in his diary on the cabinet he and general council leaders faced at 10 Downing Street on the morning of 12 May.

> I looked at them with mixed feelings – bitterness – when I reflected one of them at least would have butchered our people without compunction on any pretext which offered. I thought to myself what an anomaly it is that there should be such a thing as a governing class. I comforted myself with the reflection that some day that would be altered.[27]

Such private thoughts – not even published in his memoirs – reveal the depths of genuine anger aroused as a result of the General Strike in a man who was normally criticised by the left for being too rational and not emotional enough.

'We have had our general strike. Imperfect as it has been, mechanically and in the evolution of policy, it has been the most magnificent effort of rank and file solidarity, that the British movement has ever displayed', wrote Citrine.[28] But he added: 'Never again will the Congress undertake the custodianship of any movement without the clear, specific and unalterable understanding that the general council, and the general council alone, shall have the free untrammelled right to determine policy.' 'The outstanding lesson of the general strike of 1926 is that authority must be invested exclusively and entirely in the directing body', he added. In unpublished extracts of his diary Citrine expressed his contempt for the behaviour of Arthur Cook, the Miners' Federation general secretary, 'hasty in judgement and full of selfishness', 'inflated with a sense of his own importance although he never loses sight of his humble origin and equipment'.[29] By contrast he expressed his admiration for the stubborn but authentic and tragic resistance of Herbert Smith, the federation's blunt-speaking president. His views of Bevin were not all complimentary either. As Citrine recalled, Bevin 'did not like to suggest it but could anyone doubt that with his unrivalled experience of strikes and the fact that nature had endowed him with a constructive brain, the Deity had specially ordained him to run the first general strike in Great Britain'.[30]

Citrine's earlier analysis of the obstacles to effective trade union unity was confirmed by the outcome of the General Strike. The TUC 'is a loose aggregation of members held together only by a perception of an identity of interest in some principal matters', he concluded. 'Just what makes up that identity of interest is far too complex to analyse here – trade rivalry, craft identity, demarcation difficulties, individual union disputes, the temperaments and motives of individual men – all cause differences just as they do in any large human organisation.'[31] But he also pointed in the privacy of his diary to another enduring lesson the TUC learned from the experience of the General Strike. 'The worst thing about this dispute and possibly about all of these large disputes in my view is the implication that class bitterness and class hatred are essential to trade unions.'[32] Citrine believed that whatever the outcome, the miners who remained locked out and in dispute would have to 'learn to face the facts'. 'We cannot expect to build up our movement if opinion is to be enslaved by the yells of the mob. If we do, then goodbye to the Labour Movement as an enduring moral and ethical factor', he admitted.

'I did not regard the general strike as a failure', Citrine claimed 30 years later in his memoirs. 'Nor do I today. It is true it was ill-prepared and that it had been called off without any consultation with the unions who took part in it.'[33] But 'the fact is the theory of the general strike had never been thought out', he admitted.

The machinery of the trade unions was unfortunately not adapted to it. Their rules had to be broken to give power to the general council to declare the strike. However illogical it may seem for me to say so, it was never aimed against the state as a challenge to the constitution. It was a protest against the degradation of the standards of life of millions of good trade unionists. It was a sympathetic strike on a national scale.

And he added:

The general strike was an abnormality outside the provision of trade union rules or even British trade union conceptions It has been used on the continent of Europe before and since but always with a limited objective, albeit sometimes an entirely political one. No general strike could ever function without adequate local organisation and the trade unions were not ready to devolve such necessary powers on the only local agents which the TUC has – the trades councils.

The new direction

The experience of the General Strike and its aftermath strengthened Citrine's conviction on the way the TUC needed to evolve as a national institution. It confirmed his doubts about the use of coordinated industrial action as a weapon in any wider dispute that might involve a confrontation with an elected government. But the events of 1926 also strengthened Citrine's belief that the TUC needed to move in 'a new direction' that would transform itself into a necessary and respected body in public policy-making both in relation to employer associations and if possible the state. Citrine wanted a modernisation programme aimed at ensuring the TUC was 'indispensable to the affiliated unions; to establish a leadership which they would be willing to follow and to demonstrate the capacity of the General Council was ready to act as the general staff that most progressive trade unionists wanted'.[34] These objectives were to be reinforced by a clear-sighted determination to see the trade union movement 'exert its influence in an ever-widening sphere and not be contained within the traditional walls of trade union policy'. As Citrine explained in his memoirs as he began to establish a grip on the TUC's policy agenda in the aftermath of the General Strike:

> Events were moving fast and the widely held belief in the impending collapse of capitalism would not suffice. We must try to expand the activities of the TUC until we could establish an efficient system whereby the TUC would be regularly and naturally consulted by whatever government was in power on any subject of direct concern to the unions.

Citrine acknowledged that he could not proclaim such a strategy 'from the housetops' because he knew it would meet with stiff resistance from many TUC-affiliated unions, who wanted to protect their autonomy from any further moves to centralisation. 'There is an innate conservatism and individualism in the trade union movement, just as there is in other sections of British life', he explained. 'The central bodies of employers, just like the TUC, while always ready to guide and influence the affairs of their constituent bodies, carefully avoid bringing too much pressure and studiously refrain from interference in their members' domestic affairs.'[35] However, after 1926 Citrine pressed ahead on the 'assumption that these were already features' of accepted TUC policy and that it was necessary to 'prosecute them steadfastly not noisily'. The need for greater professional competence in the TUC's administration was not to be an end in itself but a necessary means for ensuring affiliate unions would allow the TUC to act collectively on their behalf over what he hoped would be a widening public policy agenda.

'I am not so egotistical as to assume that my promotion to this position [of general secretary] is due to any superlative personal merit of my own', Citrine told the 1926 Congress as he accepted the position of general secretary.[36] 'Long ago the trade union movement so far as organisation is concerned passed the point when the individual is all paramount. I have realised that and have attempted to apply the lessons which it brings. We are all creatures of a fate to a much greater extent than we know.' Such self-effacement helped partly to disguise his ultimate and ambitious intentions for the TUC. However, Citrine was shrewd enough to realise he would have to move with care and sensitivity if he intended to make sure the TUC general council could grow in collective stature and authority over affiliate unions. But at no stage was he prepared to risk a public confrontation with union leaders over such a fundamental issue. 'I tried steadily to take the initiative in all those questions of general policy which were of common interest', he admitted. What Citrine would really have liked to have created was a strong and dominant TUC which could act as an effective counter-vailing influence to the Confederation of Employers' Organisations and the Federation of British Industry. As he admitted in his memoirs, the real problem was not trade union structure but power – 'the power to act on policy issues in a cohesive manner'. 'This could be done only by a central body representing all the unions', he explained.

People who thought like myself had for years been talking about a general council for labour. 'All power to the general council' they declared. Such slogans seemed not only eminently desirable but just plain common sense. Alas! We did not realise how conservative a force the trade union movement could be in relation to its own affairs. Our unions could draft plans in the course of a few sessions to put the whole world right. But the general council had to be extremely careful not to try to press them into making internal changes they did not care for. We had to carry the unions with us and retain their good will.[37]

Over the next 13 years from the General Strike to the outbreak of the Second World War, Citrine sought to modernise the TUC in a single-minded attempt to turn the organisation into an indispensable Estate of the Realm, the sole representative collective voice of organised labour in its relations with governments and national employer associations. In his ambitious strategy, he worked effectively in harness with Bevin although both men's strong personalities were hardly compatible. As Bevin's biographer, Alan Bullock, explained:

> On every big issue they had been in agreement and their combination of talents in pushing a policy through the TUC was invincible. Their gifts were unusually complementary: Citrine lucid and methodical, drawing upon his famous note-books for the facts, Bevin ranging and impressionistic, throwing out ideas; the one a master of exposition, the other of conviction and imagination.[38]

It was true, as Bullock explained, that the two men agreed on the big issues without any need for them to arrange any preconceived planning on a common strategy. Somehow they found a way of working together for the greater good of the TUC despite their obvious personal and mutual antipathies. In Bullock's phrase, it was 'one of the most successful involuntary partnerships in modern politics'. But it is also clear that Citrine could also usually count on the support of a number of other substantial trade union leaders on the general council, notably Charles Duke and Arthur Hayday from the General and Municipal Workers Union and Arthur Pugh of the Iron and Steel Trades Confederation.

The political atmosphere in the immediate aftermath of the General Strike hardly seemed conducive to the emergence of the kind of close and constructive relationship between the state and the TUC that Citrine sought as his long-term objective. Whatever his private feelings might have been about healing the wounds, Baldwin proceeded to introduce highly restrictive anti-union legislation in the shape of the 1927 Trade Disputes and Trade Unions Act, which was even opposed by Arthur Steel-Maitland, his Minister of Labour. This petty and punitive measure banned civil service trade unions from belonging to the TUC. It also changed the procedure of contracting-out to contracting-in for a union member's payment of the political levy in a move designed to hit Labour Party finances. In addition, the measure outlawed any form of solidarity actions or strikes that were 'designed or calculated to coerce the government, either directly or indirectly by inflicting hardship on the community'. The legislation also limited the use of picketing in industrial disputes.[39] It was no consolation to Citrine and his TUC colleagues to know Baldwin's cabinet were divided over what it should do and might have passed an even more draconian measure to avenge the General Strike if hawkish ministers had had their way.

The TUC and the Labour Party formed a joint action committee to oppose the 1927 Act. Citrine questioned openly whether Baldwin approved his own government's Bill. 'There is a general feeling abroad that the government has been rushed into this mad act by the extreme element in the cabinet – the damn the consequences brigade. Mr Baldwin is obviously not comfortable about the position', he argued. 'The plain truth is that the government's Bill is a smoke screen behind which a gas attack on the workers has been prepared. The Bill is not a product of statesmanship – it is a nightmare of men who have abandoned reason. It has been rushed forward not to meet a national emergency but as part of the preparations for the coming struggle at the polls.'[40] Citrine suggested the measure could 'have no permanent place on the statute book for it is not an expression of the people's will, it is unEnglish in character; it was conceived and is being forced through the House in a spirit alien to that which must guide our Parliament if it is to live'.

Citrine's intemperate language did not suggest he was in the mood to become the articulate advocate of a managed corporatism between the state and the TUC in 1927. In a later bulletin he spoke in a way that belied the left-wing picture of a grey functionary in search of industrial consensus. As Citrine asserted:

> People run away with the idea that the English Tories' idea of fright-fulness is after all a mild one. They have not openly murdered workers, or set fire to their houses or bombed their villages. These things are only done abroad. That is because in England the governing class can get what they want without crude violence of that sort. They are more subtle. They can speak words to cover unfair acts. They can offer prizes while they take liberties. They can talk of conciliation while they are busy reducing wages.[41]

It is true that the 1927 Act turned out in practice to be much less oppressive to the trade unions than they had initially feared, but it was to remain a constant source of irritation to the TUC until its eventual repeal by the Labour government in 1946. Even during the Second World War Churchill was not prepared to accede to the demand that the measure should either be shelved or repealed despite persistent TUC lobbying. The Act was always regarded by the TUC as a vindictive use of state power against the interests of organised labour. For nearly 20 years it was a festering symbol of the estranged relations that continued to exist between the TUC and the government no matter what obvious improvement there was to be during the 1930s.

Despite such hostile legislation, however, Citrine was determined to promote a more conciliatory form of trade unionism after 1926 within the voluntarist framework of the British system of industrial relations. He believed the General Strike had put an end once and for all to any romantic yearnings about the efficacy of direct action that might have lingered on inside the TUC as a syndicalist alternative to the use of parliamentary lobbying and application of political pressure on governments. In the relatively calmer atmosphere of the late 1920s Citrine argued that it made sense to try and make 'the worker's organisations an integral part of the economic machinery of society'; 'to allow them to be used as instruments of social upheaval will be fatal to our hopes of ordered progress', he believed.[42] In Citrine's opinion, the moment was ripe for the promotion of his own ideas in the expectation he would receive willing support for them not just from most affiliate unions but progressive employers and perhaps eventually even a paternalistic state that Baldwin claimed he wanted to establish.

For the first time in its history, the TUC had a man as general secretary who was keen to adopt a more active and far-sighted strategy that would assist the trade unions in abandoning their normally reactive and defensive role and demonstrate their relevance as willing partners in a process of industrial rationalisation through cooperation with employers. Citrine first spelt out what he had in mind by New Unionism in a signed article, published in the *Manchester Guardian* in November 1927.[43] He believed trade unionism had 'reached the end of a definite stage in its evolution'. It had established 'a virtually unchallenged control of the organised power of the workers'. Trade unionism had 'attained a position of great authority'. 'It has become a power in the land with a growing consciousness of purpose to which increased responsibilities and obligations cannot fail to be attached', explained Citrine. The next stage in trade unionism's evolution now depended 'upon a general recognition of the changes taking place in industry and of the part which the workers' organisations were qualified to play in the promotion of efficiency, economy and scientific development in the productive system'.

Citrine tried to reassure any doubting trade unions that the new direction he envisaged for the TUC would involve no break with past practice. 'It is a travesty of industrial history to represent the unions as carrying on an incessant conflict with employers with the object of making the present system unworkable', he pointed out. It was 'almost entirely due to the unions that joint consultation and negotiation had been established across most industries and trades to settle industrial disputes'. Citrine argued that the main purpose of trade unions in the past had been to get the best out of the existing system for their members, to defend workers' living standards against employer attacks, to improve those standards wherever possible and to meet 'the dictatorship of irresponsible capitalist groups by the organisation of social and economic power among the workers'. Up until the 1920s, Citrine explained, trade unions had pursued very much a hand-to-mouth policy, responding to events without any clear and comprehensive plan in mind. But now there was a 'steady growth of conscious purpose among the unions and an equally marked tendency towards the concentration of authority in the hands of a central body representative of the whole organised movement'.

Citrine believed this development could be seen in the growing powers that were being provided to the TUC by its affiliate unions 'not only to intervene in industrial disputes in which some vital question of principle affecting the unions as a whole is involved but also empowering the general council to undertake negotiations on general basic principles and to coordinate the policy of the unions on general questions'. 'Vested with these powers, it is clearly within the province of the general council to formulate its ideas in a concrete and practical form for the guidance of the organised movement in the immediate future', he argued.

But Citrine did not envisage greater power being provided for the TUC simply as an administrative means for imposing a more centralised authority over the way trade unions behaved. He argued that what he had in mind was a more far-reaching industrial objective for the trade unions. He believed they should 'actively participate in a concerted effort to raise industry to its highest efficiency by developing the most scientific methods of production, eliminating waste and harmful restrictions, removing causes of friction and avoidable conflict and promoting the largest possible output so as to provide a rising standard of life and continuously improving conditions of employment'. Citrine wanted trade unions to become positive partners with employers in their plans for industrial change. He reasoned it would be unthinkable if trade unions were obstructive or took a merely negative attitude, because they could not prevent the profound changes going on in the organisation and control of industry and would effectively silence themselves in claiming a share in the responsibility of guiding developments.

'The way to a new industrial order is not by way of a social explosion but by a planned reconstruction in which the unions will assume a larger share of control in directing industrial changes', reasoned Citrine. He pointed to the vast changes taking place 'in technology, in management methods, in the enlargement in the scale of production, finance and organisation as well as the growth of scientific research, psychological investigation and enlightened common sense that were being applied to work out the principles of a more efficient, economical and humane system of production'. This was summed up by the term 'the rationalisation of industry', which he claimed was spreading rapidly in highly industrialised communities. 'Standardised products, simplified processes, scientific planning of workshops, labour-saving machinery, improved management techniques' were to be rationalisation's guiding principles.

The sheer scale of Citrine's ambitions for the trade unions appeared to herald a radical breach with past TUC practice. But ever the practical man of action, Citrine sought to translate his trade union objectives into reality through the development of a voluntary, practical dialogue with employers. The initiative for such a move was taken at the 1927 Trades Union Congress. On that occasion George Hicks, general secretary of the Amalgamated Union of Building Trade Workers, agreed with Citrine to use the opportunity provided by his TUC presidential address to call for the establishment of an 'industrial peace' through joint consultation between the TUC and representative employer organisations which he hoped could lead to cooperation in 'a common endeavour to improve the efficiency of industry and raise the workers' standards of life'.[44] Citrine was mainly responsible for the drafting of that part of Hicks's conciliatory speech. Unfortunately it brought an immediate but negative response from the National Confederation of Employers' Organisations and the Federation of British Industry who saw no good reason why they should want to seek a closer understanding with the TUC after its defeat in the General Strike.

However, on 23 November 1927 a more positive employer reaction came in a letter to the TUC general council from 24 senior industrialists led by Sir Alfred Mond (later Lord Melchett), chairman of Imperial Chemical Industries. He proposed that an industrial conference should be held with the TUC to discuss issues of industrial reorganisation and industrial relations. Despite predictable opposition to such an offer from the Communist Party and Arthur Cook, the Mineworkers' Federation general secretary, the TUC general council accepted Mond's personal invitation for such a meeting. The first joint session was held on 12 January 1928 at Burlington House in London. Mond headed the employer delegation while Ben Turner, general secretary of the National Union of Textile Workers, led the TUC contingent as that year's TUC president. Citrine made it clear from the outset of what came to be known as the Mond–Turner talks that 'he believed it was possible to achieve a higher standard of living even under the present system without prejudice to their conception of the future system of industry. There must be no thought of excluding any topic whatever from discussion that the workers' side thought relevant. There might ultimately evolve from this conference an organisation which could speak for the whole of industry.'[45] He added:

I am one of those people who have talked in my time as vehemently and indignantly about the evils of capitalism as anyone who has stood on Labour platforms but I recognise that a time must come in the history of the industrial movement of this country when it tries to translate into practical achievement some of the shibboleths and slogans it has uttered from Labour platforms ... I can see no joy to the workers of this country in an early collapse of the capitalist system.

Citrine believed the Mond–Turner talks could mark a turning point in relations between the TUC and employer associations. If progress was not made, then the dangers of the unions moving leftwards into a confrontation strategy would become more likely. A substantial majority of the TUC general council was not disheartened by the lack of any tangible progress after their first meeting with Mond and his colleagues and they agreed by 18 votes to 6 against to continue with their discussions. An attempt by the TUC left to question Mond's good faith because of his alleged sympathy for Mussolini's Fascist regime in Italy, failed to persuade Citrine and his colleagues to abandon the talks.

The TUC general council pointed out that the list of items on the agenda of the joint talks were 'the things the trade union movement had been claiming for years to have some voice in but for years that right had been denied'.[46] A policy document was presented to the 1928 Congress by the general council, calling for the establishment of a full-scale Industrial Conference. Among its recommendations were a call for the establishment of a national industrial council made up of TUC representatives and the two national employer associations which was to meet quarterly to discuss industrial issues. Joint conciliation boards were also favoured to resolve disputes at industry level. But the first practical aim of the Mond–Turner talks sought to secure employer recognition for trade unions based on the principle that those who participated in production should also participate in the prosperity of industry. The planned agenda was to cover a range of issues of concern to the trade unions. These also consisted of collective bargaining, security of employment, the raising of the status of the industrial worker, moves to prevent the victimisation of workers, legal regulation of working hours, the formation of works councils, the provision of company information to workers, an investigation into the potential causes of disputes, the extension of the function of industrial courts, more factory legislation, improved health and unemployment insurance, provision of machinery to enable workers to make suggestions and constructively criticise employers.

Other areas for possible joint action were to cover unemployment, the distribution of the proceeds of commodities and services with a 'high wages policy', consideration of plans for participation in industry, payment by results and minimum wage principles as well as the organisation, technique and control of industry. It was also proposed to cover industrial rationalisation – restructuring to improve efficiency, flexibility, elasticity and testing of experimental conditions, the effect of unnecessary internal competition, sheltered industries and distribution. Financial issues were to be covered, including the future of banking and credit, taxation and local rates and the financing of industry. In addition, institutional questions were to be placed on the agenda such as the possible creation of a national industrial council and a permanent standing committee to meet for regular consultation on matters affecting industry, the coordination of presentation and if necessary the provision of further machinery for continuous investigation into industrial conditions. International questions were not to be neglected either, such as the problem of competition with countries with lower labour standards, the future of trade agreements and labour conventions.

In its report to the 1928 Congress the TUC general council pointed out the trade unions faced three clear strategic options. One was to adopt a revolutionary strategy to break the capitalist system. But the report added that this had been 'decisively rejected as futile, certain to fail, and sure to lead to bloodshed and misery'. A second option was to stand aside and do nothing, telling employers to get on with their own job while the unions pursued their sectionalist aims for improvements. 'The objections to this course are that it is entirely inconsistent with the modern demand for a completely altered status of the workers in industry, a confession of failure for unions to say they are going to take no hand in the momentous changes that are taking place in the economic life of the nation', argued the Citrine-inspired document.[47]

The TUC favoured what it called 'the third option'. This aimed to provide the organisation with 'a voice as to the way industry is carried on, so that it can influence the new developments that are taking place

– the unions can use their power to promote and guide the scientific reorganisation of industry as well as to obtain material advantages from that reorganisation'.[48] Citrine fought hard to convince the delegates that they had nothing to fear from conversations between the TUC and Mond and his business allies. He described the joint document they had issued as 'a logical, common sense, sequential step in the development of trade unionism', although it would not achieve the millennium. Citrine claimed what the TUC was doing was consistent with international trade union developments. As he argued: 'World trade unionism stands at the present time for the voice of the worker in the administration and control of industry, to be heard in the councils of the employers.' But he added: 'I say emphatically to talk about exercising control of industry without meeting the employers to discuss that control, is a figment of the imagination. We cannot await the advent of the breakdown of capitalism before we start marching towards control.' Citrine faced some stiff criticism for his arguments, particularly from James Brownlie, president of the AEU engineering union, who accused the TUC general council of going beyond its remit over the Mond–Turner talks. He wanted to amend their report by postponing a decisive decision on approving it until affiliated union executives had determined what they should do. Brownlie was supported by his AEU colleague Swales and even Hicks who appeared to have dropped his earlier enthusiasm for the initiative of joint discussions. Outright resistance came from Cook and A. G. Tomkins from the Communist-dominated Furnishing Trades Association. But Bevin and Thomas both strongly backed Citrine's stand. The AEU's proposed amendment was defeated with 2,921,000 against and 768,000 in favour.

In the aftermath of the 1928 Congress, further meetings were held between the TUC's industrial committee, now chaired by Tillett, and Lord Melchett's employer group on the subject of unemployment. A joint committee was established to examine the facts. This was followed by a joint conference between the two sides held on 12 March 1929 to finalise a joint statement on unemployment. However, the Mond–Turner talks – begun with some hope of a new approach – were eventually to founder in the face of employer indifference and intransigence. Allan Smith, chairman of the Engineering Employers Federation, led a rearguard action as both the main employer bodies refused to take a positive view of such discussions. Citrine's hopes of 1927 gradually ebbed away.

Citrine recognised that a serious problem for the TUC's efforts lay in the lack of any coherent and powerfully centralised employer association to which the TUC was able to respond in an effective manner. As he noted in January 1928:

> It clearly looks to me as if it will be necessary ... that an organisation must be created on the side of the employers to which firms will receive their authority as they proceed ... There is no body on the employers' side able to speak authoritatively on behalf of the whole of industry ... We have to create a joint body (between the TUC and employers) but we have to get the authority for the separate body. This may be a long job ... It may be, of course, that the body we form will be only a purely advisory or consultative one. Nothing we say will be in the position of binding the respective constituents. I am afraid that is the position which we will be faced with for a long time.[49]

However, the lack of much progress as a result of Mond–Turner did nothing to discourage Citrine away from his modernisation strategy. He would have liked to see the acquisition of greater centralising powers over its affiliate unions. 'My own view is that the proper course for the TUC to pursue, while all the time trying to foster the idea of closer association and amalgamation as it is doing today, is gradually to absorb function after function of the unions which the unions have hitherto exercised imperfectly or not at all but which are nevertheless common to all the unions.'[50] He went on: 'If trade unionism is evolving and widening its scope, it follows that new functions will appear and it is the bounden duty of some central body such as the TUC to take over those functions and perform them for the unions, leaving the unions to pursue their traditional functions and those which they are best qualified to peform.'

Citrine continued to envisage an increasingly influential role for the TUC in the life of the modern state. He believed the TUC needed to establish a distinctive role for itself in the political economy beyond its close relationship with the Labour Party. 'We must get away from the idea that the Labour party is an alternative to trade unionism', he reasoned.

> It is evidence of muddled thinking and is simply silly. I have heard speakers urge, before the election, that all that is necessary is to give a vote to the Labour party. What is the effect of this on people's minds? Why should a man pay about 1s a week to a trade union if he can secure his emancipation by the easy means of placing a cross on a ballot paper every few years? The Labour party is not an alternative

to trade unionism. It has its own functions and is a valuable asset to us. The TUC, whether there is a Labour government in office or not, will pursue its legislative function. It will be bound to regard any government in office as a body to whom proposals have to be submitted by the trade union movement.[51]

Citrine's vision of effective and responsible trade unionism required the creation of a professional full-time staff to service the TUC's own organisation. In 1924 its head office still had a staff of only 14; by 1930 its number had been increased to nearly 40. He accepted that the general council could not

> hope in present circumstances for years to rival the efficiency, adequate staffing and the elaborate arrangements made for dealing with the employers' business. When I was told the Federation of British Industries employed over 200 people in its office, I confess I did look forward to the day when this Congress might do the same thing and the Congress might be undertaking duties for the unions which would justify the employment of that number of people but those days are a long way off.[52]

Professor Hugh Clegg described Citrine's approach as 'elitist' in contrast to nineteenth-century trade unions who had 'relied on the solidarity of the members to regulate industrial relations'.[53] Under Citrine the emphasis was focused on the skills of negotiation and those who believed that such a strategy was best carried out by full-time officials and union executive members. The spread of bureaucracy, the greater centralisation of power in the unions and the move to national industry-based collective agreements – all intensified the pressure for following the Citrine version of modernisation. Unfortunately for the TUC, in the last years of the 1920s cooperation with companies had not turned out to be a successful option because of the negativism and indifference displayed by employer associations. But this did not stop the increased competence of the TUC office to develop its activities.

However, there was another strategy raised by the TUC after 1926, which was to have perhaps more long-lasting significance. Citrine was determined to carve out an autonomous and accepted role for the TUC in the wider political economy, whatever the attitude of the Labour Party might be towards it. In an important memorandum written in June 1927, Walter Milne-Bailey, head of the TUC's new research and economic department, spelt out what this would mean in practice. The

TUC was to have its own coherent and decisive public policy strategy quite separate and distinctive from that of the rest of the Labour Movement. As Milne-Bailey argued:

> It has appeared to outsiders that the unions first set the political movement on foot in order to assist industrial methods in achieving industrial objectives but that political aims and in particular socialism have become more and more important until at length they have swallowed their progenitor and now completely rule the working class movement, its philosophy and its methods. This view is silly – for the unions have gone on negotiating and otherwise taking an active part in the day-to-day problems and administration of the industrial process.[54]

While Citrine was trying to develop a more positive role for the TUC through cooperation with progressive employers and building up its capacity to deal with public policy issues, he was also determined to establish the organisation as a respectable and responsible body in the country's industrial life by the repudiation of any Communist-dominated left strategy or a return to the syndicalist tendencies of the early 1920s. Under his leadership the TUC set its face against political and industrial extremism. Citrine's hostile attitude was most apparent in his increasingly bitter opposition to the role he believed the Communist Party was playing inside industry and many trade unions. He was certainly assisted in his personal antipathy by the 'social Fascist' or 'class against class' phase of Communist strategic thought as the Soviet Union moved more firmly under Stalin's iron grip after 1928 and compelled the British party to fall into line behind an aggressive strategy that denounced organisations like the TUC as the enemy of the working class. The virulence of Citrine's resistance to both the Minority Movement and Wal Hannington's National Unemployed Workers' Movement reflected a deep antagonism towards Communism that was to last throughout his public life. In a series of signed articles, published in 1927 and 1928 in *Labour* magazine, Citrine attacked what he described as 'the cancer of Communist influence' inside the trade unions. 'Trade unionists generally do not realise the extent to which a deliberately organised attempt has been made to capture the trade union movement and to exploit it for a revolutionary subversive purpose', he argued.[55] 'The well-known tolerance and breadth of view concerning all creeds and forms of economic theory have made it slow to join issue with Communism.' But Citrine warned: 'We have seen our movement distracted and confused by savage criticism and weakened by a wholly unwarrantable influence in our affairs.' However, as he asserted: 'The knowledge that people who pay lip service to 100 per cent trade unionism and who shout loudly about the proletariat are little more than the worn and monotonous gramophone records of their master's voice from Moscow is preventing earnest trade unionists from being deceived by the forces of disruption.' Citrine's initiative was seen by him as a wake-up call to the trade unions to face up to the dangers of Communist subversion in their own organisations. In fact, his views were shared by most trade union leaders at that time who disliked the personal abuse being thrown on them by the Communists for their behaviour during the General Strike. At the 1927 Congress delegates voted overwhelmingly by 3,746,000 to only 148,000 against, to condemn Communist efforts to infiltrate the trade unions. They did so after listening to a characteristically clinical demolition of Communism in the unions from Citrine in which he identified the links between the Minority Movement and the Communist International and made it clear he would 'fight against anything which implies a duality of loyalty to the trade union movement'.[56] In the following year some left-wing delegates tried to force a reference back of the general council's report, because the TUC had forbidden Minority Movement members from attending the annual trades council conference. But their move was heavily defeated on a show of hands without even the need for a card vote. However, despite this massive rejection of the Communists at Congress, Citrine's sense of urgency about the danger they posed to the trade unions does not appear to have been shared by all affiliates. The TUC launched an inquiry into the 'dangers of disruption'. It reported in 1929 that 92 out of the 124 affiliate unions who had cooperated with the exercise had said they had no evidence of disruptive elements in their own organisations in 'greater or lesser degree'. While only 16 said they were having a 'bad effect' on their activities, a mere 8 unions considered them to be 'serious'.[57] The TUC inquiry admitted that many unions had shown 'considerable reluctance' to supply any details of disruption. 'We are glad to report with the exception of one or two cases the disruptive elements in the trade union movement instigated by the Communist party and the National Minority Movement are having a less and diminishing influence', the inquiry concluded. It suggested the unions themselves were 'capable and equal to the task of dealing with this matter of disruptive activity in their own way'.

However, the Communist 'problem' in the unions continued to concern Citrine for the rest of the inter-war years. 'The patience displayed by the trade union movement towards the disruptive activities of the Communist party is known world wide', he told delegates at the 1929 Congress.[58] 'There is no other trade union movement in the world that has displayed anything like the patience or the reluctance in coming to conclusive measures than our British trade union movement has done.' Citrine pointed out that the TUC had only finally acted against the Communists as a last resort after 'several years of an organised and subsidised system of propaganda used against it'.

Citrine was equally critical of the attitude adopted by the Soviet Union towards the TUC. He worked assiduously for the abolition of the Anglo-Russian Committee, which had been formed in 1925 with him as one of its joint secretaries.[59] In October of that year, Citrine travelled on a TUC delegation to the Soviet Union where he was unimpressed by what he saw and unsettled by the oppressive atmosphere. When Soviet trade union leaders began to attack the way the TUC had conducted itself during the General Strike, Citrine reacted angrily. As he told delegates at the 1927 Congress, the Russians were operating

> from the conception of the absolute right of [their] movement to dictate its policy to the rest of the world. The conception of the British trade union movement is radically different. Our movement has been built up on the principle of autonomy for its units nationally and internationally and on the authority of the British trade union movement to decide its own methods of progress.[60]

Citrine's speech was later described as a 'carefully phrased, unemotional and restrained discourse, free of invective, grandiloquence or tub-thumping'.[61] Nevertheless, it was highly effective in isolating left-wing opinion inside the TUC. The four to one majority among the unions in support of the TUC's position indicated widespread backing for the decision to cut the TUC's connections with the Soviet trade union movement.

A divided movement

By the end of the 1920s the TUC was in a confident mood. It had emerged from the trauma of the General Strike and developed under Citrine's guidance a moderate but wide-ranging strategy, repudiating the left and seeking conciliation where possible with sympathetic employers. But mass unemployment, a relatively hostile state, indifferent employers and a suspicious Labour Party, were obstacles to TUC modernisation.

However, the return of the second minority Labour government after the indecisive September 1929 general election encouraged Citrine into believing this would lead to the successful implementation of a more radical economic programme and closer cooperation between the TUC and the state. In its early months of office TUC leaders were well pleased by the government's performance. But Citrine was left in no doubt from the beginning that Chancellor Philip Snowden and the Treasury were not going to take much notice of TUC pressures for action. While he was to remain personally sympathetic to Ramsay MacDonald even after the formation of the National government, and continued to be so until the former Labour Party leader's death in 1935, Citrine was less than impressed by Snowden. 'I found him to be unexpectedly pompous, rigid, devoid of imagination and frigidly orthodox', he noted in his memoirs.[62] 'He had acquired the reputation of being the financial expert of the Labour movement. He could throw figures about in the millions on the platform with the best but I found that at close quarters he was by no means so capable.' For his part Snowden hardly bothered to conceal his contempt for Citrine and the TUC general council.

Over the next two years the minority Labour government and the TUC found it increasingly difficult to reach any common understanding on what needed to be done to rescue the British economy from deflation and the icy grip of the world depression which followed the Wall Street crash in October 1929. There was trouble from the start in convincing MacDonald and many of his senior cabinet colleagues on the need to consult and even inform the TUC on policy in a manner union leaders believed to be appropriate. Citrine wanted to have regular, consultative meetings held between the TUC and the government but MacDonald rejected such a suggestion, perhaps fearing the charge of TUC dictation. Nor would the government make use of the National Joint Council between the party and the TUC to coordinate policy. Margaret Bondfield, Minister of Labour, and J. R. Clynes, the Home Secretary, even refused to allow the TUC see draft legislation of relevance to the trade unions. Moreover, Citrine was irritated by the government's inconsistency in not consulting the TUC on the appointment of union representatives to public committees and inquiries. It seemed the Labour government was as unsympathetic as Baldwin had been to acceding to the TUC's desire to secure a strategic role as an important interest group in public policy-making in line with Citrine's New Unionism.

The inability or refusal of the Labour government to respond in a positive way to the TUC began to increasingly trouble Citrine and his colleagues. No progress was made at all with their efforts to secure a repeal of the hated 1927 Trade Disputes Act and MacDonald did little to endear himself to the TUC general council by the offhand way in which he dealt with them over the issue. Nor did the government make any progress of satisfaction on the TUC's wish for a ratification of the Washington convention which proposed the introduction of a maximum 48-hour working week and an eight-hour day across industry. But the main cause for growing division between the TUC and MacDonald concerned the government's handling of economic policy and, above all, mass unemployment. While it may be true to say the TUC produced no coherent and credible economic alternative to the Treasury's orthodox approach between September 1929 and August 1931 aimed at reducing the dole queues, critics are wrong to suggest that the trade unions were neither realistic nor credible in their attitude to what was becoming the country's gravest problem. In 1929 the TUC general council agreed to Citrine's proposal to establish a ten-strong economic committee of its own under the direction of Walter Milne-Bailey, a response to the discussions being held with employers. Its first task was to draw up a memorandum for submission to the Macmillan committee on finance and industry which MacDonald had created in November 1929. The TUC followed this up by preparing economic proposals to present to the Imperial conference in September 1930. The outcome of that particular exercise provoked internal differences of opinion inside the TUC when it appeared Citrine and Bevin were prepared to, at least, examine the merits of tariff protection and question the virtues of free trade. Under the pressure of events, the TUC's economic policy thinking was going through an agonising change of direction despite substantial opposition from Labour free trade traditionalists and the Communist left. However, at the same time the TUC leadership was growing increasingly disillusioned with the cabinet's acceptance of Snowden's cautious handling of the economy, which was doing nothing to reduce unemployment. Citrine and Bevin had accepted MacDonald's request in 1929 to join his Economic Advisory Council but this turned out to be an ineffective response to the growing economic crisis even if it enabled TUC officials to consort with the economist John Maynard Keynes.

In fact, the TUC was starting to develop a distinctive economic strategy of its own. The signs of the TUC's new approach were evident in the economic committee's 1930 document, setting out the strategic options facing the UK in the face of worsening economic conditions with soaring unemployment. It suggested the country could either link up with Europe in the creation of a new trading bloc, establish a similar arrangement within the British Commonwealth or form a closer economic relationship with the United States. The committee in 1930 favoured the development of a Commonwealth bloc in parallel with an extension of the League of Nations into economic governance. This would have involved initially regular economic conferences such as the forthcoming one to be held in London. These meetings would be made up of government, employers and trade unions appointed by all the Commonwealth countries on the lines of the 1927 world economic conference. An inter-commonwealth economic secretariat was also proposed, similar to that in the League of Nations. In an appendix to its 1930 report the economic committee denied that the TUC favoured the introduction of either protection or Imperial free trade. But its critical language cast doubt on the assumption that free trade still remained intact.

> Every nation and in practice if not in theory every party has long since abandoned the notion of complete freedom of trade (which incidentally would necessitate freedom in buying and selling labour). In almost every aspect of economic life regulation and conscious control of economic factors and forces is the accepted policy. Differences only concern the amount of regulation and control. It may or may not be desirable to hold up world-wide freedom of trade as an ultimate ideal but it is not and cannot be a working aim in the immediate situation of the world today. To the trade union and labour movements it can hardly be an ultimate ideal ever, since these movements rest on the belief that there should be conscious control of economic and political factors that can be controlled in the interests of human welfare. The notion that human welfare is, by some dispensation of providence best advanced by a complete absence of restrictions on 'freedom of trade' did not survive beyond the early years of the 19th century.[63]

The TUC document proposed a number of alternatives on how groups within nation states should establish economic links and work cooperatively together for the mutual advantage of their members. This, it argued, could cover agrements for the extraction of raw materials and minerals and perhaps conditional loans to purchase particular goods. The TUC gave the example of US investment in the Soviet five-year plan as one to admire. State control of raw materials as well as restrictions on labour immigration were also proposed. The TUC then added there might be an imposition of tariffs. On that option, the document was emphatic: 'Economic theory condemns the general policy of tariffs but political rather than economic considerations are usually the determining factor … it is all a matter of expediency in a given situation.' Although the committee did not recommend protection it believed the whole question needed to be 'looked at without prejudice and in the light of present day conditions'. But such ideas, however tentatively expressed, aroused widespread opposition inside many unions. At the 1930 Congress the TUC's economic report was almost defeated when 1,401,000 voted for its reference back with 1,878,000 supporting it. Bevin argued that the report sought to put before the Labour government a proposal for 'a definite economic organisation' inside the Empire. This would be an investigative body. But he added:

> It is a departure from the old method of leaving to the City of London the operation of the old monetary and free trade laissez faire system and saying that the devil can take the hindmost and we must develop the world for profit only. It is not a question of jumping to tariffs as being a solution to the problem. Tariffs are only the froth; they are merely the kind of thing lazy minds jump to. We have taken a different way. We have gone to the foundation.[64]

Loyalty to the Labour government among the trade unions, however, remained substantial despite deep differences of opinion over economic policy and personal animosities. The TUC was furious at the way the government created the Holman Gregory Commission on unemployment insurance without its participation or even asking for its advice on the body's terms of reference. Citrine and his colleagues were equally upset by the commission's resulting recommendations which said unemployment benefit should be limited to only 26 weeks in the year, contributions raised, level of benefit cut and a means test introduced. In the event, MacDonald decided not to implement such harsh proposals but the whole affair led to a further deterioration in TUC–government relations. However, many union leaders were still reluctant to take their growing anxieties to Snowden's handling of the economy to outright public resistance. The charismatic Oswald Mosley found his direct challenge to the party leadership over its economic strategy at the 1930 Labour conference brought him little support from the trade unions. Indeed, before the onset of the August 1931 crisis, the TUC was keen to cooperate as far as possible with MacDonald's government despite its mounting worries about where it was going. As Professor Hugh Clegg noted: 'To take decisive action, the union leaders and members would have had to believe that something could be done to increase employment in the circumstances of 1930. As it was, most of them appeared to accept the depression as a natural disaster, an "economic blizzard" which they must wait to blow itself out.'[65] Charles Beard from Bevin's own union and 1930 Congress president even declared: 'A long time ago many of us gave ourselves to the Labour party and we have no regrets. For myself, I still fully trust the Labour government. Furthermore, in these times of tense danger, I stand by the captain – by James Ramsay MacDonald.'[66]

However, the TUC was not prepared to cooperate with any government in crisis measures that would have meant cutting the size of the unemployment insurance fund as well as the level of unemployment benefit. Citrine and his colleagues may have lacked the economic knowledge or political strength to provide an acceptable alternative to Snowden's deflationary approach but they knew that they could not tolerate a strategy that involved further contraction in the economy and cuts in public spending which would lead to yet further unemployment and a squeeze on the living standards of the jobless. But it is hard to avoid reaching the conclusion that if MacDonald and his senior cabinet colleagues had taken the TUC general council fully into their confidence, treated them with understanding and respect and listened carefully to what Citrine and Bevin had to say, they may have found a much more sympathetic TUC facing them when the crisis of August 1931 erupted. It is quite possible that the damaging split that was to reverberate through Labour history for the next 50 years could have been avoided with some tact and sensitivity.

Nobody in the TUC really doubted that the government faced a grave situation. But at the TUC's 20 August 1931 meeting with the cabinet sub-committee and Labour's national executive at Transport House MacDonald failed to tell union leaders the exact details of what he intended to do. Snowden informed Citrine his proposed economies would include a reduction in the unemployment insurance fund, as well as cuts in the wages of civil servants, teachers and armed forces. But no proposal to cut the unemployment benefit rates was suggested at that stage and no indication was given of how Snowden's concept of 'equality of sacrifice' would work in practice. Citrine, speaking for the TUC general council, told MacDonald and Snowden that although the trade unions were ready to 'assist the government in the national emergency that had arisen', its apparent approach to the problem was 'of a character that would only lead to the accentuation of our economic difficulties'. Later that same evening the TUC economic committee met the cabinet and proposed alternative policies. These included the call for a graduated levy on profits, incomes and earnings covering all sections of the community in proportion to the ability to pay as well as a temporary suspension of the Sinking Fund and a tax on all fixed interest bearing securities and other unearned income. Citrine himself argued personally for a break with free trade and the creation of a revenue tariff to halt the fall in prices, but the TUC general council would not agree to this, saying any such decision must await the verdict of the forthcoming Congress in September.[67]

MacDonald was unimpressed by the TUC's alternatives. He wrote to Citrine on 21 August rejecting their proposals. 'Nothing gives me greater regret than to disagree with old industrial friends but I really personally find it absolutely impossible to overlook dread realities as I am afraid you are doing', he explained.[68] But as he noted in his diary: 'The TUC undoubtedly voice the feeling of the mass of workers. They do not know and their minds are rigid and think of superficial appearances and so grasping at the shadow they lose the bone.'[69] The TUC's critical intervention had, however, proved decisive for the future of his government. It stiffened the opposition from Arthur Henderson and other cabinet members to the deflationary measures the Treasury was proposing to restore overseas financial markets' confidence in sterling. In its report submitted to its September 1931 Bristol Congress the TUC spelt out its alternative. It said it had refused to accept the Bank of England's analysis of the crisis, arguing that the August run on the pound stemmed not from the specifics of the UK economy or fear of a budget deficit, but from the borrowing and lending policy of those City of London finance houses which had been deployed to save the ailing German banks from collapse. In its 1931 autumn statement the TUC proposed a number of long-term policies to deal with the country's economic problems. These called for the modernisation and restructuring of basic industries, reducing the burden of international debt and reparations and international action to raise the world level of wholesale prices. The TUC also called for devaluation as 'the most effective means within the power of this country if we have to act alone'.[70]

Union leaders were unanimous in their opposition to MacDonald's decision to create a National government with the Conservatives and Liberals as a way out of the crisis. On Wednesday 24 August a joint meeting was held of the TUC general council, the Labour Party executive and the consultative committee of the parliamentary party on how to respond. 'The trade union leaders are full of fight', Hugh Dalton recorded in his diary.[71] All of them repudiated the creation of the National government in a joint statement issued on the following day. 'The policy of the Labour Movement for national reconstruction and international cooperation, including a reconstruction of the problems of debts and reparations, provides the only basis for the restoration of credit and re-establishment of world prosperity', it declared.[72]

Citrine and the TUC certainly played a decisive role in the downfall of the second Labour minority government. But their resistance to Snowden's austerity proposals was more than merely a matter of detail. By August 1931 many in the TUC were ready to contest the Treasury position. In fact, the National government took immediate action to deal with the crisis. Sterling was devalued and Britain left the Gold Standard. This was followed in 1932 by the introduction of Imperial preference. Those drastic changes in government policy demonstrated other options were available to dealing with mass unemployment than merely cutting benefit levels. At the 1931 Congress Citrine declared: 'The strength of this TUC lies in the fact that it can detach itself from political expediency and look economic facts in the face.'

> We were faced with the position either of accepting or rejecting the programme of cuts and leaving to trust the operation of the principle of equality of sacrifice for other sections of the community. We wanted to assist the government. None of us wanted to embarrass them more than they were obviously embarrassed at the moment. But when you are faced with a policy against which you have been fighting for years and which you know will be disastrous, no course is left open to you but unequivocally to say as the general council said – we cannot subscribe to this policy ... For years we have been operating on the principle that the policy which has been followed since 1925 in this country of contraction, contraction, contraction, deflation, deflation, deflation must lead us all, if carried to its logical conclusion to economic disaster and acceptance of this policy in the judgement of the general council would have tied us and anchored us to that principle and logically we could not later resist it when it spread to other channels.[73]

Citrine rejected the accusation that the TUC had tried to dictate to the Labour government. He insisted there had been no attempt by the TUC to impose its will but union leaders had been asked for their advice and they had merely given it. The TUC threw all its strength behind the Labour Party in the 1931 general election, but the outcome proved to be a disaster.

A new beginning

In the aftermath of Labour's defeat the TUC decided to take a much more direct role in the party's decision-making through the revived National Joint Council which was established in December 1931. The body was to act as a coordinating body, 'to consider all questions affecting the Labour Movement as a whole' and 'to secure a common policy and joint action'.[74] The TUC general council held a majority on the revamped body, taking seven seats with three each allocated for members of the party's national executive and the parliamentary Labour Party. In a memorandum of collaboration drawn up in March 1932 an attempt was made to establish strict lines of consultation between the constituent bodies. These changes were acknowledged to provide the TUC with at least the opportunity to exercise a much more effective influence inside the party than it had done during the 1920s. It is not surprising that the historian Henry Pelling called Labour 'the general council's party' after 1931.[75] But Citrine was pessimistic about the immediate political outlook. Tom Jones recorded in a letter to his sister in November 1932 that Citrine 'complained that the [Labour Party] leaders were old and safe and "official" and that no young men seemed to be coming up to take their places – the "missing generation" again'.

> Citrine has a group or groups at work on banking policy, railways, electricity, coal in preparation for the next Labour government and is hoping to get as far as to draft Bills which they can bring in at once on these subjects. Their disappointment with the last Labour government is leading them to believe they can, qua TUC and Labour Party Executive, choose PM, choose Cabinet, thrust policy into their hands in the shape of Bills and thus avoid being let down again.[76]

This did not initially guarantee agreement on a reformist domestic policy. On the contrary, in the early 1930s Labour moved briefly to the left and even moderate figures like Clem Attlee seemed temporarily to lose faith in the parliamentary system. Neither Citrine nor Bevin subscribed to such an opinion. Instead they sought to expand on the ideas the TUC had been developing during the period of the second Labour government.

The TUC's efforts in the 1930s to create a coherent and credible economic strategy were not, however, particularly successful. Citrine had been impressed by the early successes of Franklin Roosevelt's New Deal. Indeed, the 1933 Congress passed a resolution on industrial recovery that called on the National government to draw on the US experience by introducing public works schemes and taking 'all possible measures for increasing the purchasing power of the masses'.[77] Citrine was to see the New Deal at first hand during visits he made to the United States as TUC fraternal delegate to the American Federation of Labor convention in 1934 and again in 1936. He did not believe the depression would remain unsolved until the arrival of socialism but he was convinced sustained recovery would depend on international cooperation and not through the action of one country alone. As he explained in 1938:

> I refuse to subscribe to the fatalism which regards economic depressions as being outside the power of nations to control. The international trade union movement can never accept the doctrine that unemployment, with all its evil consequences and current trade depressions, is preordained and cannot be in large measure averted if only there is the necessary common sense and determination among the peoples and the governments to make the attempt. I believe that even within the capitalist system there is sufficient flexibility and adaptability to overcome the worst consequences of a trade depression, if only the broad lines of economic policy laid down by trade union and Socialist movement are generally applied.[78]

In the early 1930s Citrine was keen to put some substance into the TUC's vague aspirations for planning and state ownership of industry. Detailed policy documents were published by the TUC on the socialisation of cotton and iron and steel which were adopted at the 1934 Congress. Citrine wrote a foreword to Labour's 1936 plan for the 'socialisation' of the coal industry in which he argued that all documents on public ownership were 'considerably more than of mere academic importance, since they will furnish the plans from which a Labour government will work in reconstructing the great basic industries of the country'.[79] The public debate about state ownership of industry was concentrated on what role if any should be played by workers and trade unions in the running of private enterprises when they were nationalised.

Facing dictatorship

However, it was on defence and foreign policy that Citrine and Bevin exercised a crucial influence over the Labour Movement during the 1930s. This was eloquently reflected as early as Citrine's 1933 report to Congress on 'Dictatorships and the Trade Union Movement'. As president of the International Federation of Trade Unions since 1928, Citrine had witnessed at first hand the rise to power of Hitler and the Nazis in Germany on his visits to the IFTU's head offices in Berlin. Citrine held no illusions about the danger to European peace posed by such a radical Fascist regime. The TUC report contained a graphic account of the Nazi's ruthless suppression of the German trade union movement in the summer of 1933. But Citrine went much further than this by seeking the TUC's condemnation of all dictatorships whether they were of the right or the left. He believed the TUC must also oppose Stalin's Soviet Union. His sturdy defence of trade union freedom indicated that Citrine was not to be misled about the political realities of a country that found many uncritical admirers at that time on the British left. His hostile feelings about Soviet Russia were strengthened in 1935 when he paid his second official visit there and spent over two months travelling to different parts of the country, including the Ukraine and the Caucusus. While prepared to admire Soviet economic planning, Citrine was critical of much of what he saw in the Soviet workplace as well as in the country's housing. He published his diary of the 1935 visit which went through five editions despite hostile criticism from the Communist Party.

However, after September 1933 Citrine's main preoccupation was with the growing menace to European peace posed by Hitler, and to a lesser extent Mussolini in Italy, and on how they were to be dealt with. Citrine held little hope in the effectiveness of economic sanctions alone through the auspices of the League of Nations as a deterrent unless they were backed up by a credible threat of the use of military force. At the 1935 Congress, he went so far as to warn delegates what would be involved in any attempt to stand up to Mussolini's invasion of Abyssinia by asserting:

There is only one way of dealing with a bully and that is by the use of force. Moral resolutions are no good. It may mean war but that is the thing we have to face. There is no real alternative now left to us but the applying of sanctions involving, in all possibility, war. But I say this. If we fail now, if we go back now, war is absolutely certain. I ask you what will happen to Germany, if Italy can treat with contempt the nations of the world who have pledged their word to preserve peace? Do you think you are going to restrain a Hitler Germany from carrying out its projected plan of attack upon Soviet Russia?[80]

At the 1937 Congress Citrine again spoke out forcefully that war would have to be faced if the TUC was serious in its opposition to Fascism:

> The British people awaken to dangers as a general rule very late. In their tolerant way they do not want war with anybody and they cannot believe anybody wants war with them. But bit by bit the weakness, the hesitations and the refusals of our government to face the Fascist aggressors is disturbing our people and sooner or later we shall have a cry from the general public that the limits of restraint have been reached and despite itself the government will be compelled to act.

Citrine accepted that the best defence would be collective security through the League of Nations but he warned it might be too late for that and one or two countries might have to shoulder the responsibility of resistance to Fascism. This meant the trade unions would have to accept 'some measure of rearmament'.

> Labour is planning for power; we are hoping to become at no distant date the government of this country and when we come into power it may be that almost our first problem will be to face an international crisis. We cannot wait for that time before framing our policy and indicating to our people despite the possibilities and probabilities of misrepresentation that we have a moral duty to perform and that by recognising the disturbed state of the world, this Labour Movement will not be indifferent to the defence of its own shores.[81]

Citrine explained:

> I am no Jingoist and I am no imperialist. I was opposed to the war of 1914–1918 all the way through and I regard the prospect of war with no more equanimity than anybody here. With two sons, one 22 and one 19 years of age, I know what is in store for my boys and I ask my critics kindly not even to assume different motives from their own. We want to prevent war but we do not believe we can prevent war by lying down to aggression. Sooner or later this country will demand effective resistance to aggression. Some risks are inevitable and it is a question of measuring the relative risk and measuring the danger. I do not believe we can run away from it. The situation today demands that this movement should make up its mind and if we have to come to the conclusion that some measure of rearmament is necessary in

view of the situation in which we find ourselves then commonsense dictates that that rearmament cannot await the advent of a Labour government.

Citrine brought a realistic internationalist perspective to his hard-headed attitude to the menace of Fascism. As president of the International Federation of Trade Unions, he sought to mobilise trade unionism across democratic Europe in the cause of collective security. In his speech to that organisation's 1936 conference in London, he explained:

> To say that our movement is opposed to war in all circumstances is, in my opinion, dangerously delusive and misleading. It is dangerous because it creates in the minds of the peace-seeking peoples an illusory confidence, and it is delusive because on the principles we have laid down for our guidance in international policy, circumstances may raise in which we may find ourselves called upon to make war for the enforcement of peace and the maintenance of public law.[82]

Citrine always argued for collective security through the League of Nations but he also backed 'regional pacts of mutual assistance' which supplemented and strengthened that commitment. His idealistic and passionate resistance to Fascism belies the common image of Citrine as the cold-blooded bureaucrat. What is often overlooked is that his realism was exceptional in the Labour Movement during the 1930s. Only Bevin and Dalton really shared a consistently similar outlook. His 1936 peroration provided an eloquent example of Citrine's perception of what he believed the looming struggle would be all about. As he told the IFTU's delegates:

> It is necessary for us, not only to be on our guard against Fascism, but to be resolute and persistent in our efforts to destroy it. Fascism is growing in various forms in many of the countries represented in this assembly today. We must be vigilant to check suspicious tendencies in this direction wherever they appear. It is a crime against civilisation to allow this monstrous system to continue which deifies the state, destroys personal freedom, and the institutions of democracy and riles by contempt of the most sacred rights of mankind. Plainly a struggle to the death has arisen between this system [Fascism] and the ideals of freedom and human rights which our Movement represents. We have done much, we can proudly claim, to arrest the progress of Fascism and to relieve the hardship of its victims. We can do more to

help those in Germany, Austria and Italy carry on the struggle and brave prison, the torture chamber, and death itself, rather than suffer the degradation of life under this brutish dictatorship.

By early 1938 Citrine was predicting European war. 'Sooner or later the democratic states would be compelled in their own interests to call a halt to Fascist aggression', Citrine argued.

The tendency for nations to take refuge in isolation and to recede from reliance on collective security through the League of Nations was deplorable. It played right into the hands of the dictators. Within the framework of the League there was ample opportunity for the conclusion of agreements between nations which should be open to all to join and want to ensure that collective security would be a reality.[83]

It is not surprising that Citrine was prepared to collaborate with Conservative anti-appeasers like Winston Churchill during the 1930s and speak with them on public platforms against the government's policy towards the dictators. While it may be argued that Citrine as well as Bevin was less emotionally engaged with the Republic's cause during the Spanish Civil War (1936–39) and more favourable to the non-interventionist position than many on the British left, the TUC general secretary was prepared to modify his deeply felt anti-Communism in the wider cause of confronting the dictators. After 1937 he came to accept the urgent need for the formation of a Grand Alliance between the western democratic countries and the Soviet Union. As he told delegates to the IFTU's conference in Zurich on the eve of the Second World War:

One paramount aspect of our task is to use the utmost influence of our movement to assist in the re-creation of a genuine Peace Front ... I must emphasise particularly the importance we attach to the cooperation and collaboration of the USSR in the establishment of a firm alliance of the peace-seeking nations. It is not only essential to have the Soviet Union with us in building up an unbreakable front against aggression and to assist in the defence of every threatened nation exposed to imminent invasion and conquest. Russia's help is necessary too, in the accomplishment of the fundamental aim of organising the life of the world for peace, disarmament and improvement of social and industrial standards in all countries by measures of international cooperation.[84]

In his unyielding resistance to Fascism Citrine ensured the TUC adopted a highly moral and idealistic position. It still remains one of the proudest of the TUC's achievements in the last century.

Towards an Estate of the Realm

Throughout the 1930s Citrine sought to extend the influence of the TUC over the policies of the National government. The trauma of August 1931 did not convince him that the trade unions should return to the militancy of the early 1920s. As Beatrice Webb noted in her diary, Citrine 'pins his hopes on the national/international collaboration of capital and labour forcing up the standard of living of the workers in one country after another. He distrusts the labour politicians that have no capacity and cannot do business on equal terms with employers or financiers.'[85] 'The crisis has not attracted Citrine away from cooperation with leaders of industry', she explained. The TUC's strategy was to combine 'industrial coperation with employers' with 'a determined resistance to any big lowering of the money increases of the working class by cuts in the dole or means test etc or reduction of wages'.[86] Citrine was determined to ensure the TUC did not back away from any involvement with the National government even if it disagreed with its economic policies. This was apparent as early as 1932 when MacDonald asked him if he would nominate TUC representatives to attend the Imperial Conference in Ottawa. Citrine nominated himself along with John Bromley from ASLEF, the train drivers' union, and that year's TUC chairman. Such an invitation, coming only a few months after the August 1931 crisis, indicated that, for their part, MacDonald and his cabinet colleagues had no desire to drive the TUC on to the margins of public life although they were not prepared to acknowledge that the trade unions might be useful partners in macro-economic management.

In fact, throughout the 1930s the TUC and the state were to remain in cautious, uneasy, intermittent contact through differing levels of consultation and involvement. At no stage was there much prospect that the National government would offer Citrine and the TUC the opportunity to become a fully-fledged Estate of the Realm. Citrine's more ambitious vision was to remain unrealised. But on the other hand, it would be wrong to suggest the TUC was kept completely out in the cold. Tentative moves towards a rapprochement, or perhaps more accurately a limited *modus vivendi*, did take place between the state and organised labour after 1932.

In his classic study of the relationship between trade unions and the state published in 1934, Milne-Bailey suggested that the TUC under Citrine was already becoming 'a semi-public institution, with interests and duties transcending those concerned directly with the vocational side of life'.[87] By that time, he claimed, the TUC was recognised by the government as the body that represented the wider labour interest. The trade union movement was now 'through organised consultation and even in some cases through administrative and controlling bodies, fulfilling definite, constructive functions', argued Milne-Bailey. He went on to suggest that the country's economic evolution made it possible for the trade unions 'to supplement and even supersede their earlier, limited and on the whole negative, policies by positive, constructive policies based on a wider conception of vocational aims and functions'. Milne-Bailey argued that this would bring about a transformation in trade union institutions as the *laissez-faire* capitalist system was gradually transformed into a planned economy. Trade unions could no longer be concerned solely with job control. He believed they must be given full recognition and offered participation in the 'new capitalism'. Milne-Bailey envisaged trade unions becoming 'increasingly responsible for the entire function of labour supply and regulation'. 'The result might ultimately be that collective contracts for specified jobs became the normal method, the union allocating labour and settling conditions, including the division of the contract price', he explained. Milne-Bailey recommended the creation of joint industrial councils, works councils and the like, covering every aspect of work and welfare in individual establishments but not interfering in the executive management of the company or the technical and commercial administration of the undertaking. Milne-Bailey suggested trade unions should secure industrial representation on the boards of state-owned companies when they wanted it, although he accepted they should seek no more than a minority stake in such a structure. His aim was to see a decentralisation of power and decision-making to the trade unions. 'It is not be the ruthless forcing through of legislation and the machine-gun fire of "Orders in Council" that democratic institutions can be truly reformed but rather by the devolution and splitting-up of authority.'

Milne-Bailey rejected fashionable notions of the time such as unelected chambers of functional interests like those to be found in Mussolini's Italy. Final responsibility for public policy must always lie in the last resort with elected governments through parliament elected by citizens and not by economic or other special interests. The most he envisaged in a move to corporatism was the creation of a network of consultative bodies involving the trade unions who could give expert advice from their own special knowledge and experience. This would mean the formation of a National Economic Council to represent the country's main industrial and commercial interests, including the trade union movement. Such a body would enable parliament to be made 'continuously aware of the views and criticisms of the chief economic institutions'. As Milne-Bailey wrote:

> Either at the request of the government or on its own initiative the Council could advise on problems as they arose, propose legislation for the consideration of Parliament, criticise measures under discussion and carry on continuous investigation into economic questions generally. The trade unions, being adequately represented on this body, would feel that they were participating in the work of government in a valuable, creative way and not merely in a negative fashion, at the points where their special experience was of most use.

His proposed Council would also be given certain administrative and regulatory functions to relieve the ordinary machinery of government of a good deal of its work. Milne-Bailey envisaged the development of a range of functionalist associations that were semi-autonomous from the state with specific functions that did not usurp parliamentary democracy. The TUC general council would be recognised as 'the authoritative body to advise on behalf of organised labour'.

> As the area of interest and expert knowledge narrows, the more specialised institutions will be the appropriate advisory bodies. The trade union organisations then, will be neither agents of the state nor entirely outside bodies playing a critical and hostile role. They will remain autonomous institutions within the general framework described but with functions that link them to the state in a consultative and cosntructive way.

As the country's major industries were transformed into public services, the trade union movement would assume new functions within each industry. In Milne-Bailey's opinion the trade unions had passed through a period of the state's open hostility into a period of 'puzzled and fearful toleration'.

> The innate strength of the movement has defied suppression and won an unwilling recognition but it has not established a positive status

and constructive functions. Industrial conflict has become a menace to the state but no effective steps have been taken to resolve the clash by finding an agreed basis on which trade unionism can fit into the economic life and institutions of the community without sacrificing its independence and freedom.

In the 1930s the unions should be part of a democratic process to impose a check upon the tyranny of would-be dictatorships and compel a decentralisation of powers. There is little doubt that Milne-Bailey's analysis of modern trade unionism was shared by Citrine, even if it was not one that was welcome to the government.

Any closer relationship between the TUC and the National government, however, remained problematic. In 1935 Citrine and Arthur Pugh were offered knighthoods by MacDonald which they accepted, a move that incensed many in the TUC. Citrine faced personal censure at Congress that year for agreeing to such an honour from 'the hands of a government which is not established in the interests of the workers'.[88] Citrine defended himself vigorously in a heated debate at Congress but nearly a third of the trade union block votes went against him, indicating an undercurrent of unease that went well beyond the core of the trade union left. But Citrine was unrepentant about taking the honour. As he explained in his memoirs:

> Through us our movement had been proclaimed, both by King and government as one whose members were citizens deserving of one of the highest honours that the state could convey. How could this fail to affect the minds of the thousands who know little about trade unionism and to enhance its status and privilege?[89]

The knighthoods awarded to Citrine and Pugh reflected a growing readiness by the National government to at least provide some recognition to the TUC. This was also apparent in 1935 when Baldwin sought out Citrine's views on disarmament. It happened again during the 1936 abdication crisis Citrine and his wife were invited to Chequers for the weekend by the prime minister, keen to hear the attitude of the TUC on the delicate matter of the relationship between King Edward VIII and Mrs Simpson. Official approval for Citrine himself could also be seen in his appointment by colonial secretary Malcolm MacDonald to a Royal Commission established in 1938 to investigate social and economic conditions in the West Indies. This followed Citrine's suggestion that an advisory committee should be established by the government jointly between the Ministry of Labour and the Colonial Office to include the TUC. Public socialising by Downing Street was less in evidence with the TUC when Neville Chamberlain became prime minister in November 1937. 'He appeared at that time to be utterly devoid of human sentiment. Like Poo Bah in the Mikado he seemed to have been born sneering',[90] Citrine recollected. However, he also had to admit that of all prime ministers he had to deal with, Chamberlain turned out to be the 'frankest'. Citrine established an informal and private understanding with the prime minister which helped him to establish his authority on foreign affairs on the National Council of Labour, although it never turned him into an appeaser.

On domestic affairs the TUC made only modest progress during the 1930s in establishing any kind of influence or pressure on the government. At no stage during the period did the TUC manage to convince the Treasury to deal more effectively with unemployment in the depressed regions. However, union leaders themselves were to have less than a glorious record on that issue. For the most part, the TUC remained rigidly on the defensive, anxious to protect the unemployment benefit system from government attack and oppose the introduction of a divisive means test for those without work but unable or unwilling to indicate ways to solve the problem. At times the TUC seemed more energetic in resisting rank and file protests than pressing alternative strategies on government ministers. In 1932 Congress even refused to admit a deputation of unemployed workers into its proceedings. It was to remain hostile to the organised hunger marches and suspicious that the protests were merely front organisations for Communists and other left-wing militants. The TUC's doubts about popular agitation were not entirely without foundation. Citrine was suspicious of those who called on the trade unions to challenge the government by direct industrial action over the unemployment issue. At the 1936 Congress he confronted the left's arguments head-on by opposing an unemployment march to London. It may not have been a popular case to expound but Citrine made it all the same. As he told delegates:

> When you have brought some thousands of men at very considerable expense down to London you have shot your bolt ... at the end of it what is there? There has been march after march in the post-war period on the House of Commons and at the moment of speaking I cannot recall any considerable impression that has been made upon the House by that sort of demonstration. I may be wrong but I do not recollect it. If others do, they have a better memory than I have. We

decided we must confine our activities to what might be called the agitational aspect of the question. We decided as citizens, as politicians, as trade unionists, we would raise our voice wherever we could against the regulations and try to convert the general public to our point of view. That, in the long run, will be the soundest course. If we cannot by reason and by argument, convince the people of this country that the unemployment regulations are inequitable and that they mean misery and poverty for hundreds of thousands of our people, we can never expect their backing if we try to force Parliament by extra-constitutional means.[91]

In fact, the TUC with other organisations made some headway in convincing the government to reform its harsh administration of unemployment assistance but Citrine was surprisingly reticent in his memoirs over the TUC's unimpressive record over the unemployment issue.

But after 1936 the TUC began to stage a significant recovery. Trade union membership began to grow again, partly helped by the TUC's own emphasis on recruitment campaigns. This was not always appreciated by affiliate unions. Citrine wanted the TUC to help organise a drive for unionisation among women as well as service workers in London's outer suburbs, but this was turned down by the unions. However, the TUC focused activities on encouraging union organisation among nurses, young workers, domestic servants and white-collar staff, linked to efforts to secure protective legislation for them. The TUC's Youth Charter called for the introduction of a 40-hour working week, minimum wage rates for 14–16-year-olds, provision of training facilities for the young and the abolition of apprenticeship premiums and fee-charging agencies. The TUC also mobilised action in support of statutory holidays for workers.

In September 1938 the TUC celebrated its 70th birthday. Citrine took that opportunity to assess how far the organisation had changed during his period as general secretary. 'The tendency nowadays is for unions to look more and more to the TUC for guidance and help, not only in matters of major trade union policy, but in many of the matters which are more particularly of domestic concern to individual unions', he claimed. Citrine believed the General Strike, like the Great War, had shown the trade unions the 'necessity for unity of command'. But he went on to deny that the general council enjoyed any powers in excess of anything with which the TUC affiliate unions had endowed it. As Citrine explained:

The TUC exercises and can only exercise only such authority as the unions are ready voluntarily to delegate to it. This, in turn, is conditioned by the depth of conviction which they may have that the authority already vested in Congress has been wisely used. Any attempt by the general council to usurp an authority which has not been freely conceded, would be fatal to the continuance of the trend which is steadily developing to make the general council a really effective general staff for trade unionism. The general council is unlikely to try to usurp any powers which have not been willingly and consciously conceded to it by the affiliated unions and thus impede and frustrate the steady development which will one day make the general council a really authoritative general staff.[92]

Citrine would have liked to see the creation of a TUC general council that could respond more swiftly to political, economic and social events. He insisted it was not always possible to have consultations in the extended manner the TUC rules provided for.

Someone has to take responsibility for making decisions, and in the nature of things on matters of broad policy, the general council of the TUC must assume this duty. It is a natural corollary of this that the general council must be able to gain access to the essential facts and data and must be supplied with the most accurate information upon which to base its decisions.

He pointed to the growth of industry-wide collective bargaining and the widening and broadening of arbitration, conciliation and dispute settling machinery. This trend required trade unions to grow more professional with the appointment of specialist officers able to argue effectively before joint industrial councils, conciliation boards, industrial courts, senior civil servants and ministers. Citrine believed the older generation of union officials, who had lacked much formal education, were limited in what they could achieve. But now the trade unions had at their disposal 'people whose educational qualities, cultural background and trained minds were equal to the best which employers and governments could command'. This did not mean, he hastened to add, that a university education was a substitute for 'those natural qualities of initiative, resourcefulness, common-sense and other characteristics which are summed up in the word personality'.

Citrine was keen to emphasise in 1938 how much the individual trade unions were equipping themselves for the new world with large administrative offices and modern techniques of management. 'Many of us have known at some time or other in our younger days the general secretary of a union who was doing the work of an office boy in opening envelopes and licking stamps', he recalled.

There are very few general secretaries today who can afford the time to indulge in these hobbies. Go to a modern, well-equipped trade union office and you may easily imagine you are in one of the most efficient commercial offices in the kingdom. Internal telephones, dictaphones, buzzers, synchronised clocks, noiseless typewriters, electric duplicating machines; all these meet the eye.

One of Citrine's achievements was to encourage such modernisation, not merely as an end in itself but as a necessary means to enhance the role of trade unions in the eyes of those they had to deal with in government departments and company boardrooms. As he explained:

Many a government official or leading industrialist has visited a trade union office for the first time in a slightly supercilious mood but has gone away rather surprised and chastened. The absence of unnecessary noise and bustle, the efficiency of the staff, the arrangement of the offices, impress him. And this is good psychology because we are rather apt to judge on first impressions. Anything which gives the impression that the trade union movement is old-fashioned or inefficient is detrimental to the interests of the workers as a whole.

In 1938 Citrine claimed the trade unions were 'more powerful and influential than at any other period of their history' because they had proved they could adapt to new conditions. He envisaged them becoming not only more effective collective bargainers on pay and benefits but also securing greater influence 'in the problems of industrial management and the actual conduct of industry itself'. 'Gradually the trade union movement is embracing within itself the technicians, administrative and supervisory workers as well as the craftsmen and manual labourers. Sooner or later the democratic control of industries will come within the realm of practicality.'

On the outbreak of war the TUC under Citrine had clearly grown in its national influence and importance since his election as general secretary. Its own report on its activities during the first six months of 1939 revealed its close involvement in the rearmament programme, the making of air raid precautions and the introduction of national military service. The TUC's position was undoubtedly helped by the impressive expansion which was then taking place in trade union membership. Between September 1937 and September 1938 TUC net affiliated membership increased by half a million. The TUC indicated this improvement was due partly to 'the growing appreciation by every section of the community of the valuable part which a well-organised, democratically-controlled trade union movement can play in national affairs', as well as the spread of a more favourable image of trade unionism through modern techniques of propaganda and publicity.[93] But the TUC was also concerned to emphasise the importance of recruitment in trade union expansion. 'From first to last we have to organise, organise, organise', declared its report. The TUC offered assistance in developing demarcation agreements between affiliate unions to avoid destructive competition and it initiated trade union recognition agreements.

But the TUC's power and influence continued to be severely limited by what its affiliate members were prepared to tolerate. Citrine tried by stealth to acquire greater centralising control but he was always well aware of the restraints imposed upon him by the structure of trade unionism. This did not, however, mean that he could not lead. The passing of the years had enhanced his own personal authority on the general council. But the TUC remained much more of an 'ordinary pressure group' than a fully-fledged Estate of the Realm. This was mainly because governments between the wars did not envisage a dynamic role for either the TUC or employer associations. The Ministry of Labour's purpose was 'not to transform national organisations into governing bodies but individual industries into self-governing entities over which government could judiciously watch in order to safeguard the public interest'.[94] There was little enthusiasm for the kind of responsible public policy unionism envisaged by Citrine and Milne-Bailey. This is why Bevin was exaggerating when he claimed in his 1937 Congress presidential address that the TUC had become 'virtually an integral part of the state and its views and voice upon every subject, both international and domestic, is heard and heeded'.[95]

The Chamberlain government declared war on Nazi Germany on Sunday 3 September 1939 as delegates gathered in Bridlington for the TUC's annual Congress. It was decided to confine proceedings to two days. Citrine spoke with a passion and authority of the coming conflict. He told his audience in particular of what the war would mean for the working class:

I remember the period of 1914–1918 and the glowing promises held out. I would be a traitor to myself if I enunciated phrases of that kind. I believe the working class in this as in every other country, will attain such a measure of success in the prosecution of its ideals, as it is powerful enough and determined enough to work and fight for. I make no promise beyond this. If this movement of ours is solid and united, we may emerge from this great struggle a finer people, a better people, a people who can shake the hands of other nations with mutual confidence and hope, that this terrible holocaust into which we have been plunged will be a thing of the past, never to be repeated. No one can foresee the destiny of nations. No one can predict at the outset of a conflict what may emerge. Dark and evil forces may show themselves in this period. But it is for us to keep our eyes fixed firmly on the goal which Labour has always had before it and to ensure that when finally Nazism has been defeated, when the power of the aggressors has been crushed, we emerge as a Movement with better prospects and greater power than we have ever known previously.[96]

With only two dissenting voices Congress delegates voted overwhelmingly to back the declaration of war against Nazi Germany. Citrine and the TUC had been vindicated by the turn of events. Since February 1933 Citrine had consistently warned of the dangers of Nazism. The man and the institution he served were as one. As Congress delegates dispersed from Bridlington in that first week of the war it was to be the start of what turned out to be the Labour Movement's finest hour in the twentieth century. Citrine deserves to remembered as a man who played a crucial role in preparing the TUC for the testing times ahead. Under the anvil of war, Citrine's TUC was to come into its own.

2
Ernest Bevin, Walter Citrine and the TUC's War, 1939–1945

You will have claims made to you that individuals won this war, but who did win it? The soldier, the sailor, the airman, the civil defender, the men and women who had to endure the shelters night after night through the blitz and the bombs; the men and women in the factory, in the mines and in the fields; those who gave up their homes to work, toil and sweat to produce the munitions of war – the sailor who sailed the seas and brought us our food; the mine-sweeper who cleared the channels. Indeed they are so numerous that they can only be summed up in the words 'all of us' working in a great spirit of cooperation.

Ernest Bevin[1]

The influence of the trade unions has been enormously strengthened during the war and at no period in British history has the contribution which the organised workers have made to the success of their country been more widely and readily recognised.

Sir Walter Citrine[2]

You took on the most difficult task in the government and triumphantly overcame all difficulties.

Clem Attlee to Ernest Bevin[3]

The events of the Second World War transformed the TUC into more of an Estate of the Realm than at any other time in its history. In the victorious summer of 1945, Prime Minister Winston Churchill and Labour leader Clement Attlee both paid fulsome tribute to the TUC's contribution to the defeat of Nazism. 'We owe an immense debt to the trade unions and never can this country forget how they stood by and helped', declared Churchill. 'The strength of Britain has been that of free men and women, working as they have never worked before and willingly accepting the restraints which were necessary to win the war.'[4] Attlee told TUC delegates in Blackpool that September as prime minister of the first majority Labour government: 'This Trades Union Congress of 1945 takes its place among the victory parades of the forces of the United Nations.'[5]

Under Citrine's leadership a united TUC and its affiliate unions rallied valiantly to the defence of Britain. When it was given the opportunity by the state to participate to the full in the war effort, organised labour mobilised effectively for action in the workplace. The Workers War in Britain is a story that remains to be told in any detail.[6] But the activities of organised labour in conditions of total war were not only vital to the successful military campaign against Fascism. The trade unions also played a crucial part in the formation of an implied understanding reached between the state and the people forged in 1940 and which was to grow in intensity in the construction of the post-war world.[7]

The key to the TUC's achievements during the war lay with the redoubtable figure of Ernest Bevin. From Chamberlain's declaration of war on the Sunday morning of 3 September 1939 the TGWU general secretary was to argue in an increasingly impatient, frustrated and angry mood for all-out military mobilisation against the enemy. Bevin was very much a proletarian patriot. He recognised the freedom of the British working class was in deadly peril, that Hitler and Nazism threatened to extinguish all the liberties the country had acquired over the centuries. As David Marquand argued:

> Bevin's Ministry of Labour took over the Treasury's traditional role as the most important economic department. From that vantage point he did as much as any single person to win the war. In doing so, he also left an indelible imprint on the post-war settlement. Thanks to full-time full employment, the balance of economic power had, in any case, shifted massively in labour's favour. But the shift might have been temporary. Bevin's achievement was to make sure that it would last.[8]

Bevin's ministerial role was certainly appreciated by Conservative colleagues who served alongside him in Churchill's war cabinet. The prime minister himself had enormous regard for Bevin, whose massive figure can be seen in old newsreels standing right next to Churchill on the balcony of the Treasury before rejoicing crowds in Whitehall on VE day. 'Bevin is an immense figure in the country. A man of great ability and force of character', wrote Lord Beaverbrook, minister of aircraft production, to a friend in October 1940. 'He is the strongest figure in the trade union movement, which is one of the keys to our war effort.'[9] By February 1942 he believed Bevin was the 'strongest man in the present cabinet' after Churchill.[10] Such flattering sentiments, even when he expressed them to Bevin, did nothing to cool Bevin's antagonism towards him. But there is no doubting the dominant force that Bevin brought to the war cabinet. Bevin's ultimate success was forged, however, through the strengthening of that peculiar alliance with Citrine that had characterised the TUC's leadership in the years after the General Strike. It was Bevin's relationship with the TUC that ensured an effective mobilisation of the workplace for the war effort.

During the early period of the war that ended with Hitler's invasion of France and the Low Countries in May 1940, Bevin and Citrine complained almost constantly about what they regarded as the sluggish pace of government preparations for conflict and criticised the persistent indifference or neglect of many ministers towards consulting and involving the TUC in any systematic way with government war plans. At his meeting with the prime minister on 4 October 1939 Citrine complained that the trade unions 'were being deliberately held at arms length by the government which was trying to limit the scope of consultations to what it considered to be "labour questions"'.[11] Citrine explained to Chamberlain that TUC representatives had 'no intention of being treated as distant relatives and were not going to be told those functions were something that lay within the field of the employers and the advice of the trade unionist was not wanted upon them'. He went on to argue that

> in wartime there was no room for an unorganised person. If he chose to remain outside their associations he should not have the licence to break their agreements. There was an obligation on the government to ensure that agreements between employers and trade unions (if the joint bodies so desired) should be made applicable in the industry generally.

From the start of the war Bevin and Citrine made it clear they wanted the TUC to become directly involved in consultation and decision-making, not just with the Ministry of Labour and National Service but with other domestic departments such as the Home Office, Transport and Health. However, their cause was not helped by the behaviour of the employer associations who were foot-dragging and making it difficult to develop closer tripartite relations with the TUC and the state despite the war demands. 'Unless the general council knew at the commencement what sort of powers they were going to have they were not going into it', Citrine informed Chamberlain.

On 16 October 1939 Citrine held a further meeting with the prime minister to try and ascertain what the government believed should be the 'status of the trade unions during the war'.[12] Chamberlain assured him that all government departments would be instructed to establish 'the most complete understanding and cooperation' between themselves and the trade union movement. There would be 'no difficulty in arranging that the TUC and its affiliate unions should be properly consulted'. Two days later the prime minister announced the formation of a National Joint Advisory Council under the auspices of the Ministry of Labour and National Service, made up of 15 TUC representatives with a similar number from the British Employers' Confederation. At the TUC's insistence the new body was not to confine itself simply to dealing with labour questions. Its terms of reference were wide, although it was made clear that the NJAC would not be able to intervene directly in the domestic affairs of any specific industry but it was agreed it was allowed to deal with 'matters in which employers and workers have a common interest'.[13] Bevin was unimpressed by this apparent gesture of the creation of such a tripartite institution. 'I am bound to confess that whilst we may have representation, the effective control of the departments is by people who have in the main been drawn from the employing interests and whose approach to big problems is influenced by those interests', he complained in his union's journal in December 1939.[14]

'It must be appreciated that in their heart of hearts the powers that be are anti-trade union', confessed Bevin.

The Ministers and Departments have treated Labour with absolute contempt. Yet without the great trade union movement the forces cannot be supplied with munitions nor the country with food. The principle of equality has not yet been won – equality not merely in the economic sense but in conception and in the attitude of mind of those in power. We do not desire to be invited to serve on any committee or body as an act of patronage. We represent probably the most vital factor in the state: without our people this war cannot be won nor the life of the country be carried on. The assumption that the only brains in the country are in the heads of the Federation of British Industry and big business has yet to be corrected for, as a matter of fact, most of the delays and unpreparedness so apparent today are due to the reliance of the departments of state upon a very limited advice of people who, after all, live in a very narrow world indeed.[15]

As late as April 1940 Bevin continued to feel a 'good deal aggrieved' by the government, arguing it was still not prepared to take the TUC into its confidence. He believed the trade unions were

tolerated so long as they keep their place and limit their activities to industrial disputes and are willing to bury all their memories and feelings and assist the nation willingly when in difficulties and go back to their place when the war is done. But there will have to be a great recasting of values. The concept that those who produce or manipulate are inferior and must accept a lower status than the speculator must go.[16]

The lack of rapport between the Chamberlain government and the TUC was apparent in the antagonisms raised by the Treasury's predictable calls on the trade unions to restrain the wage demands of their members in order to contain the danger of inflationary pressures. On 6 December 1939 Sir John Simon, the Chancellor of the Exchequer, addressed the NJAC and demanded a 'slowing down of wage increases'.[17] Citrine challenged his assumption that 'equality of sacrifice' was being practised in industry. In the face of rising prices, the trade unions would be placed in an 'impossible position' if their negotiators held back and saw living standards fall, he complained. 'I pointed out that the general council had no authority to control the activities of the unions in regard to wage applications and it would be resented were they to attempt to do so.' The TUC general council argued that it was possible to hold inflation in check, but only through 'rigorous' controls on profits and prices and the introduction by the government of 'an efficient system of rationing' to 'equalise the burden of the war'. The TUC was concerned that employers should not be able to take advantage of the war to increase their profits at the expense of the workers. On official enthusiasm for a national savings drive to fund the war effort, the TUC insisted any savings made by workers should not be used against them in future wage negotiations and should be disregarded when any worker applied for unemployment benefit or public assistance. A number of meetings were held between the TUC and the employers to attempt to reach agreement on a joint statement on wages, but this proved impossible.

Total war

Such feelings of suspicion and doubt between the TUC, the government and employer associations were swept away after the crisis of May 1940. Chamberlain was forced to resign after a massive Conservative backbench revolt against his handling of the war in Norway, and Winston Churchill emerged as prime minister of a coalition government. The new administration was to include a substantial number of representatives from the Labour Movement. The TUC general council met in emergency session in Bournemouth on the Sunday afternoon of 12 May on the eve of the Labour Party conference to decide what its attitude should be to the coalition proposal. Citrine told them the National Council of Labour had agreed Labour should join the government under any other prime minister but Chamberlain. He added that he had turned down a specific proposal that he himself should join the cabinet. However, Bevin accepted the offer of a ministerial position with the TUC's full approval. Attlee promised the general council that if the Labour Party joined the government there would be no repetition of what had happened in 1931. He assured union leaders he 'intended to maintain regular and intimate contacts with the industrial movement in such ways as they felt necessary. They felt that they would be failing in their duty to both the political and industrial sides of the movement if they did not do this.'[18]

Bevin lost no time in mobilising his Ministry for action. By the time the National Joint Advisory Council met him on 22 May 1940, a week after taking office, he had drawn up his radical programme for workplace mobilisation. He told the TUC and employers' leaders that the government intended to legislate emergency powers for itself which it would hold in reserve to use only when required. These would involve state direction of labour, the banning of strikes, an end to the profit motive, state control of industry, the introduction of a production council and labour supply board with local committees. Communal feeding in the armaments factories was to be established by the state. Women were to be drafted into war work and government centres were to be opened to train both employed workers and the jobless. Despite the potentially draconian powers envisaged to put Britain on a total war footing, Bevin assured union leaders that he wanted to preserve in wartime conditions as much of the voluntarist system of industrial relations as he could. 'The government had come to the conclusion that with the goodwill of the TUC and employers confederation, they could maintain to a very large extent intact peace-time arrangements, merely adapting them to suit these extraordinary circumstances.' Bevin asked the trade unions to take added responsibility and for workers to become members of a union.[19] Citrine assured him that the TUC 'to the best of their ability would do what they could to extricate the country from the danger it was in'. As he explained to affiliate unions, the Emergency Powers (Defence) Act 'placed the whole resources of the nation, in money and manpower, at the service of the state. To that extent but with aims far different from those of its foes, Britain has become a totalitarian state.' But Citrine and his colleagues accepted the gravity of the crisis facing the country required such autocratic behaviour by the government. Although he insisted the TUC would seek 'certain safeguards' for workers, he acknowledged this was 'not a time to haggle and make conditions'. Citrine and his general council colleagues were to be provided with permanent and regular weekly contact with Bevin through the creation of the Consultative Committee. Composed of seven general council members led by Citrine and seven employer representatives, the Committee was to prove a vital and effective consultative forum for the TUC in particular in dealing with the wartime agenda in close liaison with the government and employer bodies.

At the moment Bevin laid out his plan to the TUC leadership, British forces were being evacuated from the beaches of Dunkirk and the clutches of Hitler's conquering army. It was a time that the TUC – in what was also its finest hour – committed itself without question to the fighting of total war. On the morning of 25 May the TUC held a special conference of trade union executives in London's Westminster Hall to decide what its attitude should be to the new political situation. Bevin, in his new position as Minister of Labour and National Service, spoke in Churchillian vein to the assembled delegates. He concluded his passionate speech with memorable words:

> I have to ask you virtually to place yourselves at the disposal of the state. We are Socialists and this is the test of our Socialism. It is the test whether we have meant the resolutions which we have so often passed. I do not want to get worried too much about every individual that may be in the government. We could not stop to have an election; we could not stop to decide the issue. But this I am convinced of: if our movement and our class rise with all their energy now and save the people of this country from disaster, the country will always

turn with confidence forever to the people who saved them. They will pay more attention to an act of that kind than to theoretical argument or any particular philosophy. And the people are conscious at this moment that they are in danger.[20]

Later that same day Bevin broadcast on the BBC World Service to workers across the world.

We are used to liberty, to debate, to argue, but practically the whole people have put it on one side. They have rallied with a great one-ness to defy this ugly beast, this brute. They say he shall not conquer, neither shall he force us to surrender a single inch of the British Empire to his aggression and is it not true that his defeat by the allied forces will cause the greatest sigh of relief that the world has ever known?

Bevin highlighted the sweeping new powers over citizens acquired by the British state as testimony to the national will for victory. 'For the first time in history, every penny, every inch of land, every item of wealth, factory and workshop is now at the disposal of the nation. Private individuals can be compelled to subordinate any private interest or gain for the common weal.' But Bevin emphasised that the mobilisation of labour was not to be achieved in a coercive manner. On the contrary, the British people had 'placed themselves upon the altar of civilisation itself in order to preserve it against this brutal aggression'. He was proud to tell his world audience that the trade unions would 'voluntarily assist' in the reorganisation of the workplace.

They are going to use their branches and their resources to assist in the necessary disciplining and control for us. With their great experience they will help to organise and carry out the necessary mobility of our people. That great trade union movement with its foresight and wisdom has taken the opportunity of demonstrating to the world that it does not merely exist to fight for wages and hours of labour alone, but as the call has come, to show their capacity to save the nation and in the saving of it they will win the gratitude and confidence, not only of their own people but of every lover of liberty throughout the world.[21]

It was apparent from the very start of the war that both Bevin and Citrine were well aware of the opportunities the conflict provided for the TUC in helping to raise the status and power of the working class, not just for the duration of hostilities but for when the peace eventually came. Bevin argued that now was the moment for turning workers into citizens, as he had sought to achieve for the dockers 20 years earlier before the Shaw inquiry. 'We are the last great class to rise in the world', he said. 'Throughout the world the day of the common man has come.'[22]

Bevin's steadfastness was equalled by that of Citrine. As the TUC general secretary told delegates:

> I am not accustomed at these conferences to appeal to anything but your reason. I do not try to appeal to your emotions. I try to direct my thinking and your thinking along practical cold lines. I only want you to remember that this conference has assembled at a more dramatic moment than any within the history of our movement. We have never been menaced in the way we are menaced today. Within a very few miles of the English coast now the Germans are massing forces which in the inevitable course of events will show their effects upon this country in the very near future. We must accept the period of strain, we must accept the testing time which will show the calibre of every one of us. These are moments when I am sure our trade union movement will not resent these abnormal measures which have had to be taken by the government to deal with this situation. The manner in which these regulations will be applied will determine the degree to which this government of ours is ready to maintain the democratic traditions of our movement.[23]

Citrine argued there was no time available to them for prolonged discussion. The unions needed to trust the TUC in the crisis and endorse what the general council had done. A resolution was passed by acclamation, backing the TUC's decision to give 'full support to the necessary measures that must be taken to protect our people against these dangers by organising the entire resources of the country and striving to the utmost to defeat the forces of aggression'. It also added that the unions had 'complete confidence' in the general council and its representatives on the newly formed Consultative Committee 'in the fullest assurance of their determination to preserve the powers and functions of the trade unions and to endure the maintenance of the hard-won liberties of the workers'.[24]

Union leaders representing the TUC were to sit as of right on new tripartite committees and joint consultation machinery established mainly by Bevin to organise workplace production for the war effort. Citrine's declared wartime aim was to achieve 'a watchful though cordial collaboration' between the TUC and the government.[25] As John Price, head of the TGWU's research department explained:

> Organised labour will henceforth be satisfied with nothing less than full partnership in the state. The war has brought out more clearly than ever before the country's dependence upon the mass of working people. At a critical moment the call for that assistance went forth. By helping to save the country, they will find their own salvation too.[26]

Citrine accepted that the trade union movement would have to accept some restrictions on the liberty of workers as well as the 'curtailment and temporary abrogation of many of labour's cherished rights'.[27] But he insisted the TUC would keep a 'vigilant eye upon the exercise of the power vested in the government, continuously through its multiplicity of advisory committees, and by direct representation which sought to curb any bureaucratic impulses to impose unnecessary restrictions on the community'. However, there was always one area that the TUC insisted should remain outside direct government control. Citrine made it clear to Bevin and the Treasury that the trade unions would resist any attempt by the state to regulate wages. A joint statement was published by Citrine and the leaders of the main employer organisations – Sir John Forbes Watson and Sir Thomas Phillips – which was circulated to union general secretaries on 8 June 1940. This called for the continuation of existing machinery for collective bargaining. Where an issue over pay and conditions of employment could not be resolved, both parties were to be given the option of using arbitration with a final appeal to a newly formed National Arbitration Tribunal appointed by Bevin. This was to have the power to ensure that any eventual pay settlement should be made binding on all those concerned. At the same time the TUC and employer associations agreed that 'in this period of national emergency it is imperative that there should be no stoppage of work owing to trade disputes'.[28]

In response to Bevin's promise that pre-war working practices 'temporarily surrendered during the war period' would be restored, the TUC general council insisted such changes were to be registered with local labour supply committees and employment exchanges on the grounds that if these were not recorded 'any machinery for ensuring their restoration would be futile'.[29] It was also agreed that no workers would be allowed to take any holidays if this interfered with production in essential war industries. Further changes involved adoption of frequent rest periods, the introduction of two or three shift systems where practicable and the restoration of a day of rest once a week 'at the earliest possible date'.

The Consultative Committee's agenda in the crisis months of 1940 included drawing up plans to defend factories from air attack, the welfare of munition workers and the control of employment through employment exchanges or recognised trade union machinery. On 19 July Bevin issued the famous Order No. 1305, outlawing strikes or lock-outs unless the dispute had been reported to him and 21 days had elapsed without his having referred the matter to independent arbitration. The TUC chose eight of its own representatives to sit on the National Arbitration Tribunal. Breaches of the executive order would bring three months' imprisonment or a £100 fine on summary jurisdiction, with six months in jail or a £200 fine for an indictment. 'Offenders were to be prosecuted as individuals as action could not be taken against the organisations to which they belong.'[30]

Bevin was heavily influenced in his actions by the TUC's own proposals on the registration of trade union practices across industries to facilitate their rapid restoration at the end of the war. Agreement was reached on the number of hours to be worked to prevent fatigue or reduced output because of excessive overtime. It was also proposed to reduce the length of the working week to 55 or 56 hours as soon as this was possible and one day of rest a week was to be introduced. Such measures presumed an increase in the existing labour force by 20–25 per cent, and it was suggested that this could be achieved through more training or a transfer of skilled and semi-skilled workers from other industries into war production and the use of volunteer part-time employees. Bevin was keen to ensure that rank and file trade unionists as well as union officials were closely involved in such developments. In the Ministry of Supply area machinery, for example, trade unionists would chair board meetings on a rota with employers. Even the trades councils were to be mobilised in getting the long-term unemployed into useful work.

Of course, for all its potential powers, Bevin was not operating a centrally imposed manpower strategy. In his 1981 Bevin centenary lecture, Jack Jones, a future TGWU general secretary, explained that Bevin's wartime achievements were centred on two main themes: first, the maximum mobilisation of manpower: second, the recasting of social values and the permanent alteration of the status of working people. These two themes fitted together, as being the only way to win the war. As far as Bevin was concerned, it could not be won by totalitarian methods. Britain had to stick to government by consent in order to secure the willingness of people to make sacrifices greater than those that could be obtained from them by compulsion. And this consent was closely tied up with consultation and respect for the dignity of the worker. This philosophy did not exclude coercion but confined its use to those occasions when the time was right and it was generally acceptable to those at whom it might be directed.[31]

The hoped-for success of the direct involvement of the trade unions through TUC machinery at national, regional and local level in the promotion of the war effort in alliance with Bevin's mastery of the Ministry of Labour and National Service was acknowledged in a memorandum published by the Ministry of Information on 30 May 1940.

> Britain's war government has tapped a new source of public spirit, energy and experience by drawing upon the trade union leadership to assist in organising the country's industry and manpower for war production. Within a few days of Mr Ernest Bevin's appointment as Minister of Labour his fellow countrymen realised that a strong and forceful personality had entered the field of industrial organisation. Qualities of intellect and character which trade unionists have had ample reason to trust were suddenly put to the test of a great emergency. And the promptitude, breadth of view and grasp of detail shown by the new minister when he unfolded his plan of operations convinced the public generally that Mr Bevin's reputation amongst his own people did not exaggerate his powers of organisation.[32]

Bevin was in an understandably belligerent but confident mood when he addressed the September 1940 Congress, but he was also already looking forward to better days. 'In the past we have made a claim, we have asserted that we have the ability to work out the destinies of nations. Today we are doing it. Today we are devising the plans. Not me. The suggestions are pouring out at every conference that we attend.' He argued that the 'rising mass of labour'

> must be the dominant factor in a new democratic world. If the boys from the secondary schools can save us in the Spitfires, the same brains can be turned to produce the new world. Democracy does not mean to me a mere question of voting at elections. But a complete broadening, right down to the humblest home, of every opportunity in a democratic state. Neither can there be any limitation to a narrow class from which servants of the community can in future be drawn.[33]

Bevin ended his address with a stirring peroration that brought congress delegates to their feet:

> Go back to your workshops and – whatever the difficulties may be which we have to overcome in this great trial – use every endeavour you can whether in equipment, whether in armaments, or in the export trade which is necessary to find the money to buy our equipment, in the turn-round of shipping, or in any occupation in which you may find yourself, to go forward as a great industrial army in this great and terrible total war. And at the end it shall be said that Labour by their skill, their crafts, their courage, their devotion, saved a great people.

The Bevin–TUC entente was often to come under fierce attack from opponents in government who did not believe that the practice of free collective bargaining could be tolerated in wartime economic conditions. The pressure for state intervention into wage negotiations grew ever stronger, especially inside the Treasury during the summer of 1941. However, the TUC continued to resist any such suggestion. Bevin and Kingsley Wood, the Chancellor of the Exchequer, met the general council on 2 July 1941 to discuss the issue. Wood wanted the TUC to make a 'reasoned statement' over pay with the British Employers' Confederation that would support wage stabilisation. Bevin was opposed to this. As he told the TUC:

> There was a great demand they should freeze wages. That he knew was inviting industrial trouble. In the last war lost time was colossal but the improvement in this was not due to the Arbitration Order. It was due to the organised relationship which has grown up over the last 20 years. It had been steadied by this additional machinery but largely it was the growth of trade union organisation and employers and with a sense of responsibility on both sides.[34]

Wood and Bevin both acknowledged that since the outbreak of war the existing joint working machinery for wage negotiations had operated successfully and wage rate increases had been reasonable. 'The authority of the unions in the day to day adjustment of wages and conditions has been maintained', they agreed. 'The freedom of opportunity to make claims and to have them discussed has enabled industrial peace to be maintained.' Moreover, the government claimed it was the policy of the government to avoid any substantial modification of the machinery for wage negotiators and to leave the various voluntary organisations and wages tribunals free to reach their decisions in accord with their estimate of the relevant facts. Among these facts was the consideration that the purchasing value of existing and future wage rates depends largely on the maintenance of price stabilisation policy and that efforts to increase wage rates would defeat their own object unless they were regulated in such a manner as to make it possible to keep prices under control and to avoid inflation.

Bevin's years as Minister of Labour and National Service were to provide the opportunities for 'large numbers of working people to climb out of subservience'. The union activist in the workplace, for the first time, was given legally enforceable security from dismissal by an employer. With the coming of full employment, shop stewards were provided with both a framework for action and the power to negotiate. As Jack Jones recognised, Bevin made sure employers were given no alternative but to bargain with trade unions. The introduction of Order 1305 had opened the way to an extension of workplace unionism, even if it could be seen rightly as a breach with beloved voluntarism. Despite this Bevin was as determined as possible to uphold the traditional system of British industrial relations, despite the powers he had acquired to act in an arbitrary manner. 'There is nothing quite like it in the world. It is a form of industrial democracy and capable of tremendous expansion', he explained. 'I am quite satisfied that in the main those operating this machinery will, during this period of crisis, act as trustees for the nation and will act with a full sense of responsibility.'[35] In personal notes written in December 1941, Bevin reflected that the maintenance of the principle of collective bargaining 'was the most certain method to carry us through the war with the minimum of industrial troubles'. But there was another reason why he defended the traditional system so vigorously against opposition from his cabinet colleagues. Bevin wanted the regime of compulsory national arbitration to continue after the war. He believed it had been the trade union's disengagement from such an arrangement after the end of 1914–18 conflict that led to setbacks that weakened the Labour Movement between the wars. The persistence of Order 1305 was crucial, he believed, to avoid either the return of inflation or deflation. This is why he wanted to see it persist for at least six years of peace. Bevin even floated the idea of creating a wages commission that could involve dealing with cases of union recognition. The continuation of the Essential Work Order was also favoured by Bevin to avoid any return to pre-war employer practices that obstructed trade unions. Bevin also raised the question of whether the Factory and Welfare Board he had created should be 'embodied in the state as a permanent institution'. It seemed that the prospect of a benevolent and pro-worker post-war state had modified even his enthusiasm for voluntarism.

However, the relationship between Bevin and the TUC during the war years often proved difficult. Citrine was keen to ensure that the trade unions did not become subservient to the state under pressure. 'It is fundamental in a self-governing democracy that the people themselves take the initiative in those things which most vitally concern them', he told the 1941 Congress.[36] 'It is imperative that our people should not get into the habit of looking to people above them to solve their problems for them.' He reminded his audience that he had been determined from the outbreak of the war to ensure that the TUC acted to 'restrain the inevitable development of bureaucracy', to ensure they 'were going to retain trade union independence, to retain the maximum of our liberties irrespective from what quarter the encroachments came'. Any state control of wages would certainly have undermined the TUC's purpose. 'If we were to subscribe to that, following very short-sighted advice, we should strike at the fabric which has led to this country displaying a national unity excelling anything in our history.' Citrine assured Congress that the TUC had 'no right to interfere with the wage-fixing machinery devised and constructed by its separate organisations'.

> It is basic to trade unionism that the unions, with autonomy and experience in the separate industries, must devise the form of machinery they want. We certainly have some responsibility for the guiding general principle and I hope that we shall not dodge that but the final judgement must be left with the organisations directly concerned.

'Our cooperation with the government is such that we maintain our right to act as a free and independent trade union movement for our fight is for freedom and democracy', Citrine explained in an analysis of 'wage regulation in wartime' which he wrote on 18 December 1941.[37] He recalled that a strong stand on the principle of consultation with government had taken place on the drafting of state regulation which sought to stop employers being able to advertise for or recruit labour except through a public employment exchange. The TUC did not object to a ban on advertising but it opposed with the employers any ban on existing means of hiring labour.

Real danger for conflict also came from the TUC over Bevin's 1941 Essential Work Order. This looked like a potentially threatening state intervention into workplace relations, although the TUC was closely involved in its drafting. Under its provisions an employer could not dismiss a worker, nor could the worker leave his or her job without giving seven days' notice. An appeal system was introduced with strong union representation to prevent abuses. But Citrine still insisted that this Order must not lead to the imposition of fixed hours or wages. 'This is a matter we insist must be determined by the negotiating machinery within the industry, consisting of unions and employer organisations', he wrote.[38]

By the end of 1941 the trade unions – thanks to the alliance between the TUC and Bevin – had grown into an indispensable force in the effective mobilisation for total war. 'In every field of industry the trade unions are developing ever closer and more amicable relations with organised employers', Citrine noted. 'Association with government departments has been mutually beneficial and the advice of the trade union movement, through the TUC, is sought not only on industrial topics but also on matters affecting the life of the country generally.'[39] The range of topics on which the TUC was consulted by the state looked impressive – compensation for air raid victims, control of food, clothing rationing, price regulation, air raid precautions, the shopping problems of married women workers, the length of holiday periods. 'These and a thousand and one other matters are all brought before the TUC for advice and guidance from time to time by government departments', Citrine explained on 12 December 1941. 'So in the heat of the present world conflict the TUC is forging stronger links with government and employers so that democracy may be stronger now and when victory is won.'[40]

Preparing for peace

Both Bevin and Citrine never lost sight of the need not only to promote the war effort but also to prepare for the peace that would follow Fascism's defeat. From the early stages of the war the TUC was concerned to play its part in making preparations for the creation of a better world. It was not only Bevin's conviction that the working class had been provided with an opportunity to demonstrate their indispensability through practical action, but also that organised labour must ensure there would be no repetition of what had happened to organised labour after 1918. Citrine explained in 1942:

British trade unionism looks forward to the post-war period with confidence and hope. Out of the struggle and sacrifices of years of war is being born a determination in all sections of the community for a better world. What its exact shape will be no one can at present foresee but men of common sense and goodwill are resolved that war and international rivalry shall be replaced by a system of friendly collaboration and properly organised relationships, which will bring to mankind, a greater measure of security and happiness than has yet been possible.[41]

The first tentative steps for peacetime reconstruction really began in the TUC during 1942 when formal discussions began between Citrine and his TUC colleagues and Arthur Greenwood, the minister responsible for the peacetime agenda, and Minister without Portfolio Sir William Jowitt. The TUC was keen that the employer organisations should also be closely involved in the process and the two sides of industry proposed the creation of a joint advisory committee on reconstruction. On 18 December 1942 a joint council including both sides of industry was established under Jowitt's chairmanship. Its stated aim was to 'secure a mutual exchange of views between representatives of labour and industry and the Minister without Portfolio on important issues of general policy arising out of post-war reconstruction'.[42] Union leaders insisted the joint council should 'not in any way limit or interfere with the right of the TUC to make a direct approach to any minister or department of government on any particular question of post-war policy'.[43] Citrine was a member of the council along with senior union leaders, and the head of the TUC research and economic department, George Woodcock, became its secretary. In its initial meetings the council wrestled with the problems that would arise in the transition period between the ending of hostilities and the conversion of the economy from war to peace. The TUC believed it would be impossible to avoid shortages and dislocations unless 'measures of public control over prices, production, distribution and consumption' continued 'as long as circumstances required'. 'Inflation and deflation must equally be avoided and the price level stabilised. Industrial raw materials must be controlled and properly allocated', said the 1943 Congress report.

Demobilisation of the armed forces and of civil defence workers must be arranged with due regard to the circumstances and the objects of transitional policy. Public and private investment must be controlled and directed. Consumer rationing must be maintained and if necessary extended.[44]

It was TUC pressure that also led in February 1942 to the government's creation of an independent inquiry to examine the future of social insurance under the chairmanship of William Beveridge. A year earlier on 6 February 1941 at the height of the Blitz, a TUC delegation had urged Malcolm MacDonald, the Minister of Health, to carry out a 'comprehensive examination' of the existing social insurance system with the aim of devising a better scheme for implementation as soon as the war was over.[45] After some months of deliberation the Ministry of Health announced on 22 May 1941 that the matter should be dealt with by an inter-departmental committee on social insurance and allied services to be chaired by Beveridge, who at that time was an under-secretary in Bevin's department. This was turned in February 1942 into a full-blown investigation. The TUC was to be the first organisation to submit detailed evidence to Beveridge. This called for the creation of an inclusive cash benefits scheme covering unemployment, sickness, maternity, non-compensatable accidents, invalidity, old age, blindness, death, widowhood and orphanhood. Those eligible to participate would consist of 'all gainfully occupied persons irrespective of income'. The TUC recommended a flat rate of benefit starting at £2 a week plus dependants' allowances. Contributions would be divided between half from the state and 25 per cent each from employers and insured workers. In addition, the TUC favoured 'a comprehensive national medical service' that was 'available to everybody in the state'. While the TUC argued that the 'whole aim and purpose of social service is completely inconsistent with the furtherance of commercial interests and there should be no room for that in the new scheme', it believed the trade unions 'with their long and honourable tradition of service ought to be preserved so that the benefit of their experience and goodwill can be utilised in administration on behalf of the state'.[46] The TUC also envisaged a role for local authorities as the 'medium for translating into action national policy in their localities for such services as may be decided'. The TUC met Beveridge on two separate occasions to discuss their recommendations. Beveridge argued in his memoirs that the TUC 'in general agreed' with him, except over industrial accidents which they believed should have higher levels of benefit. Beveridge said that he succeeded in convincing the TUC in principle to discriminate between the short- and long-term cases of incapacity through accident.[47] His personal relations with the TUC were much more amicable than they had been with the wider trade union movement during the Great War. The Beveridge Report won immediate support from the TUC general council when it was published on 19 December 1942 and it was seen by many trade union leaders as a vindication of their initial demands. The only genuine point of disagreement between them concerned Beveridge's belief that workmen's compensation should be dealt with separately from other benefits. The 1943 Congress displayed its enthusiasm by passing a motion that welcomed Beveridge's report as 'a constructive contribution to the establishment of social security' and deplored the government's 'hesitating attitude' towards its implementation.[48] The TUC demanded that 'preparation of legislation should commence immediately in order to give effect to the principles of the report with the least possible delay'.

The TUC also showed a strong interest in the future of education after the war as early as September 1942 when Congress backed a detailed memorandum on the subject. In his introduction to the document, Citrine envisaged the creation of a new scheme of secondary education to ensure older children aged 11 and over were given a fair chance to become 'worthy citizens of a democratic society'.[49] The TUC called for a school building programme, a raising of the school leaving age from 14 to 16, abolition of fees in secondary schools, the end of all private education and a reduction in class sizes. The TUC also called for the introduction of continual half-time education for young workers on two half-days a week release to the age of 18. 'Some may ask whether in these days of immediate stress we can afford time to consider education after the war', Citrine wrote. 'The answer is that if we do not consider it now and if we do not have our plans ready and the necessary legislation on the statute book when hostilities cease, educational reform may well find itself left far behind in the welter of urgent problems which will then beset us.'[50] The 1943 government White Paper on education fell far short of the TUC's proposals. 'They are the very minimum of reform necessary and express the hope that some improvements may be affected', complained the Congress report.[51] However, the TUC gave a warm welcome to the 1944 Education Act. 'For the first time in the educational history of this country it is proposed to lay the legislative foundations on the basis of which a comprehensive and coherent system of educational provision can be built', it argued.[52] But the TUC was critical of the lack of any firm government commitment to the raising of the school leaving age.

The TUC was also keen to establish a wide-ranging reconstruction programme for when the war ended. At the 1943 Congress delegates passed a composite resolution calling for the preparation of a 'general plan' for the post-war revival of the country's basic industries linked to a commitment to full employment, a degree of national ownership or control over each industry, public control and direction of raw materials, the output of finished goods, prices and quality standards and what the 'place and responsibility' of unions and the TUC should be in such a plan.[53] Bryn Roberts, general secretary of the National Union of Public Employees, who moved the motion, pointed out that the national crisis of war had 'compelled the application of socialistic principles and these had under actual test, even under the most unfavourable circumstances proved more effective and efficient than free enterprise'.[54]

The resulting 1944 interim reconstruction report remains a seminal document in the TUC's history. Its blend of hope and caution reflected the idealistic but also practical spirit of the times. Under Citrine's influence the report also laid out a general philosophy of trade unionism that was to resonate through the difficult years of peace. The TUC emphasised that its ultimate commitment was to the maintenance of a free and democratic society in which trade unions were not subject to state control or legal restraints on their right to frame policy and pursue activities in support of that policy. 'As voluntary associations of workpeople they must, in their policies, interpret the wishes of workpeople and their actions must be designed to protect and advance workpeople's common interests. Otherwise, though they may continue to exist as organisations, they will cease to be trade unions', it was argued.[55] However, the TUC accepted that this did not mean that trade unions could behave without any self-restraint in their legitimate pursuit of collective bargaining if full employment was to be achieved in peacetime. The report acknowledged that the key point was how the trade unions intended to use their freedom of action as collective bargainers. 'It is clear to us that no government can guarantee full employment unless they can be assured that the steps they are taking or propose to take, will not be rendered ineffective by the failure of other quite legitimate but powerful interests including the trade union movement to make their actions conform to the achievement of the same objective.' The TUC suggested that it could not be committed in advance to the particular means to achieve the desired objective of full employment, but if the government could guarantee price controls and seek similar commitments from the trade unions on wages, there would have to be a positive response. 'In those circumstances it would be the duty of the trade union movement to give suitable guarantees about wage settlements and reasonable assurances that such guarantees would be generally observed.' But the TUC also made it clear in its 1944 interim report that it was

> not in any circumstances inviting the state to impose a system of compulsory arbitration in wage disputes or to make it a criminal offence on the part of workmen to refuse to accept the terms and conditions of a wage settlement. We would in all cases insist that reliance must be placed upon the ability of unions to secure the general compliance of their members and that the possibility of individuals or small groups refusing to conform to general settlements should not be made the excuse for the imposition of legislative sanctions.

The tortured issue of state regulation and voluntarism was highlighted in particular in an appendix to the 1944 report which set out the TUC's answers to the questions that had been posed to the trade unions by Beveridge over the achievement of full employment and 'rising standards of living in a free society'. Beveridge had wanted to know whether it was 'inevitable' in a seller's rather than a buyer's market that wages and prices would spiral upwards and lead to inevitable inflation, and if a steady demand for labour would fail to produce full employment unless labour was willing to be more mobile than it had been, and whether this was feasible. Was it possible, in other words, to secure full employment without compromising trade union freedoms?[56] The TUC was unequivocal in its response. As it argued:

> We are bound to insist that in all circumstances trade unions should retain their present freedom from legal restraints upon their right to frame policy and pursue activities in support of that policy and should even be given greater legal freedom in those respects than they now possess. As voluntary associations of workpeople, they must in their policies interpret the wishes of workpeople and their actions must be designed to protect and advance workpeople's common interests. Otherwise though they may continue to exist as organisations, they will cease to be trade unions.

No satisfactory conclusion was in fact reached during the important exchange of views between Citrine and Beveridge in early 1944 after the publication of the government's own White Paper on employment. Citrine told him that the unions remained 'resolutely opposed to any method of wage fixation by decree' as they had been from the beginning of the war. He tried, however, to assure Beveridge that 'it would be possible through the collective organisation of the TUC to prevent too great a surge of wage demands from individual unions'.[57] The difficulties of trying to reconcile free wage bargaining with the state's commitment to 'full' employment were to grow after 1945. But the TUC played a key part in establishing a national consensus that placed the achievement of full employment as a high priority in government economic policy.

For Bevin, who did not really approve of Beveridge's attitude, the coalition's 1944 employment White Paper was a strong sign of the coalition's determination that there would be no return to the dole queues, means tests and the human misery of the inter-war depression. In a speech welcoming its publication he told the Commons of a meeting he had had with soldiers of the 50th Division embarking for the beaches of Normandy.

> They were going off to face this terrific battle with great hearts and great courage. The one question they put to me when I went through their ranks was 'Ernie, when we have done this job for you are we going back to the dole?' (HON MEMBERS: Ernie?) Yes, it was put to me in that way because they knew me personally. They were members of my own union and I think the sense in which the word Ernie was used can be understood. Both the Prime Minister and I answered: 'No you are not'.[58]

But Bevin was also convinced that the official commitment to full employment would require a much more interventionist role for the state with a 'new code of conduct for industry'. For its part, the TUC was doubtful whether any future state direction of the movement of labour after the war was possible for more than a limited period of transition.

> The trade union movement will never surrender its bargaining powers or undertake to use them for any purpose other than those of protecting and advancing the interests of workpeople. It cannot commit itself in advance to the relaxation or modification of any of its practices nor can it give pledges as to its future actions in the absence of firm undertakings about the policy of the government and the obligations to be entered into by all other parties.[59]

The TUC recognised the need for balance. It saw that its task was 'at one and the same time to inspire the government to pursue a proper employment policy and to protect workpeople against unnecessary encroachment upon their freedom of action'. However, despite this, Citrine for one believed 'a price must be paid' for full employment. The TUC general council wanted a return to individual freedom for labour as soon as possible once the war was over. But unless the trade unions developed an alternative voluntary scheme for supplying vital labour a continuation of compulsory powers by the state looked unavoidable, Citrine reasoned. However, his sensible views were rejected in October 1944 by the general council. There were clear limits to how far the TUC would be allowed to go in devising a national economic strategy.

A similar caution was also imposed on the TUC by affiliate unions on any reform of trade union structure in the name of closer unity. The 1944 TUC interim report on the subject turned out to be little more than a reassertion of the principles laid down in the TUC's examination of the problem back in 1927. Citrine accepted the TUC may have gained more authority and influence over its affiliates, the state, employer associations and the general public during the war so that it could adopt and pursue a united TUC policy but he also acknowledged the TUC could not exercise any dominant power over its members. 'It is not always recognised that the TUC cannot compel its affiliated unions to make substantial changes in their organisation', argued the report.

> Each union is autonomous and is at liberty to accept or reject the advice of the general council as it may feel disposed. It is clear, therefore, that in the absence of power to enforce structural changes, the maximum the general council can do is to persuade unions to adopt such measures as in the experience of the council may appear necessary.[60]

This meant the cause of industrial unionism was not going to succeed in the British trade union movement. The best the TUC could hope for was to encourage more unions to amalgamate with one another. Moreover, the TUC recognised the value of existing structural diversity which reflected 'generations of industrial experience' with roots going deep into the lives of the workers. The trade union movement could not have survived, it argued, 'unless it had met the essential needs of the working class. Nothing must be done to destroy the stability that has been gained over these many years.' While 'basic structural changes' were 'impracticable', the TUC had to make the best it could of existing realities.

However, the report also acknowledged the unity the TUC had achieved during the war would be much more difficult to sustain in peacetime conditions. And yet this would be crucial if the TUC really hoped to acquire 'a voice in determining post-war policy nationally and internationally'. As it explained:

> The question the Movement will be called upon to answer at many stages and on many subjects will be as to whether the trade union movement alone, in a changing world, can retain its pre-war ideas of organisation. This question may be even more pointed when vested interests are being assailed in plans for the reorganisation of industry.

The TUC accepted that many employers sympathetic to working with unions wanted the unions to strengthen their authority over their members to ensure closer collaboration with management. The report admitted 'that internal conservatism' within trade unions was 'responsible for some of the obstacles with which the development of maximum trade union efficiency is confronted'. 'Practical experience shows that the obstacle to greater cohesion is the tendency to struggle for the union or the theory of organisation, in which members have an interest or a loyalty, rather than for the trade union movement as a whole.'

In black type the TUC's report highlighted what it saw as the basic problem:

> The outstanding fact is that the only solution to our problem is that the unions themselves must strive for closer unity and resolutely pursue that end, probably making some sacrifices on the way, until it is achieved. That fact has been known for a long time. But it has still to be faced. The trade union movement in a changing world cannot retain its pre-war conception of organisation if it is to prosper and efficiently fulfil its ideological and practical functions.

Instead of concentrating on trade union structure, the report suggested that it was best to examine trade union functions. Here Citrine laid out his blueprint for a modern union movement for post-war Britain. In the negotiation of wages, hours and conditions of labour, trade unions would need to use research, statistical and specialist technical services and work together on common claims, thus avoiding self-destructive competition. 'There is nothing revolutionary in the proposals', admitted Citrine. 'In the main the suggestion is that there should be a speeding up and further development of the adaptations which have already been found practicable and necessary.' It would be wrong to suggest that the

TUC's approach in 1943–44 amounted to a missed opportunity. But it remains hard to reconcile the TUC's awareness of what would be required in the wider political economy to secure trade union objectives on employment and industrial participation with its cautious view of what was possible in the face of trade union autonomy. However, the 1944 document hinted at future developments and made it clear the TUC would have to modernise itself and could not go back to the world of the inter-war years.

When the general election was called in July 1945 after victory in Europe, the TUC issued a 'call to the workers' urging them to vote for the Labour Party. This self-confident manifesto reflected the advances it had made during the war. It emphasised they should do so first of all because of the need to prevent a 'hasty and ill-considered removal of public controls' which would lead to soaring prices, 'an artifical boom, inevitably followed by an industrial slump as widespread and severe as any experienced in the years following the last war'.[61] The TUC painted a lurid picture of what might happen to the wages, salaries and savings of workers in the event of a Conservative victory. It warned that controls would be necessary to prevent economic and industrial exploitation and 'as a means of enlarging the boundaries' of workpeople's freedom. The TUC accepted that there could not be wholesale nationalisation of industry, but it called for the public ownership of coal and power, iron and steel and internal transport services as an 'immediate necessity'. It also called for the introduction of a 40-hour working week without loss of pay and two weeks' paid holiday for all workers. A Labour government would back social security and a national health service for everybody. The TUC accepted that there might be a need for a continued direction of labour, though this would be relaxed 'to the greatest possible extent consistent with the national needs of post-war reconstruction in order to reinstate the personal freedom and the rights of the individual citizen for which the Labour Movement has always contended and for which this war was fought'. The TUC also called for raising the school leaving age over three years to 16 and the abolition of all fee-paying schools. It added that Labour would also ensure the repeal of the 'iniquitous' 1927 Trade Dispute and Trade Unions Act to allow freedom of association for all workers.

The extent of the TUC's growth of power and influence that had taken place during the Second World War was spelt out by Citrine in his final address to the 1946 Congress on receipt of his gold badge as he moved on to the National Coal Board after 22 years' service with the TUC. 'The authority of the TUC is now in the industrial sphere of organised workers not only unchallenged but unchallengeable', he told delegates. Citrine recalled when he joined the TUC in 1924 the parliamentary committee and the newly formed general council had relied on the 'personality and eloquence of particular trade union officers to extricate the Congress from very complicated situations'. But over time the general council had acquired a self-confidence which ensured that it got its way with delegates by commanding respect. At the same time Congress itself was less likely to be swept away by oratory and was more concerned with policies based on facts and analysis. 'We have passed from the era of propaganda to one of responsibility', he added.[62] Indeed, in 1946 the TUC stood at the peak of its national authority and influence. In war as in peace, the Bevin–Citrine alliance ensured that the TUC had stood the test of the greatest threat that Britain faced in modern times. The praise it received across the political spectrum was well deserved. The TUC – despite its internal weaknesses and hesitations – had at last become a respected and effective national institution. In their differing ways but with clear-sighted objectives Bevin and Citrine had demonstrated their practical common sense and commitment to the mobilisation of the trade unions through the TUC – from the shopfloor to Whitehall – in the Workers War.

3

Trade Union Freedom and the Labour Movement: Arthur Deakin, Frank Cousins and the Transport and General Workers Union 1945–1964

No union has contributed more in organised strength, in practical wisdom and in imaginative vision to the success of the Labour party than the Transport and General Workers union.

Clement Attlee[1]

Brothers, we have got to recognise the difficulties that confront us and act with a sense of responsibility, while expressing our determination to secure those conditions that will make for a reduction in the prices level and increase the level of the wages that we get.

Arthur Deakin[2]

The general executive council of my union firmly believe that its job is to improve the standard of living of our people. We are not satisfied even to maintain it. We know the economic struggle that the country is facing but we also know that we are governed by a body which advised us that we were coming into an era of prosperity in an atmosphere of free for all. We have said and we mean it that if it is a free for all, we are part of the all.

Frank Cousins[3]

The Transport and General Workers Union was always the colossus of the Labour Movement from the moment of its formation through mergers in 1922 under the visionary leadership of Ernest Bevin.[4] During the period immediately after the Second World War, it became the largest trade union in the western industrialised world, claiming over 1.3 million members by the middle of the 1950s. The TGWU's massive block vote of 1 million in the 1950s out of a total conference vote of just over 6 million was used ruthlessly to dominate policy-making at party conference as well as to decide who sat on most of the National Executive Committee and the all-important Conference Arrangements Committee. Labour leaders always tried to make sure the TGWU was on their side in their inner-party battles. In power and influence, it towered over the other trade unions affiliated to the party. Only the National Union of Mineworkers enjoyed comparable strength and that union's importance went into serious decline during the 1950s in line with the loss of jobs in the contracting coal industry. The pivotal role played by the TGWU in TUC and Labour Party politics, however, was not simply due to the sheer size of its mass membership translated into a huge block vote. Its strategic position also owed a great deal to the strong character and robust opinions of the union's successive general secretaries.

Bevin deliberately created a highly centralised trade union, designed to unify the often conflicting sectional interests that existed between its disparate members. Its sense of purpose and direction therefore came primarily from the personal abilities of the man who reigned at the top of the union. The authority he wielded was strengthened enormously by the fact that the post of general secretary was the only one in the TGWU elected through a branch ballot vote of the entire membership. 'The general secretary represented the unity of the union', explained Alan Bullock in his biography of Bevin. 'He was the man who held it together and resisted the particularist tendencies of the trade groups. It was to the general secretary that the executive looked for guidance in formulating policy and under his supervision that the officers carried out the executive's decisions.'[5]

The union's unique structure reflected Bevin's personal domination. He used it to turn himself into the indispensable figure both in the modernisation of the TUC with its general secretary Walter Citrine after the 1926 General Strike as well as in the return of the Labour Party to the mainstream of national politics in the aftermath of the 1931 election disaster. Without the TGWU's moderating influence, it is doubtful whether Labour would have accomplished even a limited electoral recovery during the years leading up to the outbreak of the Second

World War. However, the TGWU often looked to the outside world as little more than Bevin's creature. He seemed to control or at least dominate its internal proceedings through both the union's general executive council and the biennial delegate conference by the sheer force of his dynamic but overbearing personality. But in May 1940 Bevin was seconded from the TGWU by Winston Churchill to join his coalition government as Minister of Labour with the task of mobilising Britain's workers for total war against Nazism. He turned out to be one of the great successes of that administration in the eventual achievement of victory. After 1945 Bevin, as Foreign Secretary, was an impressive guarantor of Labour's peacetime social revolution with its commitment to full employment, the creation of a national health service and the nationalisation of key industries like coal, the railways and iron and steel.

Deakin and the social settlement

The history of the TGWU between 1945 and 1964, however, suggests that the union did not require a larger than life figure like Bevin in order to exercise effective power and influence over the rest of the Labour Movement. Both Arthur Deakin, general secretary from February 1946 until his death on May day 1955, and Frank Cousins, who held the post from March 1956 until June 1969, were to demonstrate in their contrasting ways just how important the TGWU continued to be after Bevin's departure in ensuring the party's political success as well as its internal cohesion.

Deakin's posthumous reputation has suffered badly, especially from the hands of his own union. He is invariably portrayed by the TGWU as a tyrannical figure of 'darkness', an anti-Communist autocrat who tried to dominate the union with a rod of iron against an increasingly restive rank and file hostile to wage restraint. 'In running the union Deakin resembled a small businessman in outlook, rather than the leader of hundreds of thousands of industrial workers', wrote future TGWU general secretary Jack Jones, who disliked Deakin's right-wing anti-Communist Labour politics, perhaps more than his autocratic style of running the union.[6] But Geoffrey Goodman – no enthusiast – wrote in his biography of Frank Cousins that Deakin was 'a strange mixture'. Outwardly he was a 'hard, ruthless, blustering, bully-like man', but behind the 'iron mask was an unexpectedly sensitive and generous human being'.[7] Michael Foot – from a hostile Bevanite perspective – described Deakin as 'a fierce, breezy, irascible, stout-hearted bison of a man who genuinely believed that any proposition he could force through his union executive must be the will of the people and more especially the will of Ernest Bevin whose requirements he had normally taken the precaution of finding out in advance'. Foot also believed he 'lacked Bevin's redeeming powers of imaginative rumination'.[8] It is true Deakin was no Bevin but then there has never been anybody else like Bevin in the trade union movement. However, when judged by any other standard, Deakin turned out to be an impressive and effective general secretary who maintained the TGWU as a powerful and responsible force in a period that turned out to be, but perhaps did not seem so at the time, Labour's golden age. It is no exaggeration to assert that it was the TGWU and the TUC under Deakin's leadership that helped to save the Attlee government from economic disaster. Between February 1948 and the summer of 1950 Deakin – at first with understandable reluctance and then with characteristic enthusiasm – took the lead inside the TUC in trying to restrain pay demands among the rank and file at a time of full employment.

Deakin was one of the most belligerent champions of Labour's postwar social settlement. Professor Hugh Clegg believed Deakin equalled Bevin in his courage and 'came near to him in force of character', while sharing most of the same values, although he lacked Bevin's genius for 'an intuitive grasp of situations and problems and how they could be handled'.[9] Philip Williams described Deakin in his biography of Hugh Gaitskell as: 'one of those vigorous, boisterous, extroverted and intolerant working-class characters whose bullying and crudity are readily excused by intellectuals who like their politics but never forgiven by those who do not'. But Deakin belonged to that small group of postwar national trade union leaders who 'in the precarious economic situation after the war used their great bargaining power with restraint'. Despite persistent left-wing criticism, Deakin and others like him, wrote Williams, 'improved their members' real standard of living substantially without imposing the arbitrary injustice of inflation on the poor and weak and they made it possible under the Attlee Cabinet to reconstruct the economy and lay the foundations for lasting prosperity on which future governments failed to build'.[10]

Deakin was acting TGWU general secretary during Bevin's absence at the Ministry of Labour between May 1940 and July 1945. It was under his leadership that the TGWU grew in membership during the Second World War. There is no reason to believe he was anything less than competent and diligent both in managing the union and acting on its behalf in the mobilisation of the organised working class under crisis conditions. The shopfloor war effort owed much to the work of the trade unions, and not least to the TGWU. Deakin played a key role among that remarkable generation of Labour Movement leaders who helped to defeat Nazism and prepare for post-war reconstruction. Whatever his personal feelings might have been towards Bevin, Deakin remained publicly his faithful and able lieutenant. But it was in the immediately post-war period that he came into his own and out from under Bevin's massive shadow. Deakin proved to be a passionate and loyal champion of Labour's cause whether the party was in government or opposition. It is true he would often wield his union's huge block vote at party conferences to obstruct the party's increasingly vociferous left-wing. In alliance with Will Lawther, president of the National Union of Mineworkers, and Tom Williamson, general secretary of the General and Municipal Workers, Deakin became a pivotal figure in the so-called TUC Junta. This group acted as a formidable praetorian guard, protecting the Labour leadership from its party enemies. The total vote of their unions amounted to nearly a third of the votes in the party conference. The unswerving support given by the TGWU leadership to the post-war Labour government, both inside the TUC as well as the party, was undoubtedly a crucial factor in consolidating its overall achievements. Vic Allen in his portrait of Deakin went so far as to suggest he occupied the role Walter Citrine had played when strategically minded TUC general secretary until his departure to the National Coal Board in September 1946. He was 'the central figure of a small but influential group of union leaders whose unions accounted for almost half the total affiliated membership of the TUC'.[11] During the period of the Attlee government it was Deakin – with occasional interventions from Bevin at the Foreign Office at times of national crisis – and not the mediocre TUC general secretary Vincent Tewson who played the dynamic role in the development of that vital political and social network of power and influence, which was established between senior cabinet ministers and union leaders and underpinned the stability of the Labour government. Deakin was delighted at the degree of access to government departments that the trade unions gained for the first time during those years. 'We have an open door in relation to all state departments and are thus able to get our difficulties examined in such a way as would not have been possible with any other party in government', he told Allen.[12] Deakin was an active member of a number of tripartite organisations that continued to function after the war including the National Joint Advisory Council and the Joint Consultative Committee. The Economic Planning Board, established in 1947, also provided senior union leaders like Deakin with the direct opportunity to influence government policy.

But the TUC did not enjoy unquestioning access to ministers. There was no general TUC right, for example, to be consulted on the drawing up of legislation for taking private industries into the state sector. As Norman Chester wrote in his official history of nationalisation: 'The TUC and the unions found the fact that a Labour government was in power did not eliminate the need for formal consultative machinery. Indeed, at first they had to fight hard for the principle of being consulted on those matters which were directly within their sphere of interest.'[13] But for the most part the TUC and the government managed to work in harmony together. The common understanding between the ideology and instincts of the party and the trade unions during those years owed much to Deakin's steadfastness under external as well as internal union pressure.

Kenneth Morgan suggested 'the Labour government's unity was based, more than at any other time in its history, on the projection of a traditional programme of protection for the working class and recognition of the unions as a new estate of the realm'.[14] This did not mean the government–trade union relationship was not without its strains. Some cabinet ministers, notably Emanuel Shinwell as Minister of Fuel and Power and Herbert Morrison, Lord President of the Council, were less than punctilious in drawing union leaders into the policy-making process or even keeping them informed on what they were doing. No formalised structure of liaison was created to keep the government and the TUC in close touch as occurred in the 1970s. As a result, the TUC complained about the lack of ministerial consultation over key decisions on a number of occasions. But in a very deep and personal way the emotional ties between the party and the big trade unions like the TGWU remain crucial for any understanding of the strengths and weaknesses of the Attlee government.

The importance of Deakin to the success of the special relationship between the party leadership and the unions can be gleaned from a variety of contemporary sources but especially from his many verbal interjections at the union's biennial delegate conferences, in his signed articles in its monthly journal – the *TGWU Record* – and above all in his quarterly reports to the union's general executive council. Despite his bluster and notoriously short temper Deakin could be a persuasive and thoughtful advocate of what was a new kind of trade unionism shaped by Citrine and Bevin before the war. This sought to transcend the industrial politics of collective bargaining and to concentrate on extending the power and responsibilities that Deakin believed organised labour ought to exercise in the interests of an economic strategy that sought full employment, more social justice and greater equality. The resulting social contract of the 1940s may have fallen far short of the centralised national coordination practised successfully by Social Democratic governments in Scandinavia with their trade union allies during that period but it still represented a significant modification to the traditional British system of voluntarism, where trade unions – outside the exigencies of wartime conditions – sought to keep the state out of their bargaining activities with employers. The impressive unity displayed by the 'contentious alliance' between 1945 and 1951 was based on a shared sense of working-class solidarity. By contrast the tangled relationship between Labour governments and a more decentralised trade union movement during the 1960s and the late 1970s was to prove much more difficult to sustain than in the Attlee years. Of course, the social circumstances of the period immediately after the end of the war encouraged greater working-class cohesion. Faith in voluntarism and rank and file support in the trade unions for the first majority Labour government in history was of crucial importance in ensuring the defence of its achievements. But it would be churlish to ignore the enormous contribution that proletarian patriots like Deakin made to Mr Attlee's overall performance.

Deakin himself always took collective loyalty to the Labour Movement seriously. As he explained in his quarterly report to the union's general executive council shortly after the party's 1945 election victory:

> We must realise the new government will require all our assistance and understanding in the tasks that lie ahead. Very clearly, if we are to bring about economic security and a great measure of social reconstruction it will be necessary for everyone to pull their weight; in other words, we have got to work well to live well.[15]

The TGWU had strengthened its own position in the parliamentary Labour Party at the 1945 general election. Not only was Bevin appointed foreign secretary. Others from among the union's sponsored MPs were also given senior posts in the new government with Sir Ben Smith as Minister of Food and W. J. Edwards Civil Lord of the Admiralty. In addition, the TGWU was proud to proclaim three of its sponsored MPs were also parliamentary under-secretaries at the Home Office and Colonial Office and a parliamentary secretary at the Ministry of Health. As many as 39 of the Labour MPs in the 1945 parliament were directly sponsored by the TGWU. But it is true the proportion of union-sponsored Labour MPs in the parliamentary party was lower than it had been before, consisting of only 120 out of the 393 sitting on the government benches.

From the early months of the Labour government Deakin called on workers to demonstrate their loyalty to their trade unions as well as the new political order. 'Nothing could be more fatal to the restoration of our economy and to the creation of the new wealth we must have if we are to have higher standards of living than a repetition of the unofficial strikes we have witnessed during the past month, particularly in the docks', he told his general executive council in December 1945.[16] He attacked unofficial strikers in the Port of London, suggesting their behaviour played 'into the hands of reactionary elements'. Deakin believed in what he called 'an orderly society' through an acceptance of voluntary negotiation based on collective bargaining through industry-based joint councils.[17] He understood and sympathised with the Labour government's efforts to restore Britain's war-shattered economy to peacetime conditions. Deakin urged the union's members to back the 'great drive for exports' and to show the 'greatest possible measure of loyalty, self-discipline, patience and restraint on the part of the public generally'.[18] 'If we are to make up the goods in short supply and at the same time develop our export trade to the greatest possible extent, it can only be done by a measure of control within a planned economy', he explained in his spring 1946 executive council report. 'If we fail to do this then I am convinced that we shall repeat the errors of those fateful years between 1921 and 1933 which followed from the false prosperity arising from our failure to grapple in a practical way with the conditions that obtained at the end of the first world war.'[19] Deakin warned his members of the economic rigours that lay ahead and said he was disturbed at the way in which they accepted 'the propaganda carried on against the continuance of controls'. 'Whilst this form of restraint is naturally irksome and repressive in war-time it is, in my view, very necessary and we should accept for a considerable period of time ahead that orderly approach to our economic problems which will enable us to gradually get back to our normal trade both in the home and export markets.'

Deakin was never Labour's fair-weather friend. He believed his union must defend and fight for the party against its innumerable enemies in bad as well as good times. However, he was always keen to try and ensure the political and industrial objectives of the Labour Movement were kept separate. Deakin never held a high regard for most politicians and was keen they should keep their noses out of internal trade union affairs. This often led to an apparent confusion. At the 1946 party conference he moved a resolution urging the Labour government to 'require all employers to negotiate the introduction of the 40-hour working week with the trade unions' in line with TUC policy. During his speech Deakin suggested the trade unions did 'not want to use the political organisation' of the party to secure a reduction in working hours, arguing that it could be 'best achieved through our industrial machine and through the usual channels of negotiation'.[20] However, Deakin went on to demand that George Isaacs, Minister of Labour, be given enabling powers to force employers and unions to bargain together over the working hours issue. This would enable him to tell both sides of industry: 'Get together. Shorten the hours of work within a reasonable period of time.' Deakin argued that a shorter working week was 'an indispensable condition to our industrial progress and to the promotion and maintenance of high efficiency in industry'.

But as an increasingly important figure on the TUC's economic committee, Deakin was also painfully aware of the mounting economic troubles confronting the Attlee government. He welcomed the TUC's growing involvement in discussions with the Treasury on macro-economic policy. 'The trade union movement at this time is developing a wider sphere of activity and is required to assume a greater degree of responsibility than at any previous time in its history', he told his general executive council in his fourth quarterly report for 1946.[21]

It might be said that the function of the trade union movement is changing considerably. We are no longer confined to the limited function of dealing merely with wages and ordinary conditions of employment. Trade unions have a part to play in the planning of that economy which will provide full employment and rising standards of life, developing a relationship within socialised services which calls for a new approach and understanding with an acceptance of responsibility to the masses of the people. The acquisition of power leaves us with no middle course. We must face up to the fact that power carries with it responsibility.

At times, Deakin often gave the mistaken impression that the TGWU was almost alone in carrying all the responsibilities for the management of the post-war economy on its massive shoulders. As he explained to his executive council:

We are now facing the most critical period following the war. The government cannot alone solve those pressing problems with which we are faced. Production and nothing short of maximum effort on the part of all concerned will bring about those conditions which will enable us to produce the goods we require and maintain those services which are essential to our national development, with the realisation of our policy of full employment and rising standards of life. We must face up to our responsibility, leaving our members in no doubt whatsoever that it all depends upon them. There must be no side-stepping of responsibility or refusal to face up to the obvious. Nothing else but an all-out effort will pull us through.[22]

Deakin was prepared to go a long way in his support for the government with his calls for higher productivity and improvements in workplace efficiency. As a member of the Anglo-American Council on Productivity, established by Chancellor Sir Stafford Cripps in 1948, he was an enthusiast for a better utilisation of labour, the introduction of new production techniques and more industrial investment. Nor was Deakin opposed to a revival of the joint production committees, which had been so important in mobilising industrial performance during the war. 'This type of joint consultation is essential and should be developed', he wrote in the *TGWU Record*.[23] But he argued this should be done without involving such bodies in wage bargaining. Deakin remained ferociously hostile to unofficial strikers and sought to prevent the breakdown of recognised industrial relations procedures, especially in the docks where he found himself at loggerheads with the union's militants in ports like Liverpool, Hull and London. He was always suspicious of the behaviour of shop stewards, regarding them as too often a disruptive and disobedient Communist menace and with the coming of the Cold War as part of a wider political conspiracy to subvert the economy.

As President of the World Federation of Trade Unions between 1946 and 1949, Deakin also became increasingly aware of the Soviet Communist domination of that organisation, particularly over the Marshall Plan. In early 1949 Deakin and the TUC walked out of the WFTU and helped in July to form a new anti-Communist international body – the International Confederation of Free Trade Unions. It was during the same year that Deakin also led the way to suppress Communist activism in the TUC and affiliate unions, not least in his own where an estimated nine Communists sat on the TGWU's thirty-four-strong general executive council and three of the eight-strong finance and general purposes committee were Communist Party members. At the union's 1949 biennial conference Deakin took the lead in having Communists and Fascists banned from holding full-time office in the TGWU. Such illiberal behaviour reflected the emotions of the time. International events such as Stalin's blockade of West Berlin and the capture of power by the Communists in Czechoslovakia did much to alienate Labour Movement sympathies for the Soviet Union.[24] But Deakin's anti-Communist tirades were over-zealous and simplistic, especially during the unofficial dock strikes of the period. The most authoritative account of that industrial conflict carried out by K. G. J. C. Knowles suggested Communist strength was due mainly to weaknesses in the TGWU's structure which failed to articulate genuine grievances. 'The history of all these strikes reveals not only a resentment by the dockers of the tight discipline necessitated by decasualisation of the industry but also an enduring suspicion of their own main union which seems to have been aggravated by union participation – however defensible – in the managerial functions of the Dock Labour Board', explained Knowles.[25] A study of the internal affairs of Deakin's union by a young American Joseph Goldstein, published in 1952, characterised the TGWU as 'an oligarchy at every level of its structure, failing to elicit the active participation of its members'.[26] Although any similar analysis in other unions would have probably revealed the same representation problem, it is clear that the TGWU was suffering from atrophy, although it seems improbable to believe the rank and file was to the political left of Deakin, at least on international issues. However, his anti-Communism was often extreme and unconvincing, even by the standards of his day. He even blamed a Communist 'fifth column' for the loss of some Labour parliamentary seats in the 1950 general election such as Bexley, Govan, Shipley and Glasgow Scotstoun.[27]

Deakin was by no means a sturdy champion of freedom in industrial relations despite his hatred for Communism. He was quite ready, for example, to throw his formidable support behind state regulations to control the movement of workers to meet supply bottlenecks caused by labour shortages. He also accepted the continuation of the National Arbitration Order 1305 imposed by the government in 1940 after the end of the war. This was supposed to outlaw strikes through the imposition of compulsory arbitration. Deakin also favoured other forms of government control to manage the economy such as the regulation of trade, rents, dividends and profits. He was an enthusiastic supporter of the Labour government's industry nationalisation programme, at least until 1949 when he began to favour a temporary halt in the cause of consolidation rather than further state ownership of the means of production.

But for a long time Deakin remained implacably opposed to any form of wage restraint based on even indirect government action. As late as the summer of 1947 he continued to oppose the idea of a national incomes policy which was still at that time a popular cause on the Labour left. 'I know there are people crying out for a wage policy, that is, a revised version of the Marxist theory – to each according to the service rendered to the state', he told the union's biennial conference.[28] Employers also favoured a wages policy, added Deakin pointedly. They did so because it would help them to increase their profits at the expense of workers' pay. 'Neither point of view is acceptable', he declared. 'No point of view which strives to secure that one industry or a section of industry shall get a privilege over the others, will work or prove acceptable to our people in this country.' Deakin was keen to see an improvement in annual labour output but he did not believe this should directly involve any intervention by the state. 'The question of incentives, wages and conditions of employment are questions for the trade unions and the sooner some of our people on the political side appreciate that and leave the job to the unions the better the battle for production.' However, he also told the 1947 Labour Party conference that his union would continue to oppose any suggestion of a national incomes policy. 'We will have none of that. Under no circumstances at all will we accept the position that the responsibility for the fixation of wages and the regulation of the conditions of employument is one for the government.'[29] Deakin's views on voluntarism may have been instinctive and traditional but they were based on hard, practical experience in representing TGWU members. There could be no state intervention into collective bargaining that would involve any preferential treatment for some workers with skill and who were in demand at the expense of the rest of the working class. 'The people I represent are not prepared to play second fiddle', he warned. 'Any attempt to alter the method of negotiation within industry would be fatal. You will not get the necessary production in the next eighteen months if you destroy confidence in our negotiating machinery, in our established procedure in industry.' Deakin pleaded with delegates at the 1947 party conference to reject a statutory incomes policy. 'It would be disastrous, it would create chaos and conflict amongst the rank and file and this would be destructive of the economy of the country.'

In a debate on a left-wing motion from Rushcliffe constituency party calling for a comprehensive policy from the government on wages, hours and the distribution of the national income, Deakin expressed his hostility to any state involvement in pay determination. As he explained:

Do we want a pay policy in this country that attempts by a declaration to determine what is the right wage in a particular industry? Are we seeking to set out the order in which wage policy shall be applied to industry? If you accept this policy then you will rue it. We shall quickly reach that inflationary stage which we have sought to avoid. You will have such strife and conflict within your ranks that no power can restrain the demand for wages and the production of those conditions which will result in inflation. What we have got to strive for is to make wages of real value, increasing the purchasing power of the wages we have got. By that method we shall strike a balance in our industries which will enable us to build up a standard of life to get the goods so necessary at this time.[30]

As late as October 1947 Deakin continued to resist the idea of wage restraint emanating from the state. In a speech as TUC fraternal delegate to the American Federation of Labor in San Francisco, he told delegates that the British government had established a new section of the Minsitry of Labour to collect and collate wage data with the intention of presenting such material to wage tribunals and other negotiating bodies to help them assess the sense of wage claims. 'We are not prepared to allow this to go further than a fact finding apparatus', he added. 'We should resist any claims on the part of the government concerned, even to offer an opinion as to whether a particular wage claim should be conceded or turned down.' But Deakin added that the British unions themselves needed to consult among themselves on pay and develop machinery to do this. At the same time the government would have to act more decisively on keeping down price increases to avoid an inflationary spiral.[31]

It was therefore with genuine reluctance that Deakin dropped his instinctive opposition to any form of government intervention over pay bargaining. However, as chairman of the TUC's special committee on the economic situation, he knew full well just how close the British economy was coming to collapse by the end of 1947. Deakin and his TUC colleagues were kept fully informed by Hugh Dalton and then by Stafford Cripps as Chancellor of the Exchequer about the country's perilous position. The tone of his quarterly reports to the union's executive council do not suggest Deakin needed much convincing that this was no time for complacency or self-congratulation. 'We shall not find any solution to our present difficulties by burying our head in the sand and refusing to face up, in a realistic way, to the intricate and serious problems confronting our country at this time', he explained to members.[32] But Deakin – like other loyal national union leaders – disliked the government's lack of consultation before publishing its White Paper on personal incomes, costs and prices in February 1948. This threatened vaguely to introduce direct state intervention in wage bargaining unless the unions stopped making pay demands that might add to business costs and lead to price rises. It is true the document did not propose the introduction of a full-blown national incomes policy like those of the 1960s and 1970s, but it did represent a significant breach in the voluntarist tradition of pay bargaining. Unfortunately the emphasis was on wage self-restraint alone and the government did not seek to use the opportunity to develop a wider strategy of manpower planning with long-term objectives. The White Paper warned no wage rises were justified that were not earned through a 'substantial increase in production'. It added that the government would be guided by that principle in its own behaviour as an employer. The White Paper also argued that any rises in production costs due to wage increases should not be taken into account in any proposed price rises. Under such pressure and with obvious misgivings the TUC agreed, at a special conference of affiliate union executives in March 1948, by 5,421,000 votes to 2,032,000 against to cooperate with the government on wage restraint. However, the size of the minority trade union vote was a clear warning that many unions resented what they believed to be a government-imposed policy which would restrain their freedom to negotiate freely with employers. In fact, the TUC was successful during intensive negotiations with Cripps in winning reassurances from the Treasury that the new wages policy would still enable low-paid workers to gain higher rises, allow companies in undermanned essential industries to meet labour shortages through better pay offers and recognise the key role of intra-industry wage differentials based on craft skills, training and experience. On the face of it, those caveats could have been loopholes that might have led to the early collapse of the policy. But in practice Deakin and other national union leaders issued restraining instructions to their negotiators that proved effective in holding back wage rates, at least for a time.

In his quarterly report in the spring of 1948 to the general executive council Deakin explained his own conversion to the need for wage restraint. 'We must have a measure of stability in relation to wages and prices and take those steps which will avoid inflationary tendencies', he argued.

This means trade union executives have got to accept a measure of responsibility and guide policy. It is not sufficient to be swept along in a clamour of wage increases. If we accept a position of that kind it simply means that we would be assisting in creating those conditions which would ultimately destroy the real influence of the trade union movement.[33]

Deakin's loyalty to the TUC's national wages policy was also evident at the 1948 party conference. Defending the government's economic strategy, he praised Labour's welfare reforms and called for absolute support for ministers.

Let us make up our minds that we say nothing which will prevent our people from pulling their full weight. I would say to the political theorists: 'Beware of stepping out in such a way that you hinder rather than help the programme of the government at this time'. I know there is a disposition on the part of some of our friends in the political movement to make specious promises and to say we must change this and the other but we must have regard to the economic facts.[34]

It was Deakin too who moved the key composite motion on the control of wages, prices and profits, calling on the conference to welcome the government's economic strategy as long as it was based on a determination to stabilise the cost of living. He did so by emphasising the assurances the government had made to the TUC over dealing with excess profits. Deakin was sensitive to the charge that he had changed his position over wage restraint because of his unthinking loyalty to the government. 'I do not want anyone to tell me that I have changed my ground; that I was opposed to a wage policy', he insisted.

I was and still am in relation to any proposal which would leave the government with the responsibility for fixing a minimum standard of life. We welcome the policy for the reason that it leaves us freedom for negotiation and some of us have not been unsuccessful up to the present in securing the consideration that was our entitlement even in the face of the White Paper.[35]

Deakin pointed out that the government's policy provided 'an opportunity for claims on behalf of people who increase their productive capacity'. 'We recognise the difficulty of the government. A change over in principle of the character involved in this policy cannot be accomplished overnight', he admitted. 'We have to be a little patient.' Deakin made it clear he expected the TUC 'as the responsible instrument for the negotiation of wages and conditions' to keep a 'tight hold on the position and see to it that the assurances and the guarantees given to them were fully carried out'.

By the late summer of 1948, however, Deakin was less defensive in his support for the wages policy and lectured his executive council on the changing role of the trade unions in their relations with the state. As he told them in his August report:

> The trade union movement is faced with problems which need a reorientation of our point of view. With Labour in government, socialisation of industry, control and supervision of industry, the incidence of taxation and of governmental policy designed to limit the activities of the money interests, we must condition our approach to the changed conditions with which we are faced. We have got the power but with it we have the responsibility calling for clear insight and a conception of the new order. The trade unions have an ever-increasing importance in developing the new social order. We must act with wisdom and discretion, not at any point sacrificing our principles or the interests of the people we represent but in a constructive manner and with a sense of dignity and understanding.[36]

Deakin believed that the TUC wages policy had helped to save the British economy from collapse. As he told his executive council in his last quarterly report for 1948:

> Whilst the question of wages, profits and prices has inevitably caused us some concern and poses a policy which is not readily understood it would not be too much to say that the restraint that has arisen from the acceptance of this policy has possibly saved us from a depression and a worsening of our standard of life which could, and would in my opinion, have followed any refusal on our part to face up to practicalities.[37]

By the time of the 1949 Labour conference Deakin had become a passionate advocate of pay restraint, condemning its critics for 'arguing a policy of despair'. However, he continued to battle for the protection of the low paid even in a period of wage restraint. 'We believe there is justice due to the people engaged in vital services who are contributing substantially to the economic recovery that is taking place. They are entitled to more consideration than they are getting.' But Deakin was convinced the government's restrictive approach remained necessary. 'If you lift the limit at this time you create a condition which will react very unfavourably upon the minds of wage earners', he concluded. 'Are we striving to attain the policy that this Movement has declared so long or are we striving to create chaos and confusion? Do not forget there are people who say we cannot succeed unless we produce that condition where unemployment and under-employment prevails. That is a distinct challenge to our purpose and unity.'[38]

It was during his passionate defence of the TUC wages policy at his own union's 1949 biennial conference that Deakin explained why he believed the unions had faced no credible alternative but to respond to the government's pleas for a restraint on their wage demands. As he told the delegates:

I do not say there is an easy way, any early solution to the problems with which we are confronted, but at least I am satisfied of this, that if we take the same course, exercise restraint, accept a measure of stability, I am perfectly sure that we shall avoid those economic consequences that attended our efforts in 1922 to 1932. Seared in my soul is a remembrance of the want, the suffering and privation that came our way following the depression of 1922, bringing with it those vast tracts of depressed areas and a great army of unemployed.[39]

It was Deakin's personal fear that the current economic troubles could well precipitate a return to the desperate conditions suffered by the working class during the inter-war years that shaped his attitude. His 1949 speech to the biennial conference on the need for voluntary pay restraint was one of the most impressive he ever delivered to the union. He called for loyalty to Labour at a time of national crisis. As Deakin explained:

It is no use anyone trying to fool you at this time and say that we can promote and succeed with extravagant wage claims or even modest wage claims in some of the better paid industries with which we are dealing. In point of fact I am going to be brutally frank this morning. I doubt whether at this time we can get wage increases at all. I am going to be no party to misleading the members of this organisation into a belief that we can do those things in face of the circumstances which confront this country at this time. That, I suggest to you, is not leadership. It means that you are fooling people into the belief that you can do things which you cannot. You are creating a condition of unrest in the minds of people which is absolutely and completely unjustifiable. I am not a person who advocates a policy of despair. I believe we have achieved solid results during the years when Labour has been governing this country ... I want to see that position consolidated. I know there is a popular idea running around that you have to keep people in a continual state of agitation if you are to maintain their economic position. I do not believe it. I believe that if you do that, if you follow that line of country, you are rendering lasting disservice to the people whom we represent.

In the aftermath of the government's September 1949 devaluation of sterling, Deakin told his members 'there was an even greater need for trade unions to exercise restraint in their right to pursue wage claims'. He was convinced there was no alternative but to tighten up the TUC's existing voluntary wages strategy. 'Unless we accept a measure of restraint within the limits proposed by the TUC then we have not even a fighting chance of averting the crisis which faces us', he added.[40] But the mood among many unions was growing hostile to any more self-restraint in pay bargaining. They only backed the national wages policy narrowly by 4,263,000 votes to 3,606,000 when it was tightened up after devaluation. The new policy argued that wage rates must be held stable while the interim retail price index, which then stood at 112, remained between an upper and lower limit of 118 and 106. If the figure reached either limit, then the TUC said there should be a resumption of voluntary bargaining. The formula also insisted sliding scale arrangements, which provided back-dated adjustments to cover rises in living costs, should be suspended. The policy was supposed to last until January 1951, but within a few months it was no longer credible as union after union rejected it in the face of rising prices and pressure from their activists. By June 1950 the TUC had more or less abandoned its own restraint policy, leaving it to the 'good sense and reasonableness' of the unions to determine the size of their wage claims. Deakin continued to exhort support for the national pay policy but his was becoming an increasingly lone and beleaguered voice. The 1950 Congress buried any further commitment by the unions to wage restraint by refusing to accept further support by 3,898,000 votes to 3,521,000 against, despite Deakin's assertion that its opponents favoured a policy of 'smash and grab'.[41] It was the first defeat the TUC general council had suffered since 1945 but reflected through trade union structures the disintegration of solidarity in many workplaces.

Was the temporary trade union self-sacrifice important in preventing an economic collapse? In his authoritative history of British economic policy during the period, Sir Alec Cairncross acknowledged that between June 1945 and June 1947 average hourly wage rates increased by 9 per cent in the first twelve months and by 8.5 per cent in the second. Over the next nine months to March 1948 wages grew on average by almost 9 per cent. But from then until the September 1949 devaluation the annual rate of wage increases actually fell to 2.8 per cent and dropped further still to not much more than 1 per cent in the twelve months following devaluation. By contrast, retail prices rose during that same period, with a sharp 5 per cent annual growth rate in food prices in the period up to devaluation. 'That money wages rose so little when real wages were stationary or falling and unemployment was down to 300,000 is striking testimony to the influence of the trade union leaders', concluded Cairncross.[42] Kenneth Morgan has written of the 'remarkable abdication of their roles by the unions, unqiue in times of peace. The general effect of the wage freeze policy was remarkably successful in the fragmented, adversarial world of British labour relations and a political triumph for Cripps.'[43] To Peter Hennessy it was 'a measure of the never-to-be-repeated unity of the Labour Movement in the late 1940s'.[44]

But it is also true that the trade unions could not continue to restrain the wage demands coming from their members indefinitely despite pleas by government ministers about the need for moderation in the national interest, particularly when the economy began to deteriorate with an increasing balance of payments deficit and the threat of inflation due to soaring world commodity prices after the onset of the Korean War. Deakin may have convinced himself that wage moderation was vital to the achievement of economic success but he found it increasingly difficult to assure many negotiators in the TGWU that this was any longer a sensible strategy to pursue in the face of shopfloor frustrations. Throughout 1950 and the first ten months of 1951 the Treasury continued to yearn for the formation of some kind of institution like a central wages board to oversee pay trends without compulsion. Deakin may well have gone along with this proposal if the government had decided to introduce such a policy but it is unlikely the TUC would have agreed to it even if Labour had won the 1951 general election. Overwhelmingly, members of the TUC general council accepted they could no longer uphold a so-called national wages policy. Deakin was unhappy at the growing opposition to wage restraint inside many unions. But he acknowledged that the TGWU could not stand against the tide. 'We cannot permit the interests of our members to be lost sight of in the general trend of events', he told the executive council in August 1950.[45]

> If the Movement will not exercise restraint and good sense it is too bad. On the other hand, we have a job of work to do on behalf of our members. If the great measure of stability that we have secured is undermined, then those who have advocated a policy of disregarding economic facts will have something to answer for.

Deakin continued to believe the TUC's rejection of the principle of restraint was 'a great mistake'. From his sick bed in the Manor House hospital in November 1950, he insisted that while the union would accept the TUC position, this 'did not mean the end of wage restraint'. 'It simply means a shifting of responsibility', he explained. Instead of the TUC, the affiliate unions would have to pursue restraint in their own way or there would be a 'policy of drift' which would precipitate 'an inevitable collapse of the nation's economy'. Deakin expressed opposition to submitting 'fantastic wage claims'. 'The sensible line to take is to submit open applications where considered justified, leaving it to the ability and wit of the negotiators to produce the best possible result.'[46] He believed a 'smash and grab' policy never achieved anything of lasting value. It only creates a feeling of 'you wait until our opportunity presents itself and we will get our own back' which is not the right atmosphere within industry.[47] Deakin was also as convinced as ever that 'to merely strive for increased wages which quickly disappear as a result of increased prices is no solution to the working-class problem'. 'What we must all be fearful of is creating that condition which will result in an uncontrollable inflationary spiral. If this happens, then I feel nothing can save us. The clock would be set back for many decades; in fact, we should not recover during the lifetime of the present generation', he told his executive council in June 1951.[48]

Despite the genuine difference of opinion over pay between the government and the unions, Deakin made a rallying call for unity at the pre-election 1951 party conference. 'We have had our grouse but at the bottom of the hearts of our people is the recognition that never before in the history of government in this country have we had a better deal than we have had from the Labour government during the last six years. We know as trade unionists, how great is the value of the support and consideration that we have had.' Deakin expressed trade union appreciation for government successes in maintaining full employment and introducing measures of social justice.[49]

Deakin on the defensive

Labour's narrow defeat at the polls was followed by a period of bitter inner-party conflict in which Deakin played a prominent role. He seemed to devote much of his time to an endless and negative struggle against those he saw as his implacable enemies on the left. In alliance with Williamson and Lawther, he sought to defend Attlee and his government's legacy against the challenge from the brilliant but mercurial Aneurin Bevan. At the raucous 1952 Morecambe party conference Deakin provoked uproar among delegates with an outspoken attack on the Bevanites in his speech as TUC fraternal delegate. He accused them of forming an inner party caucus and 'creating a mistrust which will destroy the confidence of the people in the Labour party as an effective instrument of parliamentary government'. Deakin called for a 'complete disbandment' of the party's 'dissident element'. He bellowed over a rising chorus of boos; 'Let them get rid of their whips; dismiss their business managers and conform to the party constitution. Let them cease the vicious attacks they have launched upon those with whom they disagree, abandon their vituperation and the carping criticism which appears regularly in Tribune.' He said they needed to realise that ordinary trade union members and the party rank and file had 'no time or use for such tactics or for their disregard of those principles and loyalties to which our Movement has held so strongly throughout the whole course of its existence'.[50]

Later at the same conference Deakin erupted in fury against a left-wing attempt to win support for the use of industrial action for political purposes. The following exchange, recorded in the annual conference report, speaks for itself:

> *Deakin*: 'I think it is time conference came down to earth on this matter and appreciated the significance ...' (at this point the speaker was interrupted by shouts from a section of the conference).
> *Chairman*: 'Will delegates please listen to the speaker on the rostrum.'
> *A Delegate*: 'We have heard him once.'
> *Mr Deakin*: 'You know you would listen if you wanted to get money from the trade unions.'
> *A Delegate*: 'Who is buying his way now?'[51]

But Deakin was unintimidated by the delegates and concluded with the assertion that the trade unions would not back any incitement to foment political strikes. 'We believe in parliamentary democracy. We know perfectly well who has got to carry the baby when trouble of that character comes and if you want to destroy the future prospects of this party and delay the day when Labour is returned to the government of this country, then pass this resolution.'

Not even the Morecambe conference went so far as to encourage the use of political strikes to confront a democratically elected government but Deakin's extraordinary behaviour reflected the belligerent mood of the trade union right, forced on to the defensive in the face of growing resistance to the party leadership from many constituency activists. Morecambe's aftermath was significant because it revealed Deakin's preference for whom he believed should succeed Attlee as party leader. At a speech in Stalybridge, former Chancellor of the Exchequer Hugh Gaitskell questioned how many Communist or Communist-inspired delegates had been attending the Morecambe conference and called for an end to 'the attempt at mob rule by a group of frustrated journalists', with the restoration of the 'authority and leadership of the solid, sound, sensible majority of the Movement'.[52] Such robust remarks impressed Deakin and he began to mobilise trade union block votes behind Gaitskell. This led to Gaitskell's triumph over Bevan for the party treasurership in 1954, seen as a necessary stepping-stone to his election as party leader over twelve months later. Without Deakin's strong support, Gaitskell may have found it more difficult to make an impact among the trade unions. It is true that union backing was not a prerequisite to be elected party leader at that time. The parliamentary Labour Party held the exclusive franchise. But Gaitskell's close relations with union leaders like Deakin, Williamson and Sam Watson of the Durham miners strengthened his support on the party's centre-right and especially among the trade union group who made up an estimated third of the Labour MPs who almost all voted for him.

Although he might have suggested the unions should not interfere directly in the party, Deakin believed the trade unions should not restrain themselves from expressing their collective opinion on party policy. 'The trade union point of view must be considered at all times and the trade unions be given the opportunity to take full part in developing those policies which we regard as of prime importance to the members we represent', he told delegates to his union's 1953 biennial conference.[53] 'We are not prepared to accept the view that all the sense and judgement rests in the political movement of this country. We have hard experience, we are not mere theorists. We have got to face hard, matter of fact, day to day problems.'

However, while Deakin remained resolute in his defence of the party's right-wing leadership, he was not ready to welcome or participate in any public debate on how Labour should modernise its policies to regain political power. Deakin was never a revisionist. He continued to articulate a traditionally pragmatic trade union position. He did not show much obvious interest in a wider employment agenda either. It is true he opposed the shopping list approach of the left to the nationalisation of specific industries and favoured a period of consolidation before any more were taken into state ownership. But this did not mean that Deakin was ready to question Labour's traditional commitment to nationalisation.

On the other hand, Deakin was not prepared to oppose the Churchill government on principle on everything they did. Indeed, Deakin and the other right-wing members of the TUC Junta established friendly relations with the prime minister and the conciliatory Sir Walter Monckton, Churchill's Minister of Labour. Deakin remained anxious about the dangers of any wages free-for-all in a time of full employment. 'There still prevails in some sections of our movement the idea that all they have to do is to continually seek wage increases regardless of consequences', he told a conference of tin-plate workers in May 1954.[54] He insisted that the Labour Movement had 'moved on from the propaganda stage to the point where we must of necessity be prepared to accept a great measure of responsibility ... Our duty is to take care of the wages and well-being of the members we represent, to do that as effectively as possible and not to allow at any time political considerations to obscure our day to day responsibilities.'

Deakin opposed the suggestion that trade unions should seek to maximise their bargaining strength whenever possible by taking advantage of any shift in the industrial power balance. As he told his union's Irish delegate conference in Belfast in October 1954:

It should not be the policy of any single trade union or group of unions having a privileged position to pursue policies to the disadvantage of the interests of the community. If the trade unions are to maintain that influence and position in the economy which they claim, the pattern of their policy must be related to the needs of the community at large in addition to serving the interests of the people they represent.[55]

Deakin insisted that under his leadership, the TGWU would continue to exercise restraint and not pursue wage claims to exploit the position of a particular group or for the sake of it.

But this did not mean he was ready to discuss the possible creation of an incomes policy under any future Labour government. As he told his executive council in June 1952: 'It is not practicable to switch over to a firm policy of fixing wages on a national basis by relating the wages paid in one industry to those operating in another, without creating a measure of industrial unrest which would add considerably to our difficulties at the present time.'[56] An attempt was made at the 1952 Trades Union Congress to create a review of wage-fixing and negotiating machinery, with the aim of deciding whether it was 'desirable' to have greater coordination 'with a view to providing greater equity and fairer relativities'. Although TUC chairman on that occasion and therefore unable to speak himself, Deakin made his views known by telling the mover of the motion it would be a 'sheer waste of time' for him to exercise his right of reply to the debate.[57]

But Deakin also found himself pushed on to the defensive in his advocacy of voluntary wage restraint in the national interest and in opposition to what he saw as the growing dangers of wage-push inflation through workplace extremism fuelled by militant shop stewards. In his final years Deakin seemed to be a bitter, frustrated man at odds with the times. He grew increasingly critical of the mass media which he believed was unfairly giving the TGWU a bad name through abuse and misrepresentation. But he was also exasperated by what he regarded as the wrecking tactics of the Communist Party inside the union. Deakin was determined, as far as he could, to ensure the union's industrial activities were kept rigidly separate from its political aspirations. 'I will be no party under any circumstances so far as I can influence the position, to sacrificing the industrial welfare of our people on the altar of political expediency', he told a Scottish delegate conference in July 1954.[58] By the time of his fatal heart attack, however, Deakin sounded like an embattled figure from another age, defending a post-war social settlement that was starting to disintegrate in some industrial sectors under the pressures imposed by militant workplace bargaining and full employment.

Cousins and the new militancy

In fact, within seven months of his death Deakin's union began to move in a quite different political and industrial direction. This had little to do with any spontaneous rank and file revolt. The election of the left-wing Frank Cousins as TGWU general secretary in March 1956 was more the result of fortuitous events than due to an uprising from below.

Deakin's chosen successor had been the emollient and moderate Jock Tiffin, but he was already a sick man when elected and he died soon after taking office in December 1955. By that time Cousins had already been appointed to the key position of assistant general secretary by the union's executive council. No doubt, ability played an important part in his meteoric rise to the top of the TGWU but as Geoffrey Goodman explained, if Harry Nicholas had not been found inadvertently in arrears with his membership subscription he would probably have occupied the second most important post in the TGWU after 1948 instead of Tiffin and would therefore have been groomed to succeed Deakin in 1955.

From the moment of his surprise arrival at the top of Transport House, Cousins began to move the union away from what he regarded as the political excesses of Deakinism. This did not mean democratising the TGWU's structure. As general secretary, Cousins was as keen as his two predecessors to ensure he held on to all the power and authority that came with what was the most important trade union job in the Labour Movement. Indeed, Cousins was viewed with some initial suspicion not only by the party's right-wing but also by the Bevanites. Bevan himself never found Cousins an easy man to deal with, suspecting he was a syndicalist at heart. His acolytes Richard Crossman and Barbara Castle were more sympathetic but somewhat equivocal about the Cousins approach. Indeed, the TGWU general secretary – described as the 'awkward warrior' by his sympathetic biographer Geoffrey Goodman[59] – found himself very much a solitary figure both in the TUC and the Labour Party. He was unpredictable and awkward, quick to take offence and often difficult to fathom. It is untrue that the TGWU under Cousins turned left-wing on every issue over night. While his union could no longer be relied upon to be part of any praetorian guard protecting the leadership, it was not a consistently reliable supporter for a left-wing agenda either. As Martin Harrison explained: 'The problem that Mr Cousins and his union set the party is not that they have gone into systematic opposition but that their support can no longer be depended on as it was in Deakin's day.'[60] Certainly the TGWU was now a source of genuine anxiety to Gaitskell as he sought to find a way for the party to move out of the political wilderness. Cousins and his union became quickly the bogeymen of the right-wing tabloid press and were therefore seen as a liability and not an asset in Labour's hopes of electoral recovery.

Cousins also turned out to be as much an autocrat as Deakin. It is debatable whether his strongly held left-wing political beliefs were shared by the majority of his union's rank and file. Certainly his emotional commitment to unilateral nuclear disarmament did not reflect the views of the union's membership. And yet he was able to change TGWU defence policy within two years of his election as general secretary. The union has remained in favour of unilateral nuclear disarmament ever since, even into the age of Tony Blair.

Cousins was determined to exercise control over Labour MPs who were sponsored by the TGWU. David Buckle, the union's district secretary in Oxford for 27 years, records in his autobiography his interview with Cousins when he sought his union's financial support as a parliamentary candidate. On that occasion Cousins made it clear that he expected Buckle to give him a personal undertaking that he would neither ask any questions nor make any speech in the House of Commons if elected on any matters relating to the TGWU or industrial relations without first consulting him. Buckle replied that he could give no such assurance because he would regard himself as the representative of the constituency which elected him and not a delegate of the TGWU.[61]

However, perhaps the most important difference from the Deakin years came with Cousins's outspoken repudiation of any form of wage restraint. The change of attitude in the TGWU was clear from the general executive council's declaration in December 1955 with its opposition to any form of wage restraint. 'We are not prepared that our members should stand still whilst the government continually hand out largesse to those who are more favourably placed', acting general secretary Cousins explained in the union journal. He made it clear the TGWU in future was not 'prepared to accept the principle that the proper living standards of the members of the unions shall wholly be dependent upon higher productivity'.[62] Cousins burst dramatically on to the public scene with a militant speech to the 1956 Trades Union Congress that upset many on the TUC general council with a blunt repudiation of wage restraint. 'We accept that in a period of freedom for all we are part of the all', he told delegates.

> We are not going on the rampage. We are not going to use our organisational strength to prove that the TGWU are first and the rest can get where they like. What we are saying is that there is no such thing in this country as a place where you can say 'wage levels stop here' and that we ought to be content even if things remain equal.[63]

His speech may seem confused when read today but it left the distinct impression that Cousins and his union were in the mood for a wage confrontation with both the government and employers. However, his TUC declaration was of more symbolic than substantive value. It made it clear that Deakinism, with its emphasis on responsibility and cooperation with employers over wage bargaining, was at an end. From now on, the TGWU would adopt a much more aggressive wages offensive in line with the angry frustrations of the shopfloor. In practice, Cousins turned out to be much less combative than his threatening rhetoric might have suggested, at least when it came to confronting employers across the bargaining table. The 1958 London Transport bus strike turned out to be a seminal event in the humbling of Cousins as a trade union militant when his members went down to humiliating defeat after the TUC general council refused to throw its weight behind their cause.

Cousins was to enjoy much more success as TGWU leader inside the Labour Party. It was soon clear that he had little time for the efforts of the modernisers who wanted to make Labour more electorally popular. Cousins was an old-style authoritarian Socialist who believed unquestioningly in the state nationalisation of large sectors of industry. 'We still think of nationalisation as an instrument of economic power for the government', he told his union's biennial conference in 1957. 'We do not think it right that industries which have the power of control over the livelihood of the people should be subject to the whims of the persons engaged in them only for the sake of making profits and able to determine our standard of living, leaving us in the position of redressing the balance through our trade union organisation.'[64] As he assured the 1959 party conference: 'There are five or six million people who are socialists in embryo waiting for us to go out and harness them to the power machine we want to drive.'[65] Cousins may have endorsed the party's moderate 1958 statement on Industry and Society but he was at the forefront of the opposition to Gaitskell's ill-fated attempt to revise clause 4 of the party's 1918 constitution. The TGWU even voted, though alone, against the compromise statement of aims that ended that particular crisis.

Cousins was also more party political in his advocacy of unilateral nuclear disarmament, although it remains difficult to fathom what he actually wanted to advocate. His emotional hostility to all nuclear weapons was self-evident and so was his belief that Britain should set an example to the world and abandon its own nuclear deterrent. What remained unclear was whether Cousins also wanted Britain to withdraw from the US-dominated North Atlantic Treaty Organisation, demand the closure of all US nuclear bases in the country and declare itself to be a neutral country. Initially, Cousins called for an end to all hydrogen bomb tests for ever, an immediate pledge that Britain would not be the first to use nuclear weapons in the event of a war and that a future

Labour government would ban the manufacture of nuclear weapons. In a letter to Gaitskell in June 1956 he suggested it was 'absolute nonsense' that he wanted both a unilateral renunciation of the bomb and an end to Britain's NATO membership.[66] A month later his union's conference voted for a composite resolution that called for resistance to all missile bases in the country and the prevention of all planes carrying nuclear weapons using UK bases.

It is true that during the spring and summer of 1960 a number of unions joined the TGWU in the unilateralist camp, including the shopworkers' union, USDAW, and the AEU engineering union. But Cousins was muddled over what he favoured. In his 1960 conference speech he tried to explain to delegates whether the unilateralist strategy meant Britain would have to leave NATO. 'If the question is posed to me as simply saying, am I prepared to go on remaining in an organisation over which I have no control, but which can destroy us instantly, my answer is Yes, if the choice is that. But it is not that.'[67] Cousins and the TGWU continued to oppose the party's defence policy, but after their defeat over the issue after Gaitskell reversed the Scarborough decision at the 1961 conference, it seemed unlikely that they would be able to stage another successful offensive. In fact, the political differences between Cousins and Gaitskell narrowed during the autumn of 1962 when the two men found themselves in full accord on their anti-European Common Market stance. For the first time since Cousins's accession to the TGWU leadership, it seemed that the union and the party were in harmony. Nonetheless, the accession of Harold Wilson to succeed Gaitskell who died suddenly in January 1963 brought an even warmer relationship between the TGWU and the Labour leadership. Wilson made a speech to the union's biennial conference that summer which was well received by delegates, although he denounced unofficial strikes and outdated restrictive practices and warned that Labour would require a restraint on pay if elected to government.

Cousins was ill at the time and could not preside over the 1963 biennial conference but his views about incomes policy was the subject of difficulty for the Labour leadership. On this issue, however, he spoke directly for his unskilled manual worker members. As he told the 1958 Trades Union Congress, the TGWU would accept no form of wage restraint. If they did they would be entitled to be called 'an industrial mouthpiece of a political party'.[68] But Cousins said they were 'trade unions representing the workers and we shall continue to do that whatever government is in power because that is democracy'. As he explained in the *TGWU Record* in October 1963: 'If we do not fulfil the purposes for which members join unions, to protect and raise their real standard of living, then the unions will wither and finally die. We can give leadership, we can persuade but basically we must serve trade union purposes.'[69] In a speech in Oxford in June 1964 Cousins expressed similar sentiments. 'It is not the intention of the trade union movement to hold back its members' wage claims if they are justified. It is our purpose to sell our labour and our skill in the open market to the best of our ability while we live under the present system.'[70] Such views were unexceptional among trade union negotiators at the time. But they suggested that under any elected government, even a Labour one, not only should organised labour be allowed to practise collective bargaining free from state interference, but it must not even agree to any voluntary wage restraint. However, Cousins was prepared to accept what he described as a 'planned growth of wages', perhaps more through a willingness to ensure unity on the eve of the general election than any genuine change of attitude to pay policy.[71]

Cousins told the 1959 TGWU conference that he believed 'the most important thing in our lives was to elect a Labour government determined to carry out a socialist policy'.[72] However, his behaviour as general secretary compelled the party leaders to reassess what the relationship between Labour and the trade unions ought to be. As Gaitskell explained to the 1959 Trades Union Congress:

We are comrades together but we have different jobs to do. You have your industrial job and we have our political job. We do not dictate to one another. Any leader of the Labour party would not be worth his salt if he allowed himself to be dictated to by the trade unions.[73]

For his part, Cousins in 1956 had assured the party conference that 'I told you last year not to tell the unions how to do their job and I am certainly not going to tell the Labour party how to do its job.'[74] In practice, he violated his own recognition of that tacit understanding over spheres of influence that implicitly determined how the party and the unions conducted their affairs. On one occasion he told Tony Benn that he had 'always wanted to form a trade union political party'.[75] The very public conflict between Cousins and Gaitskell helped to highlight the difficult nature of the party–union relationship. Allan Flanders, in his brilliant essay on trade unions and politics written at the height of the conflict over defence, explained the nature of what he called 'that silent self-denying ordinance practised by the trade unions within the Labour party', which Cousins had brought temporarily into question.[76]

But it was not so much the controversy over defence that threatened to bring the party–union marriage into question. Under both Deakin and Cousins the TGWU revealed the more fundamental tensions that lay at the heart of the party–trade union connection, focusing on the nature of collective bargaining in a market economy in relation to a party committed to planning, social justice and economic growth. The two men did not share common political views on most issues. Deakin was a working-class patriot, who believed in the mixed economy, order and responsibility and managed his union with increasing difficulty in the face of rising shopfloor discontent. Cousins was a muddled, emotional but incorruptible man of integrity who often seemed more interested in developing a political than an industrial agenda. Both men were authoritarian, hostile to dissent within their union and convinced of the rectitude of their own positions. They also shared an understandable pride in the power and influence that the TGWU was able to exercise over the rest of the Labour Movement. They also held similar instinctive and traditionalist views about voluntarism in industrial relations. They were not modernisers, though sympathetic to the challenge of automation and the need for greater productivity. They were above all both believers in free collective bargaining. Deakin's passionate views on that subject between July 1945 and February 1948 were mirrored by those of Cousins after 1956. It is true that Deakin came to support wage restraint and persisted with his concern to hold back sectionalist demands even when the Labour Party was in opposition. He seems to have genuinely convinced himself that a wages free-for-all would ignite inflation and wreck the economy, plunging the country back to the dreadful conditions of the inter-war years with the return of mass unemployment. Cousins was uninhibited, at least in theory, about the need for TGWU members to be part of the all. In his often angry way, he reflected the frustrations and aspirations of a growing number of manual workers in what was becoming the age of affluence. Although in practice he was no militant, perhaps chastened by the searing experience of the 1958 London bus strike, Cousins remained instinctively hostile to any form of national incomes policy. He was persuaded to join Harold Wilson's cabinet in October 1964 as Minister of Technology. But after much frustration with political life, he resigned in July 1966 in protest at the government's decision to introduce wage restraint in the midst of a financial crisis. Returning to his union, Cousins prepared the succession for Jack Jones but he did not launch a raging campaign against the incomes policy in the period up to his retirement in 1969.

The history of the Deakin and Cousins years reveal how difficult it was to reconcile a belief in economic planning and collectivism under a Labour government with free collective bargaining in a segmented, decentralised market economy. Labour leaders from Attlee to Wilson sought to find ways of reconciling that contradiction. Despite their genuine loyalty to the party and the principles of democratic Socialism, both Deakin and Cousins showed the severe limitations imposed on them by industrial realities to unify their trade union and political aspirations with a coherent strategy. Even the implied Social Contract of 1945 that did so much to ensure the cohesion and self-confidence of Mr Attlee's government could not withstand the fissures produced by an industrial relations system that thrived on inter-union competitiveness and sectionalist pay bargaining. This was a dilemma which was well explained by Professor Jean McKelvey, an American academic, in 1952. She wrote:

What the British experience indicates most sharply is the essentially conservative nature of the trade union movement. This is not meant as either praise or criticism but simply as a statement of fact. So long as unions remain independent interest groups in a free society, they must function as associations whose primary concern is that of protecting their own members. No matter how much rhetoric is used about the new functions of the trade unions, the fact remains they are sectional bodies pursuing special interests.[77]

In fact, the economic and social conditions of post-war Britain made it impossible to reconcile *laissez-faire* and statism in industrial relations. Deakin was wrong to think the problem was caused by the Communist menace among the shop stewards, although the far left was able to exploit the instabilities caused by pay bargaining in a disintegrating and disorderly labour market experiencing full employment. Deakin's increasingly frenzied appeals for responsibility and order from his rank and file members could not succeed because most of them were never going to subordinate their bread and butter demands for the needs of a Labour government in trouble. Wage restraint could work for only a limited period without provoking severe tensions and conflict inside increasingly fossilised union structures like that of the TGWU. On the other hand, it was Deakin and not Cousins who was aware of the wider demands imposed on the Labour Movement by efforts to save an increasingly vulnerable economy in relative decline from international financial pressures. In his valiant but ultimately thankless efforts to support wage restraint in the national interest as defined by a Labour government, Deakin resembled a later TGWU general secretary. Jack Jones, during the Social Contract of 1975–77, recognised the perils of hyper-inflation and the devastating impact economic collapse would have on the living standards of his members. Like Deakin, Jones was also eventually convinced that free collective bargaining was a threat not only to the introduction of democratic Socialism but to the long-term well-being of the economy and therefore of trade unionists. The two men shared a similar fear that a free-for-all could bring a return of the poverty and despair experienced by many of Labour's core voters among the manual working class between the wars. However, the TGWU in the post-Bevin era demonstrated through the calibre of its leaders that its behaviour was vital to the party's success and failures. Inside that mighty organisation the tensions and dilemmas that troubled the Labour Party over regulation and voluntarism in the immediate post-war years were debated although not really satisfactorily resolved.[78] Perhaps they never could be in a democratic society dominated, in part, by a culture of *laissez-faire* individualism.

4

'What Are We Here For?' George Woodcock and Trade Union Reform, 1960–1969

The character of our trade union movement has been moulded by conditions and not by theories. It has taken shape and its purposes and practices from the circumstances in which it grew.

George Woodcock[1]

We are a voluntary body. We have no sanctions and even if we had, we have no power to enforce them.

George Woodcock[2]

George Woodcock's time as general secretary of the Trades Union Congress from September 1960 until March 1969 is often characterised as a period of unfulfilled promise, a lost opportunity for the trade unions to modernise themselves and become a necessary partner in the management of the British economy. An undisputed if insecure Estate of the Realm, the TUC in the 1960s was given the opportunity to become a crucial institution in helping to resolve the country's economic problems, so it was argued. However, the TUC failed to seize the challenge. Woodcock himself is often blamed for what happened. 'He is a cynical man – maybe if you get to the top in the trade union movement you have to be cynical, but not as much as he is', Anthony Wedgwood Benn, then Minister of Technology, wrote in his diary.

He once made a speech saying that life was full of shoddy compromises and I think, early on, he had a conception of how the trade unions should develop and be run which never came to reality, partly because history was not ready for it and partly because he did not have enough drive. It has made him very bitter. He is also a terrible old bore.[3]

George Brown, a man who, when Secretary of State for Economic Affairs, Woodcock initially admired for his energy and optimism, took an equally unfavourable view of Woodcock's role at the TUC. 'He is a most up and down fellow; even in his most enthusiastic comments, he sounds rather like an undertaker. One day he would be for it but the next day while he was still for it, he now saw all the snags and possibilities', complained Brown.

Woodcock was always sure I was in too much of a hurry – that if only one would do things in a fairly leisurely way over the next fifty years, then one could bring it about. He professed to be well aware that you had to make 'shoddy, shabby compromises'. It was only naive fools like me who thought you might do something rather better.[4]

Richard Crossman, senior cabinet minister in the Labour governments of the 1960s and one of Woodcock's former tutors at Oxford, was relieved to see him go. Of Vic Feather who became TUC general secretary in March 1969 on Woodcock's retirement, he wrote in his diary: 'He is far more vigorous and far less neutral than Woodcock, far more solidly pro-Labour and pro-government.'[5] Barbara Castle, impatient of trade union ways when Secretary of State for Employment and Productivity, was exasperated by Woodcock who had given her the impression he agreed with her 'In Place of Strife' proposals to reform the trade unions. Woodcock had told Denis Barnes, the department's permanent secretary, that he believed 'Barbara has done a first-class job of work. 'The policy is excellent – very skilful.' As she noted in her diary, 'It will be the day when he says that to the press and I will believe it when I hear it.'[6] She was tired of union leaders saying one thing in private and another in public.

Woodcock could irritate even friendly Conservative government ministers who wanted to help him as much as they could to draw the TUC into an acceptance of wider public policy responsibilities. Reginald Maudling, expansionist Chancellor of the Exchequer under Macmillan in the early 1960s, testified to the 'cordial relations' he established with the TUC General Council, not least with Woodcock. But he was taken aback by Woodcock's sardonic sense of humour. 'I remember him once saying – "Well Reggie, I have come to the conclusion that if achieving greater productivity means getting up half an hour earlier in the morning, I am against it". Could there have been a better incapsulation of the views of the English people at that time?', ruminated Maudling.[7]

Many of his contemporaries came to regard Woodcock as a strange, cautious, introspective, intellectual figure, ill-equipped to become the moderniser of the trade union movement. More Hamlet-like philosopher than ideologist, he appeared to stand aloof and somewhat apart from the pragmatic, earthy and tough world of trade union power-brokering. Woodcock was the first to recognise his own personal limitations. 'I was a little bit of an austere person at the TUC. I hope not grumpy but a little remote', he confessed in retirement.

Woodcock admitted:

> There is a tendency in these big organizations for people to want to do the fixing with you behind the scenes and that was why I shied away a little bit from people. I preferred not to fix. If there was anything to be done it should be discussed by the appropriate committee or by the TUC General Council without any prior commitment with any member of the committee ... I never made any friends in the sense of personal friends. I took the view you were there to advise the General Council as a whole and your advice should never be tinged by your belief that you had blue-eyed boys on the General Council.[8]

But Woodcock had his coterie of admirers, especially among national newspaper labour editors such as Eric Wigham of *The Times* and Geoffrey Goodman, then of the *Daily Herald* and later of the *Sun*. John Cole at the *Guardian* was a particular friend. In his memoirs he describes Woodcock as the trade union movement's 'last, best hope to avoid its later unpopularity and decline ... He had a mind of great clarity, illuminated by a powerful imagination and human sympathy.'[9] Not all labour editors were so sympathetic. Peter Jenkins of the *Guardian* believed Woodcock became TUC general secretary 'too late' in life. He had grown 'gravely introspective, radical in thought but cautious (some alleged plain lazy) when it came to action'. Jenkins portrayed him as 'deracinated, sick in his heart', a man whose abilities and sense of purpose had 'atrophied'.[10]

However, it was Woodcock – more than any other trade union leader of his generation – who sought to prepare and challenge organised labour into playing an increasingly demanding role in a post-war economy where governments committed themselves to the creation of economic growth, full employment, high public spending, and the development of a welfare state based on universalist principles of provision. He agonised over what the relationship of trade unions should be with a democratic state that extended responsibilities for managing the economy. Woodcock tried to discover how trade union autonomy could be reconciled with industrial efficiency and innovation, how unions ought to practise voluntary restraint in pay bargaining to prevent the outbreak of damaging wage-push inflation. He wrestled with trying to balance the defence of trade union custom and practice with the need for unions to accept workplace reform and help improve labour productivity. During the 1960s Woodcock attempted – but only sporadically and perhaps always unduly aware of the obstacles to change – to find answers to such crucial questions. If he failed ultimately to do so, it is arguable that this was as much the fault of the times and the peculiarities of the British industrial relations system as his own weaknesses and personal idiosyncrasies.

The formative years

Woodcock's difficulties in office undoubtedly stemmed, at least partly, from the comparative lateness of his arrival as TUC general secretary. He had spent 13 years in the shadows as the frustrated assistant secretary to Sir Vincent Tewson, a mediocre consolidator, whom Woodcock openly despised. Woodcock was indeed an extraordinary man. Born in 1904 the son of a weaver in Walton-le-Dale outside Preston in Lancashire, he left school at twelve to work in the trade of his parents. A keen footballer, he almost turned professional, but then illness struck him and he was confined to bed for many months. It was during that crucial formative period that Woodcock read his way out of weaving. Through diligent hard work he won a scholarship to working-class Ruskin College, Oxford, in 1929. From there he advanced to New College where he secured a first class honours degree in politics, philosophy and economics. Surprisingly, he did not believe he suffered from any class prejudice. 'I thought Oxford was a wonderful place as though it were built for me', he recalled. 'It was ideally the kind of place that I wanted.' He thrived on the tutorial system. 'At no point anywhere, either among the undergraduates or among the dons did I ever get the impression of a distinction based on class', he claimed. 'I was aware of a distinction in my maturity and experience but apart from that, at no stage was I ever made aware that I was a working man and they were of another kind.'[11]

After twelve months on a scholarship at Manchester University, Woodcock took a job with the civil service. In 1936 he was appointed head of the TUC's research and economic department after the sudden death of the legendary Milne-Bailey, taking over as assistant general secretary in January 1947. In the small TUC policy-making secretariat under Citrine, whom he admired and who influenced him enormously, Woodcock thrived. During the Second World War, the TUC played an active and crucial part in decision-making through a network of joint consultation committees that covered a wide policy area including manpower problems, productivity, trade, price and wage stability. Woodcock came to know both the economist John Maynard Keynes and the social reformer William Beveridge very well. He was heavily influenced by their economic and social thought with its strong emphasis on the need for taking personal responsibility and devotion to the concept of public service. Woodcock played a key role in the efforts to develop a tripartite reconstruction programme which paved the way for the domestic policies of the 1945 Labour government. It was during the period of total war that Woodcock began to develop his underlying views of what the TUC's role ought to be in a modern democracy with an activist state. In the late 1940s he became an often robust and influential voice at the TUC in its dealings with a Labour government in economic crisis, although he was compelled to play second fiddle to Tewson. The TUC archives reveal how young Woodcock argued its case effectively and bluntly with Prime Minister Clement Attlee, Chancellor Stafford Cripps and Ernest Bevin, the Foreign Secretary. In a note written in November 1950 he assessed the increasing importance of the TUC, pointing out that before 1940 its discussions with ministers had usually been 'ad hoc and limited to one particular matter, and employers had not been present'.[12] With the war came continuous, formalised, structured and regular discussions between the TUC, government and employers.

After 1945 the TUC made itself indispensable in economic management, industrial policy and the development of the welfare state. Its influence was especially vital in ensuring a period of voluntary wage restraint in support of government economic policy in 1948–49, although the TUC approach fell apart in 1950 under shopfloor pressure against any form of wage control. Woodcock acknowledged that the post-war state had come to recognise that it should not challenge the TUC's enhanced authority but instead should try to use it more effectively in the achievement of its own economic and social objectives. As he later explained:

From the end of the First World War to the beginning of the Second, the trade union movement had great difficulty in getting governments to accept more than a narrowly limited degree of responsibility for the level of employment, economic growth and industrial efficiency ... That attitude has changed. Since the end of the war all political parties accept – at least in principle – that it must be a responsibility of a modern government to maintain a high level of employment and to promote a constant and steady improvement in our standards of living. The TUC was not alone in trying to bring about this change of attitude. Yet the change can fairly be reckoned by the TUC as one of its major achievements of the inter-war years.[13]

A more interventionist state required a TUC response. 'A government needs these days the advice and the assistance of the trade union movement in determining the practical means of achieving desirable objectives', Woodcock explained in 1968. But for their part, the trade unions needed the government to pursue economic growth strategies in order to help their members secure more stable employment and higher pay. 'We spent years in getting government round to the view they ought to set for themselves these objectives and at this stage we cannot just stand back and say "yes, we expect you to get to those ends and we are not going to help you in doing what we ourselves say we ought to do".'[14]

However, Woodcock always retained a deeply sceptical view of the direct role of the state in the industrial relations system. His own background made him an eloquent supporter of the so-called 'voluntarist' tradition which believed that trade union freedom meant that trade unions should be allowed to pursue their basic collective bargaining purposes without fear of any outside legal or political interference.

Woodcock declared:

The attitude of the trade unions towards the government is that we should be just as lief left alone. If you do not think it is possible for you to help the trade unions then the least you can do is not to impede us. Trade unions expect of the law only that it should sustain their legal immunities.[15]

Woodcock's TUC colleagues were often irritated by his provocative suggestion that as a result trade unions were 'outlaws'.

Woodcock was always acutely sensitive to what he regarded as the ultimate purpose of trade unionism. He may have sought new responsibilities for the TUC in its relations with government but he never lost sight of the realities of collective bargaining in the workplace. As he broadcast on the BBC Caribbean service in 1959:

> The short and important point about trade unions is that their essential function is to look after the interests of the workpeople who are their members. In a democratic society it is the workpeople themselves who decide what are the interests of workpeople and it is therefore they who determine the functions of trade unions.[16]

Woodcock was not a Marxist but a devout if unflamboyant Roman Catholic, although unlike other union leaders of that faith this did not turn him into an obsessive anti-Communist. It is true that he was ready to press strongly for the expulsion of the Communist-dominated ETU as his first important task as TUC general secretary. On that issue, there could be no room for equivocation. Woodcock believed that the misbehaviour of the ETU leadership over ballot-rigging threatened to drag the entire trade union movement into public disrepute, and this was unacceptable. But in his philosophical approach to industrial relations he was close to being a Marxist in his bleak analysis of the political economy. Woodcock harboured no comforting illusions about eradicating the inequalities of power that existed between capital and labour. Comforting terms such as 'social partnership' and 'industrial consensus' were absent from his vocabulary. He argued from what he believed to be a self-evident truth – that there were always two sides in industry. The primary objective of industrial relations was to secure through negotiation practical and voluntary agreements between employers and unions based on a recognition of that unequal relationship. As he explained:

> The idea that there is a natural and close affinity of interest among all those engaged in any given undertaking or industry which, if not distorted by ignorance or greed, will almost automatically ensure a common approach to problems, is deceptive. The idea of a common purpose in industry is not of itself an illusion but it can be and sometimes is used to justify conclusions which are childish or even dangerous.[17]

The abiding relevance of trade unions arose from the existence of conflicting interests in the workplace and not simply from the traditional aim of protecting working people from exploitation by their employer: 'There are two sides in industry whose interests and objectives do not automatically coincide and differences between the two sides are best dealt with by negotiation and agreement. As long as there are two sides in industry there will be trade unions.'[18] It was a theme he returned to constantly. 'Unions and management exist – not as part of the same team but as two separate groups with different aims working in the same sphere', he explained. This did not necessarily mean endless disruption.

> All that happens is that the people involved have a clearer idea of their respective roles in collective bargaining. They accept their position and that of the other side and seek to reconcile the outstanding differences in frank negotiations. Dismissing the fantasies of what might be they concentrate on what is.[19]

Woodcock did not believe such conduct represented any stubborn resistance to modernisation. On the contrary, he believed workers were readier to accept the need for technological innovation and work reorganisation if employers bargained with their trade unions to secure their active cooperation through negotiation and joint consultation. Woodcock's view of trade unionism stemmed in part from his Roman Catholicism, although he never spoke openly about its influence on his public life. As he explained, although he did not grow up in a home that was 'in any sense of the word fanatically religious – it was part of your life. We were Catholics and we were aware we were Catholics. We didn't flaunt it on our sleeves. We just were so', he recalled.[20] But it also reflected much of his personal experience as a young weaver. It was those years of grinding poverty and exploitation that gave him a deeply held moral view of what it was to be a trade unionist.

> Throughout my life I have been impressed, perhaps I have even become obsessed, with this idea of a good trade unionist as a person with a high sense of his responsibilities. It seemed to me that even as a weaver we had an obligation to each other and if mill-managers were inclined to discriminate against trade unionists it was better for all of us to join the union and make that sort of discrimination impossible.

Woodcock believed most employers realised the 'best and most reliable workpeople were those who had some pride in themselves and in their work ... and that these people were also usually the keenest trade unionists'.[21] Woodcock's constant preoccupation with the relations between the TUC and the state was therefore underpinned by a deeply moral and conservative view of what he believed was possible under the voluntarist system of industrial relations. In his solitary eyrie in Congress House, he was as keen to devolve power to the workplace as he was to enhance the TUC's position vis-a-vis its affiliate member unions. Woodcock was more sympathetic than most national union leaders in his understanding of the rise of shop steward power and the so-called 'threat from below' during the 1950s. However, by the time he succeeded Tewson in September 1960, he was also well aware of the difficulties that lay ahead in turning his philosophical insights about trade unionism into any programme of effective action. Woodcock became TUC general secretary without any detailed blueprint for trade union reform waiting to be pulled out from his bottom drawer.

But Woodcock was conscious of the high public expectations encouraged by his arrival at the top of Congress House. During the 1950s the public image of the trade unions was deteriorating. They were no longer the admired and respected institutions they had grown to be during the war. Now they were being turned into the scapegoats of relative economic decline, blamed for economic stagnation, wage inflation, unofficial and inter-union strikes, low productivity, and obstruction to industrial change. Their critics demanded urgent change from the trade unions and if they did not respond then many urged that the state must intervene and regulate their affairs. Some wanted the TUC to acquire greater centralised power and authority over its affiliate members, to discipline errant unions and make corporatist deals with government on economic policy, as it allegedly explained the success of economies like Sweden and West Germany. Others on the left favoured 'all power to the shop stewards' and enhanced industrial democracy, a delegation of power to the workplace and an end to the rigidities of national and industry-wide wage bargaining. There were also calls from all sides for internal reform of the trade unions, to make them more professional and centralised bodies with greater financial resources.

Woodcock was sensitive to the widely diverse range of critics. He recognised the trade unions enjoyed a less sympathetic public opinion than they had done during the war and its immediate aftermath. He also believed that the courts were growing more hostile to the trade unions with adverse judgments that might eventually threaten their legal security. Woodcock believed that the main reason for such growing disenchantment stemmed from the shift in the power balance in post-war industry due to full employment. Workers were more prosperous, more secure and enjoyed an improved bargaining position in a tight labour market. Although the relative affluence of many workers could not be taken for granted, their new-found strength encouraged forms of trade union behaviour such as enforcement of closed shops and pursuit of sectionalist wage demands that the wider public found hard it to sympathise with. 'It is only when the public is generally favourable to trade unions that the unions can expect them to accept with good humour and tolerance trade union activities ... Without goodwill, the public soon loses patience.'[22] Woodcock was prepared to defend the closed shop, although he accepted it was open to abuse. He wanted trade unions to curb their excesses themselves, accept wider responsibilities and justify their behaviour by reason and common sense, not through the threat or use of industrial muscle.

Public opinion would not stand for that and would turn against trade unions, demanding that the state should restrict their activities. He had in mind the demarcation disputes, 'noisy' demonstrations and unofficial stoppages that were starting to concern the government from the mid-1950s. Woodcock accepted that national union leaders were keen to stop such militancy by an undisciplined minority in giving the unions a bad name, and he urged them to do so, although he dismissed as simplistic those who believed that such industrial unrest was due to any Communist conspiracy.

Trade union structure and the limits of self-reform

Woodcock's first priority after September 1960 was to launch a wide-ranging TUC inquiry into trade union purpose and structure 'with a view to making trade unions better fitted to meet modern industrial conditions'.[23] In an interview with Hugh Chevins, labour correspondent of the *Daily Telegraph*, he explained that he believed trade unions would have to reform their structures to respond to new circumstances and this meant launching a wide-ranging public debate about trade union purpose. Woodcock confessed he was unable to do this by throwing down a direct challenge to the affiliated unions.

> Simply to say 'I believe in big unions or craft unions or industrial unions' will get you nowhere. We must ask first of all – 'What are we here for? What is your job?' If you can get that understood then there is the lever for changes that have naturally to follow.

But from the outset Woodcock seemed full of self-doubt. 'I have got seven years in this job', he explained.

This may be conceit on my part but I really want to do something and I feel that seven years is not a long time. I want to get things moving. I want to see the TUC as a central organisation representing not only eight million affiliated members but the whole of Britain's twenty three million working people. I want to elevate the TUC to a position where it can bring influence to bear on the country's industrial and economic development.[24]

In an undated *aide-mémoire* entitled 'What Are We Here For?', Woodcock sought to articulate his thoughts.[25] 'The whole point and purpose of unions', he ruminated, 'is to protect the interests of workpeople; to advance, to safeguard. Trade unions exist to interpret workpeople's experiences; to discover their real interests; to be their advocates and to administer in their behalf.' The core of the paper concerns Woodcock's familiar preoccupation with state–trade union relations. It justifies extended quotation:

There can be no formal limits or restrictions on wage bargaining; on trade unions having the right to get as strong as they can by a system of voluntary association including the closed shop. There can be no justification at all for any external limitation of a legal or any other kind upon a union's right to organise, to formulate their policies and to pursue them as relentlessly as they can. In the past, circumstances were the limiting factor. But today there is a limit to what unions should do – can rightly do – without making it impossible for the government to do the right things too. This is what I call the practical limits of regulation that we want to find. It is not a question of form but it is the principle of the acceptance of the idea that there are limits and it is for us to see if we can define those limits. We cannot define them precisely. I am thinking about a conception at a point to which the unions are obliged to restrain the full use of their authority in a full employment society with due regard to the wider national effects of their individual actions. I am trying to achieve the establishment of an idea that there is an obligation upon unions to conform to a national policy which covers situations wider than the ones with which the unions are dealing.

Woodcock also made it clear in the document that trade unions must be concerned with much more than collective bargaining:

If unions keep using their strength to push up wages to the point at which inflation is a constant feature and a constant danger to the maintenance of our exports and of the ability to maintain our position as an exporting nation, then the only thing we can do is to induce deflation – deliberately to restrain price movements even when it means inducing unemployment to be able to do it. That is the heart of the matter. A union ought to reflect upon the imposition or the acceptance in principle of a limit to what they can do. The limit is not what they can get out of the employer without having to strike but it does involve reactions all round. If a key body in an industry or firm exploits its strength to the full, then the rest of the workers in that firm have a limit imposed upon them by the action of that key body that went ahead regardless of anyone else's interests. I am thinking of arguments that will be needed to establish what will be considered a new principle of trade unionism – that unions do not ruthlessly exploit their strength. I want to make them more powerful instruments, improve their structure, improve their knowledge of the possibilities. But if as a result of the enquiry all that we did was to improve the competence of trade unions within their preconceived field of getting the most they can for their workpeople; for streamlining their negotiations, or devolving responsibility downwards by giving full authority to people at the shop level to go ahead; if, as a result, all that we can do is to make them more dangerous in terms of rocking the national boat, then we should not have done enough. My object is not simply to improve the unions as instruments for doing what they want without reflection on the consequences of their actions.

At the initial stage of the TUC inquiry Woodcock wanted agreement from union leaders on these ideas:

> Eventually we shall have to get formal machinery, some power by which we impose conceptions but the first thing is to get the conceptions accepted as part of the belief of trade unionism ... We are not going to jump in straightaway with purely structural talk. The first thing is to establish the essential functions of trade unionism.

Woodcock also used the opportunity of his undated *aide-mémoire* to define what the TUC's relationship should be in politics. 'The TUC is in politics – there is no question at all about that', he wrote.

But we are not going to take our policy from anyone else. When I say we have to fit in with a conception of national interest, I do not mean a conception of national interest given to us by anyone else, neither by the Labour Party nor the Conservative government.

In this key document Woodcock laid out what was a bold and radical challenge to the trade unions, but his exposition remained confined to the privacy of Congress House. Woodcock never revealed to the wider outside world his vision of modern trade unionism in such a startling and perceptive way. It is also strange that he did not decide to launch the inquiry he wanted until two years after his arrival as TUC general secretary. Indeed, it was not until a meeting of the TUC's Finance and General Purposes Committee on 10 December 1962 that he explained to senior union leaders what he sought in an oratorical *tour de force* on trade union purpose that seemed to bewilder his audience.

The minutes of the occasion provide a cogent account of what Woodcock had to say. If his aim was to win support for giving the TUC a greater authority over its affiliate members in the wider interests of the trade union movement, he was to find it a futile effort. Woodcock contrasted the trade unions before and after the Second World War. As he explained:

In the pre-1939 period there was a constant striving for national agreements and a common rate. The direction of union power was upwards; unions were conscious of seeking to be nationally controlled. At that time the state accepted no responsibility and we were constant in wanting no interference ... But since 1944 successive governments have accepted the necessity for full employment: in the future it is certain that governments will continue this policy. We are adamant that government should accept its obligations in such matters as trade and finance: is there no obligation on trade unions? The TUC had an obligation to help unions by continuing to impress on the government the need for full employment, which was the greatest objective of the TUC. Surely this means that unions have an obligation to the TUC or are they to exercise complete freedom at whatever cost to full employment or whatever cost to other unions? We should not always resist government interference.

Woodcock argued that

if every union was a law unto itself with no responsibility for outside, then it was not the kind of trade unionism on which we were brought up to believe in ... There was an interdependence of the trade union movement at the present time. Men on strike can put thousands out of work.

There is a serious disparity in wages, for example, between the car industry and railways. Coordination has never been possible. Last year the nurses, miners, engineers and railwaymen showed that a common effort was desirable and we could have done a great deal for the nurses and railwaymen if the miners and engineers had held off.

Full employment had given to many unions the power to go it alone, but

unions should not appeal to man's worst instincts. It is not simply a matter of the highest possible wage; man is concerned with continuity of employment and purchasing power. The free-for-all cannot continue unabated; it will bring regulation by unemployment or legislation.

Noting the devolution of authority to local groups on the shopfloor, he insisted that:

These groups should be within the general supervision of the unions. We should not encourage workers to exploit ruthlessly their strength in some sectors; this would lead to fragmented unions. Indeed, if we concentrate on wages no one will take any notice of us on 'government' matters. In a free for all we must be part of the all but is the free for all to continue for ever?[26]

For Woodcock, the 'heart of the matter' lay in a crucial question: 'Could the unions say we look to you to press the government to maintain economic conditions, to see that the demand for labour is maintained, and yet at the same time say but the TUC can have no concern at what we do however it may affect your function?'[27] He said that he was worried about what would happen if the unions did not seek to work to change the free-for-all society. If people ruthlessly exploited their economic strength created by community action and by the TUC's action in some cases, 'the community would not tolerate the circumstances which lead for instability', Woodcock continued. Even a government committed to full employment might not accept the responsibility 'if the trade union movement ruthlessly exploited to the full its strength in separate groups'. It is important to underline the fact that Woodcock pinned the main blame on employers because they had agreed to wage increases on a 'kind of cost-plus basis'. His conclusion was grave. If this problem were not solved, the government would solve it by putting employers back into the position of having to be tough. 'Industrial discipline should not be enforced by regulation or by unemployment. If they ever came up against disastrous economic conditions, there would be nothing they could do, no matter how they organised themselves.'

Woodcock found no apparent supporters around the table for his arguments. Frank Cousins, the left-wing general secretary of the TGWU, was dismissive of what he had heard. 'It is impossible to make trade unionists into idealists', he warned Woodcock. Cousins suspected the TUC general secretary wanted more power at the expense of affiliated union leaders and, if this was so, there would be little role left for men like him. 'In a system of free for all unions must be part of the free for all. Unions should not be commercial undertakings; they should use power for the people they represent.' William Carron, right-wing president of the AEU, used the occasion to attack wage disparities between skilled workers and militant shop stewards. Nobody was ready to engage with Woodcock's philosophy about trade union purpose. His bold initiative was almost over before it had begun.

Later, Woodcock blamed himself for trying to initiate the debate about union structure ahead of that of purpose. In fact, he had not done so. But the Minutes of the December 1962 meeting suggest that he stood alone in his attempt to debate in a serious, fundamental fashion what the unions were there for. Woodcock was right to feel that moving on to union structure was a pointless exercise if no agreement had been reached about union purpose. Nevertheless, that is what he proceeded to do. Again, he failed to make any headway with the leaders of affiliated unions. In May 1963 Woodcock virtually ended the possibility of any significant advance for the inquiry by submitting a paper to his colleagues advocating industrial unionism. It should have been no surprise to him that such an argument fell on deaf ears. In 1927 and again in 1944 internal TUC inquiries had discussed the idea of industrial unionism, but without reaching any agreement. Yet now Woodcock argued in his paper:

> Industrial unionism is the only basis on which it would be possible to make continuous and substantial progress towards structural integration. Organisation on any other basis, short of a single union for all workpeople, is bound to result in diversity of structure.[28]

Woodcock did not accept that industrial unionism was a utopian proposal if the unions were 'prepared to take time, patience and flexibility' in trying to bring it about. 'It has been done in other countries and the widely held belief if we in Britain were starting from scratch we would build trade unions on an industrial basis surely implies these technical questions are not insoluble.' He accepted it might take 40–50 years to achieve industrial unionism, but believed it was well worth laying it down as a TUC objective.

However, Woodcock conceded that such a change would inevitably involve the demise of two of the largest, non-industry based unions in the country, the TGWU and the GMWU, whose mainly manual worker members were sprinkled right across the labour market. This difficulty could only be overcome, if at all, by 'a scheme framed in such a way as to allow unions to make the required changes gradually over a long period of time', he admitted. He thought the example of the British Iron and Steel and Kindred Trades Association might be considered: 'recruitment into a number of separate unions was stopped and though the unions carried on with their existing membership they were eventually superseded in the natural course of events by the new association'. His paper failed to find the slightest support among other union leaders. Cousins again lost no time in rejecting his arguments. He pointed out that his own organisation was a splendid example of industrial unionism, with 54 former unions united in one body. Not to be outdone by this, Fred Hayday of the General and Municipal Workers said his union consisted of 300 different unions.[29]

Congress House continued to discuss the nature of structural reform by looking at possible areas where the TUC could encourage trade union mergers and amalgamations. But the internal inquiry was virtually at an end by the time of the TUC's Finance and General Purposes Committee on 10 February 1964. For that meeting, at Woodcock's direct insistence, the secretariat added a section to a memorandum, calling for the abolition of the TGWU and NUGMW, with a transfer of most of their members to new industry-based organisations. They would then merge to represent miscellaneous industries and groups of workpeople not easily classified for attachment to the main industrial unions, such as chemicals, paint, rubber and plastics.[30] This was not a prospect likely to find any favour with the large unions concerned. By the time of the 1964 Congress Woodcock admitted defeat on trade union reform. 'I was perhaps wrong to speak of industrial unionism and ought to have spoken more about coordination or amalgamation leading to one bargaining unit for each area of industrial negotiations either for a whole industry or more in line with present day thinking', he admitted.[31] The inquiry into trade union structure and purpose was not entirely barren of achievement. In 1964–66 the TUC held 24 union structure conferences to encourage union mergers and amalgamations. While in 1962 there had been 182 TUC affiliates, that number had fallen to 170 four years later. In addition, union density rose by 2 per cent, and there was a net gain of 450,000 members for TUC affiliates. Yet it was a sad outcome for what Woodcock had begun in 1962 with such high hopes. He does not seem to have found the time, the energy or the organisational means to turn his insightful analysis of the trade union problem into practical and successful policy-making. A TUC office note, dated 4 August 1967, on Woodcock's main achievements ought to provide a final word on his famous inquiry. As it explained:

> In 1962 the General Secretary persuaded the annual TUC to agree to a thoroughgoing examination of trade union structure. The intention of the General Secretary was to secure by amalgamation a considerable reduction in the number of trade unions and more particularly to get unions formed on the basis of industries as against the craft basis of many of the older unions or the heterogenous spread of the general labour unions. This proved to be too ambitious or precipitous for most of the unions. Nevertheless, structural reform by amalgamation and closer association has recently proceeded on an ad hoc basis more speedily than for many years.[32]

The state steps in: Donovan and 'In Place of Strife'

'I desperately wanted all the time I was at the TUC and still want to try to get a clearer and more widely acceptable understanding of what trade unions are for', Woodcock told Harold Webb, the BBC's industrial correspondent in 1970, when reminiscing on his years as general secretary, when chairman of the newly formed independent Commission on Industrial Relations.[33] Thwarted by his failure to win over his TUC General Council colleagues, he saw the Wilson government's appointment of a Royal Commission on Trade Unions and Employers' Associations as an alternative way forward. Perhaps a broader forum could begin to answer the question, 'What are we here for?': 'I looked on that commission as an instrument from which I could get this discussion and this clear statement of trade union purpose.' This is why he insisted he should become a member of the proposed Commission chaired by Lord Donovan, the well known and respected judge. Without his presence on the body he feared the other Commission members might not deal with the crucial problem that continued to trouble him. As he explained to Webb:

> I did not think that what I wanted the Donovan Commission to do could be done simply by writing a memorandum of evidence and appearing on one or two days to be questioned by a committee over which I had not got some continuous influence. I will put it as conceitedly as that: I wanted to be there in the detailed discussions.

But Woodcock confessed to Webb that, after all, the Commission failed to address the question of what trade unions were here for:

> The Donovan Commission became mainly (though not exclusively) a commission on the structure of industrial relations, on collective bargaining. And all the things that oppressed me at the TUC – our relations with government, our responsibility shared with government for the development of our social services, education, hospitals, National Health Service and so on – those things were not touched on in the Donovan Commission. I failed to get the discussion I wanted.

But the question is – did Woodcock ever really try? He had served on the Royal Commission on Taxation and on the Radcliffe Committee on the working of the monetary system, so he knew what being on such a commission involved. From the start, however, Woodcock turned out to be a surprisingly infrequent attender at the Donovan Commission's meetings. And the Minutes of the Commission give no sign that, when he did bother to turn up, he ever raised that 'What are we here for?' question. He certainly never submitted a memorandum of his own. It was Andrew Shonfield, the incisive economic editor of the *Observer*, who produced a trenchant analysis that ended up almost as a one-man minority report. The intellectual firepower behind the mainstream work of the Commission came from the so-called Oxford University industrial relations school of Professor Hugh Clegg, Allan Flanders and Otto Kahn-Freund. It was Clegg's draft that formed the core of the final report with little sign of any involvement from Woodcock. Indeed, Woodcock and his TUC colleague, Lord Collison of the Agricultural Workers' Union, appear to have adopted a wholly negative attitude to the Commission's suggestion that it should widen its investigations to cover unofficial strikes and restrictive labour practices. This was partly due to the growing concern inside the TUC that initial evidence before the Commission seemed to be hostile to trade unions. Woodcock claimed that 'the TUC had been put on the defensive by criticisms arising in evidence heard so far; this might be an accidental result of the way evidence has so far come in since the first union had only been heard that morning and the Commission had previously been reluctant to hear individual unions in advance of the TUC'.[34] But this was entirely Woodcock's own responsibility. The long delay before the TUC itself produced its own written evidence to the Commission remains baffling. Woodcock could hardly have endeared himself to his Commission colleagues when he told them:

> The setting up of the commission could perhaps be attributed to the efforts of the TUC more than anyone else and they had had high hopes of what an inquiry which would essentially be into industrial relations might achieve; but now that the commission was receiving many (often ill thought-out) proposals, for example on the legal enforceability of collective agreements, whose object was to put pressure on the unions they were naturally wary. This inclined them to wait and see what criticisms were made before putting in their own evidence. In any case the TUC staff was under severe strain at present and this was holding up work on its evidence.

Woodcock explained that he found it quite impossible to attend meetings of the Commission more than once a week.[35]

Even more surprisingly, he now seemed keen to limit the areas of inquiry of the Commission away from his own 'What are we here for?' question. He explained to his colleagues that

> It was questionable whether it was really for the commission to deal for example with some of the vast questions raised under the heading of incomes policy. Fundamentally the commission's job was to examine industrial relations. It should not act in the belief that it could direct the two sides of industry in any particular direction.[36]

When the Donovan Commission eventually held a discussion on 10 May 1966 over the role of unions and employers in accelerating the social and economic advance of the nation, Woodcock was conspicuous by his absence. By early autumn of that year Lord Donovan was starting to lose patience with the TUC because of its continuing failure to produce any of its long-awaited evidence. He told his colleagues that the Commission was now reaching the end of its hearings of oral evidence and was about to embark on discussions on the problems before it, and these discussions would concern matters of great moment to the trade union movement. It would be unfortunate if the Commission had to do this without having had both the written and oral evidence of the TUC.[37]

When the TUC evidence did eventually reach the Commission in November 1966, 18 months after the Commission had started its work, it devoted little space to a discussion of Woodcock's 'What are we here for?' question. He wrote the first chapter of the TUC's written submission himself, but its reflections on the relationship between the trade unions and the state were rather perfunctory. Indeed, Woodcock seemed to visualise government intervention in industrial relations only as a complement or a second-best alternative to the strengthening of employer–trade union agreements. 'The government's attitude', he argued, 'was one of abstention, of formal indifference'. In any future development of the relationship the 'respective responsibilities of trade unions and government' should be made quite distinct to avoid dangers of misunderstanding.[38] Woodcock at no time sought to demand a direct TUC role in the administering of public policy. The TUC evidence was highly circumscribed on what it visualised the TUC's relationship ought to be with the state. There were few signs of the more radical analysis contained in Woodcock's earlier memorandum in 1962 on the 'What are we here for?' question.

In 1971 Woodcock reflected on the outcome of the Royal Commission. 'If the Commission failed to deal with an important question it was this question of incomes policy or more correctly the relationship of trade unions and the state', he said.

> I would have been willing for the commission to discuss all aspects of incomes policy within a discussion of the wider question. I tried, though perhaps not hard enough, to get the commission to examine the essential role and responsibilities of modern governments. But by the time we had done with 'relations between management and employees' and might have gone on to the closer examination of the role of trade unions and employer associations in accelerating the social and economic advance of the nation, the commission had had enough.[39]

And yet Woodcock had plenty of opportunity during his time on the Donovan Commission to pursue the issue that agonised him. His apparent indolence and lack of interest contrasts sharply with Shonfield's hyperactive contribution. The final outcome of the Commission's deliberations, the Donovan Report, was concerned overwhelmingly with the problem of how to reconcile what it called the formal with the informal system of industrial relations, through acceptance of a more structured approach to workplace bargaining by the encouragement of company-wide collective agreements. The document had surprisingly little to say about the role of the state in industrial relations or the impact of trade unions on the wider political economy.

The TUC's own rather churlish response to the Donovan Report hardly suggests that Woodcock was part of the final outcome. But by the summer of 1968 Woodcock seems to have grown tired of TUC General Council attitudes, no doubt due in part to his increasing difficulties in maintaining its support for relations with the Labour government over incomes policy. The General Council statement on Donovan suggested it would give further consideration to establishing basic principles to cover union admission, discipline and elections, with the TUC providing a last resort for individuals who have a complaint under existing procedures. The TUC document went on: 'The General Council would be seriously concerned by any government commitment in this particular area in advance of their own examination of the issues involved.'[40] Woodcock wrote angrily in the margin of his copy: 'Government will not, however, wait for ever or be satisfied with the pussyfooting pace of the General Council.'

Indeed, he seemed to be moving towards a sympathetic view of the need for government action to reform the trade unions. Barbara Castle, the Secretary of State for Employment and Productivity, recalls that Woodcock appeared ready to swallow whole her new radical plans. As she noted in her diary on 19 December 1968:

> On an impulse I have decided to take him completely into my confidence about what I am proposing over Donovan. He listened to my full resume in silence and then to my surprise said he didn't think there was anything there that need alarm the trade union movement. I could hardly believe my ears![41]

'I don't remember the exact words I used', Woodcock later recalled, 'But what I think I said was "well I am not surprised that we are faced with this".'[42] It was Woodcock who persuaded Barbara Castle to reveal her plans to the TUC Finance and General Purposes Committee before she presented them to the full cabinet. 'He knew I would be taking a risk in talking fully to the TUC before going to the cabinet but he was sure it would reap dividends', said Mrs Castle. 'The TUC would then never be able to say they had not been consulted fully before the government had made up its mind.'[43] Again, she recalls in her diary on 2 January 1969 that Woodcock called her 'In Place of Strife' White Paper 'excellent': 'He went on almost passionately to say I had given the trade unions the opportunity he had always them to be given and that our approach had been better than Donovan's'. Woodcock informed her: 'I wanted the Commission to be more forthcoming but I had to compromise.' However, Mrs Castle was dubious as to Woodcock's practical utility as an ally:

He clearly inferred my penal powers would act as an incentive to the unions to do the job themselves and for this reason he welcomed them and I hinted hard that he could save an unnecessary cleavage with the unions if he would only say as much. He obviously intends to help but no doubt he will do so in his own obscure way.

Nevertheless, she believed him when he assured her 'there was no violation of trade union principles in my package'.[44]

Trade unions and the making of public policy

Woodcock had always wanted the TUC to take a direct role in influencing government decisions, especially in the making of national macro-economic policy. But he recognised the difficulties of persuading the TUC General Council to become involved in such a development if this meant any abrogation of the power of affiliate unions over their collective bargaining. Trade union suspicions of the state were based on tradition and practical experience, as Woodcock accepted: 'Our movement is clannish, inbred. It prefers to stick to itself and avoid outside influences. It is a bit afraid of entanglements.'[45] The TUC's strategic shift from mass demonstrations and marches to behind-the-scenes lobbying in Whitehall departments did not take place without years of agonised debate and indecision. Woodcock's attitude was similar to that of his mentor Citrine, who, during his period as TUC general secretary, had sought to broaden the TUC's influence over public policy so that it would have 'power to act on policy issues in a cohesive manner'.[46] During the 1930s – from the 1932 Ottawa conference which introduced Imperial preference, to the 1939 government preparations for war – the TUC established a limited access to consultation. But it was the Second World War that had accelerated this process. The new mood of self-confidence and realism during those years can be detected on the pages of the TUC's increasingly voluminuous annual reports. By 1945, in Citrine's words the TUC had established the right to be heard on 'those questions of general policy which were of common interest'.[47] In reality, the practice never matched the ideal. This was partly due, in Woodcock's opinion, to the calibre of the trade union leaders who joined the multiplicity of public service posts offered to them after the war. 'Seniority, union muscle, competence. You needed one of those assets to get a job and in that order', he explained. Woodcock disliked what he regarded as the improper way in which public appointments were treated as perks of office by union leaders. He recalled receiving a complaint from John Hare, Minister of Agriculture in the 1950s, that the union nominees on the marketing boards were not making an effort. 'It was true. There was no reporting back. We never knew what they were doing. In fact they did damn all.'[48]

As TUC general secretary, Woodcock was determined to try and change such attitudes. He was also keen to encourage a more active role for the TUC in its relations with government, even a Conservative one. His aims were assisted enormously by Prime Minister Harold Macmillan's decision to form the National Economic Development Council in 1962, a tripartite forum designed to develop a wider understanding of the economy in a systematic way. Woodcock later believed that one of his greatest achievements had been to persuade the unions to agree that the TUC should participate in the NEDC at a time when state–union relations were strained by a government clamp-down on public sector pay and growing pressure for the creation of a national incomes strategy. In many ways the NEDC was the institutional expression of Woodcock's philosophy, for it gave the unions the opportunity and responsibility to play a significant role in public policy. 'It was the reflection of my attitude', he explained. 'It was the outward sign of the inward grace.'[49] Woodcock told the 1962 Congress:

> We must not as a trade union movement give the impression that we are claiming absolute, unfettered, unqualified freedom, to do what we like and to hell with the rest. That is not trade unionism, never has been. The whole point and purpose of trade unionism is for people to get together and collectively come to a common policy. That is what the NEDC is for in intention.[50]

The new body was seen as the instrument that would gradually break down the defensive attitudes of the trade unions and make them ready to take what Woodcock called 'a completely impartial, coldly analytical view of all our problems'. He visualised the NEDC playing an educative role in the modernisation of trade unions by making them much more aware of the wider concerns of the political economy beyond collective bargaining. The structure of the NEDC owed much to the strength of his own arguments in convincing Selwyn Lloyd, the Conservative Chancellor of the Exchequer, that the proposed body should be much more than a device for simply extending and regularising the consultative system' and providing the Treasury with advice.[51]

From the outset, Woodcock insisted that the six union members of the NEDC must be chosen by the TUC General Council and not the government. This was made a condition for TUC involvement in the new tripartite organisation. Moreover, the TUC nominees were to sit on the NEDC as a collective group, not as individuals, and they were to report back and be accountable to the TUC Economic Committee and the General Council. Woodcock described them once as 'the ambassadors of the movement who were engaged but not committed', because that would have suggested that union leaders were under some absolute obligation which was never possible. It was unclear where the NEDC was leading under the Conservatives. Woodcock admitted to a meeting of union research officers in November 1963, 15 months after its creation, that it remained an 'open question' how the NEDC would develop. When they had come to really difficult problems they had tacitly side-tracked them, but they were at least still together, he admitted.

'The TUC had never wanted a "talking shop", doing nothing but produce reports on the economic situation and a yearly economic survey. Economic surveys, as such, were an important and indisputable part of planning but the most important part of planning was agreeing to make things happen.'[52] The 1967 TUC assessment of his achievements highlighted the importance of his role in the creation of the NEDC. The TUC's involvement was seen as a reflection of a greater willingness on the part of the trade union movement to cooperate with governments and employers in the formulation and administration of economic policy, and in economic planning in particular.[53] The monthly NEDC meetings were useful, often informative, gatherings that dealt with the familiar long-term ills which impeded economic growth such as poor productivity, lack of workers' skill training and education, too little industrial investment and lack of financial incentives for companies. More detailed, practical work was done by what were known as the 'little NEDDYs', the sector or industry-based economic development committees serviced by the NEDC secretariat. Union officials sat on those bodies but their performance was inevitably uneven in quality. Woodcock acknowledged the difficulties this presented to the TUC itself as it attempted to support their activities with its own limited resources. Critics of the NEDC complained that the body was toothless because it lacked executive powers and was more of a talking shop than a body capable of effective action. Its early agenda was concerned with looking at ways of improving economic growth and examining the obstacles to better performance. It is true the Conservative government had no wish to strengthen the NEDC in economic policy-making in such a way that it could usurp or challenge the powers of the state and parliament, but Woodcock was much more upset by the attitude of the Labour government after October 1964, when it downgraded the NEDC's strategic role through a reassertion of executive authority. George Brown's newly formed Department of Economic Affairs and the resulting ambitious 1965 National Plan were to be the dynamos for the new growth strategy, not the NEDC. Woodcock's ambivalent attitude to the Labour Party was confirmed by his experiences of working with Harold Wilson and his ministers on economic policy. In retrospect, he believed he found it easier and more congenial to work with Reginald Maudling as Chancellor of the Exchequer than his Labour successors. 'When Labour came in they wanted to hog everything, do everything their way', he remembered. 'They met an enormous amount of goodwill and got a lot of support in the early stages.'[54] In fact, Woodcock held a low opinion of most politicians, Labour as much as Conservative. He disliked the TUC being overly committed to Labour. He wanted to establish an enhanced role for Congress House as the representative national federation for organised workers, whatever their political loyalties might be, and he never visualised the TUC as a servile wing of the Labour Party. He regarded the affiliation to the TUC of NALGO, the white-collar local government trade union which was not affiliated to the Labour Party and did not even have a political fund at that time, as one of his greatest achievements while general secretary. In the TUC's evidence to the Donovan Commission the arm's-length nature of its relationship to Labour was emphasised as a significant divergence of function. The TUC memorandum reflected:

> The existence of common roots yet distinct functions is the most important feature of the relationship. The relationship becomes strained if either attempts to capitalise on the loyalties which exist and the strength of the relationship lies paradoxically in the looseness of the ties.[55]

Woodcock made it clear that he would not have considered joining the Labour government in October 1964 even if he had been asked.

Frank Cousins was to suffer an unhappy period as Minister of Technology until he resigned in protest at the government's economic crisis measures in July 1966. In his philosophy Woodcock may have been keen to develop close state–union relations. But during Labour's years in office there was a serious lack of cohesion between the TUC and government. The absence of a figure like Bevin who could straddle the two sides was to prove a real weakness.

The rise and fall of incomes policy

The focus of friction between the two wings of the Labour Movement centred around the tangled and ever-present issue of incomes policy. This was due to the almost persistent pressure from the Labour government after October 1964 on the TUC to seek to moderate the wage claims of its affiliated unions as a way of convincing the international financial community that the UK economy was basically sound. Woodcock had always been, in his own words, very much an incomes policy man ever since September 1939. He regarded reaching common agreement over wage determination between the TUC and government as an essential part of a full employment policy. But he also admitted that union leaders were always less convinced than he was about the need for any form of incomes policy. 'All through, there was reluctance, distrust, dislike, opposition, certainly always uneasiness about any talk or any attempt to control wages.'[56]

Woodcock understood trade union reluctance to engage in wage restraint even if he did not really share such doubts or resistance himself. He failed to see how it was possible for the TUC to gain any credibility in pressing its own economic agenda with governments if it failed to address the wages question in a serious manner. To militant union leaders like Frank Cousins, the whole purpose of trade unionism was to gain more money for the members. But Woodcock recoiled from what he considered such an uncomplicated view, although he bewildered rather than convinced his colleagues over what actual role he envisaged for the TUC in the development of a permanent incomes policy. His own personal experience in the 1930s, as well as his backroom work at the TUC during the war and with the Attlee government, had strengthened his belief that wage stability was necessary in a democratic society to ensure there could be no return to the ravages of mass unemployment. He regarded a voluntary incomes policy as an essential prerequisite to prevent such a catastrophe. But Woodcock was never favourable to the idea of a statutory incomes policy legislated by government and backed with penal sanctions to be used against unwilling employers or workers. After October 1964 he spent much of his time arguing as best he could against a Labour government which increasingly believed the UK economy faced ruin unless curbs were placed on pay bargaining to prevent wage-push inflation.

But Woodcock also recognised that governments were not over-impressed by the TUC's capacity to deliver its side of any economic bargain. Ministers under stress sought TUC consent, or at least acquiescence, on incomes restraint as a matter of urgency in the national interest. Woodcock did not believe that such pressure was conducive to economic success. Union leaders might respond favourably to Labour government exhortations, but through a sense of political loyalty to the Labour Party rather than from any conviction that wage restraint made much industrial or economic sense.

Woodcock regarded incomes policy as a long-term objective, not a quick fix. It would take time to convince union leaders that a national understanding over pay was in the best interests of their members, he believed. He was opposed instinctively to wage restraint imposed by government through fiat or threat. During his years as general secretary, Congress never defeated resolutions favourable to the principle of incomes policy. 'Throughout my time we adhered to the view that an incomes policy was desirable and was compatible with proper trade union objectives', he said. 'We had perhaps disagreements sometimes among ourselves about methods.'[57] In the early 1960s Woodcock endeavoured to stimulate a mood, a sense of responsibility on pay among union leaders. But his efforts were continually challenged by Cousins. At the 1963 Congress Woodcock gave articulate expression to the need for a voluntary incomes policy and its connection to his wider concerns about union–state relations. In doing so he laid bare the tangled difficulties of resolving the problem of reconciliation between the demands of the state and the aspirations of union members which was never to be resolved. As Woodcock told the delegates:

It was entirely foreign to trade union tradition and practice for there to be any interference whatsoever at any time with unions in their right to pursue on behalf of their members claims for improvements in wages and working conditions. It is a tradition of the trade union movement. This is why we were formed. This is what we have done all our lives.

Woodcock agreed that it was wrong and certainly dangerous even to attempt to interfere with unions in this bargaining process. But then he went on to point out that as a result of the TUC's own success since 1945 in increasing its power and influence over governments in the making of economic policy, it was impossible for the unions to exclude the wages question from the public policy agenda. He asked: 'Are we when these big issues come up, to sit supine and dumb and mute, to have nothing at all to say?' In his view the days of TUC protest were over. He asserted:

> We left Trafalgar Square a long time ago. Now the TUC should use its influence in the committee rooms sitting opposite the men with power in government and this meant having to discuss pay as well as prices, profits, rents and the rest.[58]

Although he was reluctant to admit it publicly, Woodcock believed the trade unions would never move over pay and perhaps over anything else unless they were subjected to external pressures. 'Governments needed to confront the TUC with problems to which it would have to respond. Unity at the TUC came from the dangers posed to it by outside threats or blandishments.' On the other hand, Woodcock found it hard to balance that belief with his intellectual fastidiousness over any crude use of political power. In the autumn of 1965 he had to tolerate the bullying style of George Brown, Secretary of State for Economic Affairs, who had demanded that the TUC General Council must accept the introduction of a compulsory early warning system for price rises and pay settlements. Woodcock believed that no incomes policy stood much chance of success if it was divorced from any genuine commitment to economic growth and became an instrument that sought to impose deflation on working people. But out of the 1965 crisis came the TUC initiative to create its own committee to vet wage claims and settlements presented to it by affiliated unions, a move that, in the words of the then Chancellor Jim Callaghan, 'attracted favourable coverage in many countries and improved sentiment markedly'.[59] The TUC's creation of a distinctive, self-administered incomes policy involving the notification by unions of their wage claims through a vetting procedure, was a clear intrusion into union autonomy.

However, Woodcock remained sceptical of the government's broad economic strategy. In the July 1966 crisis he was inclined to call inside the TUC for a rejection of the government's proposed wage freeze. Woodcock believed it would serve the unions little purpose if they swallowed the government's package and then found it was rejected by work groups through aggressive shopfloor bargaining over which neither the TUC nor its affiliate unions could exercise effective control. However, the wage vetting process continued to provide the TUC with a semblance of influence over pay, even if the government was unimpressed by the outcome in restraining union bargainers. The 1967 assessment of Woodcock's achievements argued that the TUC had strengthened its position as the authoritative voice of the British trade union movement in its dealings with governments by its role in the development of incomes policy.[60] It emphasised that this did involve a clear TUC intervention in the domestic affairs of the unions by bringing wages and working conditions of their members into scrutiny. But Woodcock saw no point in mobilising the TUC to confront the government's incomes policy as the growing left in the unions demanded. In his last speech as general secretary to the 1968 Congress, he returned to old themes. He argued that although the TUC had to oppose government policies, there was no future in getting into fights with governments in the kind of world in which we live today. In the long run, the TUC had to work with governments. He told delegates that what Britain needed was 'a better ordered and more methodical, sensible and more just system of collective bargaining and wage settlement'. He developed his now familiar text: 'While unions existed as custodians of the principle of collective bargaining, this did not mean collective bargaining was about simply strengthening little groups to do what they like and to hell with the rest of us.'[61] But by 1968 such sentiments found limited support among union leaders. Cousins, backed by the newly elected left-wing president of the AEU, Hugh Scanlon, successfully moved a resolution that rejected any legislation designed to restrict pay on the grounds that it curtailed basic union rights. A motion that merely reaffirmed Congress support for the TUC's voluntary system was carried only narrowly by a 34,000 majority.

Nonetheless, Woodcock was successful in winning over the TUC General Council to a more systematic approach to economic policy-making which would strengthen Congress House in its relations with government. This came with agreement on the publication of an annual TUC economic review. 'The success of the TUC in making a deal with government depended upon the TUC's internal competence and their ability to have something to give as well as to take in a bargain', Woodcock told a TUC conference of union executives on 17 January 1968. 'The TUC needed to have the right to commit unions on economic policy and to speak with a union about attitudes and practices which impeded the realisation of the objectives of the trade union movement as a whole.' The TUC annual economic review was regarded by Woodcock as the culmination of a process that went back to the Second World War. He saw its introduction as an important stage in turning the TUC from being a self-centred pressure group into an organisation that could offer government 'a coherent, competent, sensible, intelligent view', reflecting the TUC's position as a 'responsible and permanent part of a civilised community'.[62] The annual review did bring a greater intellectual coherence to TUC economic thought. Long after the tedious battles over incomes policies were forgotten, that publication remained an important part of the TUC's public policy process, ensuring union leaders were better equipped to argue their case in the trade union interest against the restrictive views of the Treasury.

Assessment

Woodcock regretted that he did not serve long enough as TUC general secretary. But it is doubtful whether he would have achieved much more than he did if his term at Congress House had lasted fifteen years, rather than less than nine years. The job of TUC general secretary is almost an impossible one to carry out with success at the best of times. There are no big battalions that the general secretary can mobilise. Moreover, the general secretary is very much the servant of Congress, the collective voice of the movement. This imposes severe limits on the general secretary's capacity to lead the unions too far in any particular or distinctive policy direction. Ideally, the TUC general secretary requires powerful allies on the General Council to be effective. Citrine was able to find such a partner in the massive TGWU union leader, Ernest Bevin, after 1926. Woodcock's trouble was that he was to enjoy no similar relationship with any senior union leaders on the General Council. It is true that Frank Cousins of the TGWU was a man he respected, but Cousins's ideas about what trade unions were for were very different from those of Woodcock. 'He was an influence against me. But I admired the man', admitted Woodcock.

> He read his papers. He knew the subject and his arguments were not to be thrown away. They were not trivial. They were related to a basic belief and principles just as I believe mine were. Mine was a principle of elevating the TUC to be the voice of the trade union movement in the field of economic policy. His belief was that individual unions

existed to protect the working interests of their members. Now those two things were not immediately reconcilable.[63]

The truth is that Woodcock lacked the personal and political qualities needed to cajole and glad-hand, to flatter and manoeuvre. He was conceited about his own cleverness and scornful of those who were less intelligent than he was himself. But this made it very difficult to exercise any positive influence over the thinking of the TUC General Council, although he was respected and often feared by the able Congress House secretariat. As Woodcock admitted: 'I would float a proposal. It would be chewed over in committee, then it would go to the General Council and finally to Congress by which time it was unrecognisable from what I first envisaged.'[64] He was as much aware of his own personal failings as his critics. But it is debatable whether anybody else could have made much difference to the evolution of the TUC during the crisis years of the 1960s.

What Woodcock did, however, was to ask crucial questions about the future of trade unionism. He may not have been able to translate his own answers into effective action, but he was more aware than others about the importance of establishing a stable and credible relationship between the trade unions and the state and employers in a full employment economy. This involved a difficult balancing of interests. As he explained in 1968, the TUC performed two distinct and conflicting functions. It was there to represent the common interests of working people. But it was also established that it would not interfere in the domestic affairs of the unions. 'We have to find a way of reconciling these two apparent opposite and contradictory obligations'.[65] Woodcock warned the TUC it would have to persuade its affiliate unions to adapt their own divergent policies to conform with the commonly agreed objectives of the movement as a whole. If this was not done, then severe troubles lay ahead. Unless the TUC was modernised by the unions themselves to take on more collective responsibility, then a future government was likely to introduce industrial relations laws to restrict their activities and disengage the state from economic management with a resulting abandonment of any commitment to full employment. Events under Margaret Thatcher's premiership in the 1980s confirmed Woodcock's realistic analysis.

The August 1967 TUC briefing note on his achievements summarised the Woodcock era:

Generally Mr Woodcock has tried to make the individual unions less self-centred and more willing to make their individual policies and practices fit in with the broader objectives of national policy. The ultimate practical outcome of all this in terms of structure and practice is still uncertain but what is certain is that the trade unions have become more receptive to change during Mr Woodcock's period as General Secretary.[66]

The outcome may have fallen far below Woodcock's idealistic ambitions. The TUC, as a loose confederation of disparate interests, was at its best when faced by external adversity. During the Second World War, and in its efforts at developing credible incomes policies culminating in the Social Contract of the 1970s, the TUC was able to mobilise an impressive if temporary unity to combat with some effect the impact of national crises. But the UK's social and economic structure was not conducive to the emergence of a fully-fledged corporatist system with a TUC equipped with the centralised powers enjoyed by other western European national union bodies such as the West German DGB and the Swedish LO. Woodcock realised this full well, despite his admiration for Swedish trade unionism. He tried, in his own particular way, to persuade the TUC into shouldering wider responsibilities while always acknowledging the strength of the voluntarist tradition of industrial relations. If he was unable during the 1960s to reconcile the genuine tensions between voluntarism and regulation that lay at the heart of British trade unionism, this turned out in the end to be as much a tragedy for the wider political economy as for either the TUC or himself.

5

Under Siege: Vic Feather and the Battle for TUC Autonomy, 1969–1973

Trade unions cannot be alien groups in any country. They cannot succeed in this way. They must be of the people, by the people and for the people.

Vic Feather[1]

Victor Grayson Hardie Feather was TUC general secretary for only a relatively short time – from March 1969 until September 1973. But his brief tenure in office coincided with some of the most turbulent years in the organisation's history. Feather was outwardly a jolly Yorkshireman from Bradford with a love for compromise and conciliation as well as a zest for backstairs intrigue with government ministers, union leaders and employers. Unlike Woodcock, he was hyperactive, gregarious and had an uninhibited zest for the good things of life. It is all the more ironic that a man who thrived as an arch-fixer in a public policy world of endless negotiation should preside over the TUC during a period that was characterised by the most serious outbreak of industrial conflict in Britain since the early 1920s.

Feather had no time – according to Barbara Castle – for making the TUC, as Woodcock wanted, a 'philosophic-economic affair'. He told her on one occasion that he wanted to concentrate on organisation when he became general secretary. 'I suspect for all Vic's affability we shall get even less help from the TUC under him than under George', she commented sourly in her diary.[2] Feather happened to be one of her childhood acquaintances. He had grown up alongside Barbara in the backstreets of Bradford where he was born on 10 April 1908 and left school to work in a grocer's shop at the age of 15, while she went to St Hugh's College, Oxford. Her father, Frank Betts, had been his mentor. To Barbara Castle, Feather was always 'the pawky young Yorkshire lad of my youth'. He used to call her 'luv' and patronised her in his unconsciously sexist way. Memories of their shared past did nothing to endear him to her. In truth, Feather was widely regarded as a canny and manipulative operator, a much more accomplished practitioner of the 'shoddy shabby compromises' associated with Woodcock. He was a doer rather than a deep thinker, but none the worse for that, with a wide and diverse network of personal contacts and acquaintances built up over the years.

Feather was regarded understandably with some suspicion by the increasingly influential left-wing union leaders on the TUC general council. He had won a well-earned reputation for being a hammer of the Communists on the trades councils during his years working in the TUC's Organisation Department which he joined in 1937 under the direction of Edgar Harries. 'I could see little difference in method at any rate between what Hitler was trying to do and what the Soviets themselves were doing', he recalled.[3] 'The Communist party was quite determined to supplant a democratic system at that time by a system of dictatorship.' In 1947 Feather was made an assistant secretary and during the years of Vincent Tewson at the height of the Cold War his anti-Communism was confirmed by events. He was well-known for his behind-the-scenes work in helping to unite the trade unions in Greece against Communist influence at the end of the Second World War. Some on the left even believed – without a shred of evidence – that he was and remained an assiduous member of the British intelligence services. Feather also played a part in the introduction of free trade unionism into post-war West Germany. In the late 1950s he was a great confidential help to the anti-Communists in the Electrical Trades Union battling against the ballot-rigging of its Communist leadership.

Feather was always an energetic and friendly man. But he was frustrated by his lack of understanding with Woodcock in the 1960s. As Feather remembered of his predecessor: 'There was a kind of resentfulness or a non-committal grunt' when he sought to discuss issues with Woodcock. He saw him as a 'great fatalist' with a 'lack of interest in organisation'. 'He didn't like people. He liked ideas, arguments', said

Feather.[4] The puritanical Jack Jones noted in his memoirs that Feather was 'attracted to establishment figures like a moth to a candle'.[5] But he was a man of genuinely cultured tastes, with a special love for art. 'I liked the way he didn't play mock austere; the way he asked for a particular cigar and accepted my offer to choose the wine without being pretentious in any way', noted Barbara Castle on 23 January 1969. 'As I started to explain my aims for the trade union movement, he interrupted to say he would help in any way he could with trade union conferences. "Let's keep contact like this." I think he may turn out to be a very great General Secretary.'[6] Feather's outward-going chummy manner and extrovert personality suggested that the TUC under his leadership would be taking a perhaps more assertive role than it had done under Woodcock.

He may not have been a philosopher but it would be wrong to suggest Feather was completely bereft of any ideas of what he wanted to do as TUC general secretary. It is true that in 1966 he had attached a 22-page memorandum to the TUC's evidence to the Donovan Commission that gave a rather pedestrian account of how its organisation worked without much obvious sign of original thought or vision. But this was somewhat misleading. Feather certainly lacked Woodcock's wider understanding of the political economy. He was much more at home glad-handing trade union officials at social functions outside London than arguing with Treasury mandarins about the finer points of incomes policy, But after more than 30 years in the backrooms of TUC headquarters, mainly dealing with internal organisational and inter-union matters, he was determined to show in a very short length of time that he was just as capable as Woodcock in furthering the ambitions of the TUC.

'In Place of Strife'

From the moment he became general secretary elect on 1 March 1969, with Woodcock's departure to chair the newly formed Commission on Industrial Relations, Feather made it clear to both Harold Wilson and Barbara Castle, Employment Secretary, that, like most of the TUC general council, he did not want to provoke any showdown with the government over its 'In Place of Strife' White Paper. But he urged them to trust the TUC to reform itself and not impose what he regarded as hasty, ill-conceived legislation which trade union leaders from both left and right on the general council believed would turn out to be unenforceable. As Barbara Castle reflected in her memoirs, he and Wilson spent many an evening in the prime minister's study sipping brandy and 'puffing companionably on cigars'. 'Vic was obviously trying desperately to find a way out', she accepted. 'Indeed the most remarkable thing about the whole In Place of Strife episode was the anxiety of the unions lest Harold should indeed resign.'[7] Feather had a low opinion of her. On one occasion he recalled:

> Barbara was round the bend. Hysterical. Not listening, not discussing. Just wanting to thump down her ideas. When I was talking to Harold she was muttering away with her soup. It was a most astonishing exhibition.[8]

Feather's initial task was one of damage limitation with the government. But he found himself in a difficult position. Wilson and Castle met him on 11 April to discuss their proposed industrial relations legislation. But the prime minister reported to the cabinet that the TUC remained opposed to what Feather described as 'the introduction of criminal law into industrial relations'. He told Wilson that they were not only 'bitterly opposed to the proposals imposed by the suggested Industrial Board should in certain circumstances be collected from workers by detachment of earnings', but also to compulsory strike ballots.[9] The prime minister told his cabinet colleagues that the negative attitude being displayed by Feather and the TUC suggested it would be wrong to delay industrial relations legislation until the next session of parliament. Wilson added that the Chancellor, Roy Jenkins, ought to reveal in his budget speech that the government would propose an interim industrial relations measure and announce he did not intend to introduce any new prices and incomes legislation when the 1968 Act expired. The proposed Bill would give workers the legal right to belong to a union; compel an employer to recognise and negotiate with a union; introduce a conciliation pause before unofficial strikes and amend the present rules concerning disqualification for unemployment benefit. It was decided that instead of legislating for a compulsory strike ballot, the Bill would empower the proposed Industrial Board to deal with inter-union disputes. The cabinet discussions indicate that many ministers – even at that early stage – were keen to ensure any legislative measure that emerged must do so through consultation with Feather and the TUC, whom they believed had 'already shown signs of modifying their attitude' on some points.

But Feather did not simply want to see a few amendments to the government's planned legislation. He sought to carve out a credible and agreed TUC alternative to Castle's proposals that would win the prime minister's backing. In this he was – in the end – to achieve a high degree of success. Feather secured the approval of the TUC general council to develop a 'programme for action'. This indicated the trade unions were not simply being negative but demonstrating that they were perfectly capable of reforming themselves without any need for government intervention. What Feather proposed, however, was that the TUC should take a key role in trying to resolve inter-union disputes and unofficial strikes. At a meeting with the TUC on 12 May, Wilson sensed 'a strong desire on their part to avert a split in the movement'.[10] The prime minister conceded that under Feather's leadership they had already come a 'very long way' in their readiness to try and deal with inter-union disputes. As Wilson recorded:

> The general council was to be given power to issue an award in any inter-union dispute it dealt with which would be binding on all unions concerned. Refusal by an individual union to accept such a decision would mean that the general council could either suspend the union from TUC membership or report it to Congress with a view to disaffiliation. This had been accepted by all the unions; Frank Cousins and Jack Jones both stressed to us how far the TUC had gone.

Mrs Castle agreed, suggesting the TUC had moved 'farther and faster in two weeks than in all the past fifty years'. Under Feather's influence the TUC general council agreed to strengthen its existing rules so that it would empower them to adjudicate over inter-union disputes and gave the right to congress to suspend and expel any union which refused to accept its judgements.

However, Feather and his colleagues were unable to provide a similar unequivocal commitment, which Wilson and Castle demanded, that the TUC would also be able to deal in an effective way with unofficial strikes. Under the new policy Feather tried to convince the government that the TUC was keen to be helpful by strengthening its existing powers to make it 'an obligation' on any affiliate union that it must inform the TUC in the event of an unofficial strike that it would 'take immediate and energetic steps to obtain a resumption of work'. Feather also proposed that the TUC general council would be given the power to express its 'considered opinion and advice' on such disputes when they occurred.[11] None of this went nearly far enough to satisfy Wilson and Castle. Barbara Castle believed that it was a 'question of establishing the will of unions to deal with unconstitutional strikes instead of hiding behind them'. Feather told her and Wilson that the TUC would not be able to exert effective discipline over affiliated unions in unofficial stoppages because the only sanction available to them was the threat of being expelled from the TUC which the general council would be generally unwilling to put into effect. Wilson was at least optimistic in front of his cabinet colleagues that the TUC could be persuaded to toughen up its position on dealing with unofficial strikes. As he told them, a paragraph of the TUC's own 'programme for action' made it clear that the general council would 'require' unions to satisfy them that 'they had done all that they could reasonably be expected to do to secure compliance with a council recommendation or award'. But Wilson added that it was still uncertain 'what practical steps the general council would take if an affiliated union failed to use all its powers to get members on unconstitutional strike back to work when the council so ruled'. 'There was no assurance that in such circumstances the unions concerned would invariably use their full powers to obtain a return to work and this was the essential weakness of the present TUC proposals.'[12] Feather was told by Wilson and Castle that if the paragraph were suitably amended to 'make clear that individual unions must proceed with their full powers against uncon-stitutional strikers who refused to comply with a general council ruling that they should return to work, then they believed the government and the TUC would be very close to agreement'. For his part, Feather warned that a prerequisite for going ahead at the planned special Croydon congress with 'programme for action' was that any new legislation introduced by the government should not incorporate penal clauses against either individual workers or unions.

The most revealing confrontation between the TUC and the government took place over dinner at the prime minister's country home of Chequers on Sunday 1 June, four days before the TUC's special congress at Croydon to approve 'programme for action'. Wilson kept detailed minutes of what happened on that occasion. It remains one of the most important documents of the whole crisis and deserves to be quoted at length.[13] The meeting that evening at Chequers was small and intimate. The union leaders present were Feather, Jones and Scanlon. Originally it had been planned that Wilson would meet them alone but Mrs Castle insisted on being present and was flown back from Italy where she had been holidaying on businessman Sir Charles Forte's yacht. It was clear from the discussion that erupted over the main course at dinner that the union leaders were in no mood to respond to the prime minister's warnings of the political consequences of his government not pressing ahead with its industrial relations legislation. 'Their general view seemed to be that there was nothing in this, that the political dangers of proceeding were far greater and Jones and Scanlon who did most of the talking, seemed determined to try and warn us off our proposed course of action.' The two men made it 'quite clear that they could not agree to a greater transfer of sovereignty than was in the TUC document. Scanlon indicated that 'he was personally opposed even to the transfer of sovereignty that had been agreed'. He told Wilson that he faced a dilemma at his union's recalled national committee on the following Tuesday because he had personally gone on the record in total opposition to any transfer of the power to deal with disputes affecting AEF members to either the government or the TUC.

> He now had to contradict his earlier stance and the only credible explanation he could give, which was the true one, was that he accepted the lesser evil of strengthening the powers of the TUC in order to avoid the greater evil of legislation. He thought he would be able to carry the national committee but it would clearly be on the understanding that the AEF support to the TUC was conditional on there being no government legislation which included penal clauses.

Wilson's account goes on:

> When the First Secretary [Castle] said – but was he not in fact opposed to all legislation – he confirmed that he was. At this point he appeared to be attempting to give instructions to Vic Feather in relation to his speech at the Croydon Congress saying that in his winding-up speech at any rate he should make clear that support for the TUC was based on the clear understanding that the penal clauses would be dropped.

Both Scanlon and Jones pointed out that Feather had succeeded in avoiding a vote on their joint proposal that 'programme for action' would be withdrawn and the general council would not seek any additional powers if the government went ahead with penal clause legislation. Both men acknowledged that they would agree to a 'very weighty transfer of sovereignty' to the TUC over inter-union disputes, giving it the power to make binding awards. But they refused to increase the TUC's powers over affiliate unions when it came to dealing with unofficial strikes.

Scanlon turned out to be the main trade union protagonist at the Chequers showdown. He told Wilson and Castle that the government's whole approach to the 'unofficial strike problem' was wrong. The trouble lay with 'all strikes'. 'He indicated pretty clearly that if the government continued with this distinction certain unions, clearly his own, would tend to make more unofficial strikes official at an early stage.' Scanlon also complained that the large majority of disputes were due to management, whether over dismissals or imposed changes in working practices.

Wilson then records:

Scanlon, who had driven down from his meeting in the Midlands (organised by Engineering Voice) was full of dire warnings about what would happen in the factories if the government went ahead with the intended legislation. He implied that the kind of activists he had been talking to would see to it that a rash of strikes on May Day lines would be organised all over the country and the government would be powerless to deal with them. Working to rule; go slows; one day strikes etc were all referred to (he also seemed to think that the kind of activists he had been talking to represented the real voice of the labour and trade union movement – and was sharply corrected by me).

He also warned that the trade union movement would see to it that the fines were paid by sympathisers of the men concerned, clearly hinting at a whip round though I suspect – and this was confirmed by something I heard the next day as having come allegedly from TUC sources – that he also had in mind that some of the more militant unions such as his own would set up special funds of union money for paying fines imposed on unofficial strikers.

The whole atmosphere was one of a clear determination by Jones and Scanlon to make the legislation unworkable. After dinner the discussion continued some three hours and became very much harder hitting but also highly repetitive. No new agreements were produced but the old arguments tended to be clothed in different phraseology.

Scanlon confirmed, on being challenged by Mrs Castle he was in effect manoeuvring in order to defeat the entire legislation, that his motive in supporting the TUC had nothing to do with seeking to deal with the problem of strikes and that it was legislation he was against not strikes. He cheerfully admitted this and so did Jones, because he said the question of legislation raised a fundamental principle about unions and about the whole system of collective bargaining. Once this principle was admitted there was no limit to the extent to which it could be pushed. There was clearly some fear that an incoming Tory government would seek to go very much further but the two union leaders were totally confident on their ability to make Tory-type legislation unworkable and drew pictures of British industry stopped by a series of shorter or longer strikes in a large number of industries. They thought nothing of the argument that failure to deal with this problem would make such a government and such legislation more likely.

It was becoming increasingly clear that neither Scanlon nor Jones were prepared to accept any legislation that involved even putting the penal clauses into cold storage.

They appealed to the government to drop their plans and obviously feeling they had to offer some face-saving to the government, said the government could of course claim – as it would – that the TUC had only been stirred into action by the threat of legislation. The threat had achieved its purpose; there was no need for the legislation which could not achieve anything.

Wilson and Castle responded vigorously to this onslaught. They warned that

the unions would lose all their credibility and so would the government; that since they had admitted that their willingness to transfer a degree of sovereignty to the TUC was only for the purpose of getting rid of legislation, not getting rid of strikes, there would be a gradual erosion of that transfer; that individual unions, particularly those faced with a difficult strike situation, would be more likely to wash their hands of it, while the TUC for its part would become less willing even to use the vague powers hinted at in paragraph 42.

Wilson continued:

Feather said that the TUC never envisaged that they would go to the limit in every case, any more than the government would. I said I felt with the heat off – which they conceded had produced some results – this phrase 'decided each case on its merits' would mean that more and more cases were let go, both by the union concerned and by the TUC and this would not perhaps even be a conscious decision, though we had every right to be suspicious in view of the motives of transferring sovereignty but the hopes raised by para 42 would give way to weakness and atrophy. Feather did not attempt to argue seriously against this but simply asserted that it would not happen and a great deal of case-law would be built up and that a momentum would develop.

Jones – backed by Scanlon – argued that a dual system made up of the TUC plus legislation with the latter requiring activation by an appointed-day procedure was a non-starter because of what had happened over the prices and incomes policy and the TUC's vetting machinery vis-a-vis government legislation.

Referring to George Brown's descent on the Brighton conference (in 1965), they implied that there had been a real breach of faith in that he had gone there with the terms of no legislation if the TUC had acted. Jones was unrepentant about TGWU opposition to the TUC pay-vetting machinery as well as to government legislation.

Wilson added:

Further attempts were made to discover how far they might agree to disagree – that after their protests they should accept the legislation and should judge it – as Woodcock had done in his famous phrase about the Prices and Incomes Act – not by what it said but by how it was used. All three made it very clear that the Woodcock era was over.

Wilson then painted a lurid picture of a

lame duck government seen at home and abroad to have lost control and to be unable to govern. I said that in particular that if the TUC hoped to crack their whip over trade union group members to vote against the government it would clearly mean that the TUC, a state within a state, was putting itself above the government in deciding what a government could and could not do. They made no attempt to deny this because they said a fundamental principle was at stake. I pointed out that an even more fundamental principle was at stake, namely the right and possibility of a Labour government to govern and the very essence of democracy in this country. The first secretary raised the whole question of social democracy all over the world but from Scanlon's reaction it appeared that she was not referring to the party he loved.

Scanlon asserted the right of the trade unions to take their fight over the proposed legislation to industrial confrontation, but he also referred to the dangers of another 1931 crisis. 'I reminded him sharply that in that context I was not a Ramsay MacDonald but in the context of his previous comment I wasn't a Dubcek', noted Wilson.

At this point, they started to appeal again, almost in a wheedling tone. It would be quite possible for us to drop the penal clauses without loss of face, after all it was the threat of them which had brought the TUC so far along the road and we could claim that. Jones, supported by the others, said that in view of our tribute to the TUC, why should we not drop all legislation for this session, giving the TUC a chance to show what they could do and if necessary introduce the Bill next session. I replied their objection could be fully met by an Appointed-Day Procedure which might provide at any rate time to see what the TUC could do. But I pointed out that they were no doubt gambling on the fact that the government, having been stopped from introducing legislation this year, would find it doubly difficult to introduce it when a general election was much nearer. Furthermore once the TUC or unions concerned had tasted blood and been successful in getting the government to dance to their tune, the pressure next year from them might be all the greater.

The angry exchanges continued until after midnight, at which point Feather indicated to Wilson 'we could not take it any further'. A 'general and quite friendly conversation' ended the occasion. But then the prime minister disclosed a further talk he had alone with Feather that evening. As he wrote:

Jones had not been shown his room [the Prison room] so we all went up to install him there and I left them thinking they would want to talk together. Before I did so Feather stuffed a piece of folded foolscap in my pocket on which he had written – 'I will see you downstairs in ten minutes'. He came to my room and discussed the matter further. He was not unduly concerned but I think he felt that his suggestion of a dinner of this kind had at any rate achieved one of the effects he had intended, namely that the First Secretary and I were left in no doubt about the root and branch opposition of the leaders of the two biggest unions and the unions most concerned with the industries subject to unofficial disputes.

Feather seemed determined to keep on talking and consulting continually in the search for a settlement.
Wilson recorded:

Jones and Scanlon had to leave very early in the morning separately. Scanlon left for me on the table a letter as follows: 'Dear Prime Minister and First Secretary, Sorry we could not find basis of agreement but thanks for an enjoyable and interesting evening. H. Scanlon'.

The atmosphere was not improved two days later when Castle sent a highly formal and niggling letter to Feather on the eve of the Croydon special congress in which she expressed the government's view that his proposals on TUC involvement in resolving unofficial strikes were 'inadequate'. Feather was incensed by her intervention. He phoned Denis Barnes, permanent secretary in her department, to tell him. His message reached Wilson. 'Feather was very angry', he told the prime minister.[14]

> He asked me what was the point of the letter. Denis Barnes said it was intended to reaffirm the government's position before Thursday's congress. Feather said it was impertinent. Denis asked him what he meant and Feather replied that the government was asking for more and more from the unions and offering nothing in exchange.

He added that if the letter went to the general council it would 'hit the roof'. In Feather's view it was now 'really a straightforward issue of whether the TUC went ahead with their programme for action or whether the government pressed forward with their proposals'. Feather warned Wilson on the phone that her letter was a 'bit of a catastrophe' and if he circulated it to the general council 'all hell would be let loose'.

> His colleagues would certainly consider the letter to be pernickety, a view which he shared, and they would particularly object to the sentence suggesting changes in their proposals which would almost certainly be passed by a large majority at the Congress. They would take the view that after the Congress tomorrow they could not change a 'dot or a line' of the document.[15]

Feather told Wilson that the timing of the letter, late in the evening just before the congress, 'imparted a crisis atmosphere'. But the prime minister sought to calm him down, arguing that the letter 'did not go beyond what had been said before to the TUC and there was no significance in the timing of its delivery'. Feather said that 'he was grateful for his explanation which was most helpful'. Wilson took the opportunity to tell him in return that he took a 'gloomy view' of what Jones and Scanlon had said to him at Chequers, 'that they were reluctantly acquiescing in the TUC proposals only because they regarded them as the lesser of two evils'. In the event, Feather carried the day comfortably at Croydon, with 7,908,000 votes in favour of 'programme for action' and only 846,000 against, but delegates made it clear the unions would not accept the use of statutory penalties to deal with unions in unofficial strikes.

A frosty and terse press release from her department saying none of this was enough to persuade the government to drop its proposed legislation may have infuriated Castle who had returned to Italy, but it had been issued with the prime minister's authority. He told her on the phone on 6 June at 10.20 p.m. that 'he thought it was necessary that the statement should be issued because if there was no reaction from the government, rumours would be put forward that the government's position was weakening'. Moreover, Wilson added, it had had 'a generally good effect on the press'.[16]

Castle discussed the situation on the phone again with Wilson on the Saturday evening of 7 June. He told her that his meeting with Feather on the previous evening had 'gone rather well'. Wilson said he informed the TUC general secretary that the government faced a dilemma because it could not postpone its Bill until next year. Feather said he was against the cold storage proposal, 'but not as much as expected'.[17] He also said to Wilson that a lot of members of the general council might go along with this proposal. The prime minister told Castle that he 'did not think Mr Feather had fully grasped all that was involved in this proposal', although he had said he realised this was in the majority recommendations of the Donovan Commission but that its two trade union members (Woodcock and Collinson) had opposed it. However, Wilson and Feather agreed that the idea should not be brought up at the 10 June meeting with the TUC but held back for a later session when they might be given a choice between either the cold storage or the model rules option. The prime minister told Castle that 'he had the impression the TUC had over-reached themselves in their opposition to fines and that they were now anxious for any way out of their difficulties'.

Castle suggested as an alternative to fines that the government should take power to require unions to accept model rules which would be binding on them as a condition for their registration as trade unions. If they refused to adopt and use them they would lose their legal immunity protections from the 1906 Trade Disputes Act. Wilson told the government's management committee that he 'had been attracted by this proposal since it seemed to link in well with the powers the TUC were taking and the comments the government had made on them'. Wilson had met Feather privately on June 6 and explained what happened.[18]

He was friendly but had nothing to offer except the proposal to drop the Bill for a year and he confirmed again that even if the government postponed the penal clause the TUC would drop its proposals. When the 'model rules' proposal had been put to him, however, he had reacted well and said this could be the basis for an agreement, although his reaction might be very different when he received advice from his legal and constitutional experts.

Wilson admitted to the cabinet's management committee that he

did not yet know how the trade unions would react to this proposal. One thing which might make it attractive to them was that they were so committed in their opposition to penal clauses that this proposal might give them a way out. It was interesting that Mr Feather had 'bitten hard' on the suggestion when it was put to him and had said that at worse the proposal would split the general council. A possibility might be to put the idea to the TUC and see if it would be acceptable to them or to offer both the alternative options of cold storage and model rules and see which they would prefer. If they rejected both they would certainly lose some support within the parliamentary labour party and from public opinion generally.

The prime minister acknowledged that the TUC position had in fact been strengthened by the Croydon decision. Healey admitted that 'Mr Feather had brilliantly got over to the public that neither the government nor the TUC could have any more than a marginal influence on strikes', while the Chancellor 'agreed Mr Feather had greatly improved the public image of the trade unions and of the TUC's proposals'. Mrs Castle insisted that the government

were in a war of manoeuvre with the TUC. It was important to remember the trade union movement was not monolithic and that Mr Feather positively welcomed pressure on him from the government which enabled him to press the unions to take action which had been delayed for years and to strengthen the TUC. On the other hand, Messrs Scanlon and Jones were concerned only to manoeuvre to get the penal clauses dropped and this was why Mr Scanlon had persuaded his own national council to change their previous decision which he had personally led them to take. Mr Feather had therefore to operate through the two major unions, neither of which were genuine in their approach to this matter and so far as the TUC proposals were concerned they had given him powers which he knew he would not in the event be able to work.

Healey concurred with her analysis but believed that 'Mr Feather had been very skilful in stating quite truthfully the TUC could achieve little'. Mrs Castle described Feather's dilemma, as recorded in the Minutes:

> He was concerned that if the legislation went forward he would have to drop his proposals, but, on the other hand, he considered that if the pressure from the government was off him his own proposals would soon become ineffective. She did not think the cold storage proposals were anathema to Mr Feather personally.

Wilson intervened to say that Feather had made it clear at their Friday meeting that he would have difficulty in selling the cold storage proposals to the general council. But Castle believed they should stand firm. She told the management committee that she believed that if 'the PLP kept its nerve and if the government were able to put a "cold storage Bill" through, public opinion would begin to react violently for the government and against the TUC if the TUC then withdrew its own proposals'. 'It was important for the government to stand firm', she declared. 'She had lived through such pressure before, eg on the Fords dispute. The government had created problems for itself by losing its own nerve on major issues such as prices and incomes policy and House of Lords reform.'

Wilson said that he

> trembled to think what the effects would be abroad and on sterling if the government simply withdrew its proposals with nothing in their place. It should be remembered we were dealing with people who had spent all their life negotiating and were masters of brinkmanship. Although the TUC had gone on record against the cold storage proposal he did not believe this was necessarily their last word on the matter. Mr Scanlon had come out strongly against penal clauses during the Fords dispute but at the end of the day he had agreed to penal clauses. If the government continued to press hard it might get agreement on the cold storage proposals. In any case it would be a great mistake to accept defeat now, even though it was true that the TUC had the great advantage of the overwhelming support of trade unions for their proposals while the government were in a weak position not only with the PLP but also inside the cabinet. If the

government gave up the fight now it would be clear they had no will on the issue. They could, however, still get the proposals through if the nerve of the PLP held.

Crossman said that 'if the government played on the nerve of the PLP and the nerve broke we should lose all the ministers identified with the present policy. This was therefore an important matter of calculation as the government should not play into the hands of Mr Callaghan who would then become Prime Minister with Mr Crosland as his chancellor.' Wilson retorted: 'Whoever became Prime Minister in that situation would not be able to survive a month because of overseas reaction and an almost certain run on sterling.'

Castle was convinced the TUC would come to accept the government's cold storage proposals if Labour MPs backed them. Her officials told her that about 2 million of the 9 million possible congress votes at Croydon would have accepted them if they had been presented to delegates. She mentioned that the GMW and the ETU would have voted for them. 'This was not a bad foundation to build on at this stage', Castle suggested. 'She had not the slightest doubt that if the government were able to get the cold storage proposals through the House, the whole atmosphere would change and the position at the TUC in September would also be completely changed. Basically the government were suffering from a lack of nerve in the PLP.'

Wilson summed up the position:

> The main issue to be faced was what chance was there of getting anything out of the TUC. The government was not in so hopeless a position in the negotiations with the TUC since Mr Feather was most anxious to continue the negotiations and had himself suggested that the meeting on Monday should be played short and that acrimonious dispute should be avoided. He had also said he would hope to form a negotiating committee which be on constant call and which would include Mr Scanlon and Mr Jones and had agreed to meet the government again later in the week.

Wilson believed that it 'would be useful to offer the TUC as many alternatives as possible for if they subsequently were seen to have rejected the White Paper proposals, a toughening up of their own paragraph 42, the cold storage proposals and the model rules, they would not be in so strong a position and might well have less sympathy and support from the PLP'. But he added that he was ready to consult with the TUC after the Bill had been introduced, and even beyond September's congress.

> We could offer to reach agreement with the TUC on the model rules so that the penal clauses would never in fact come into effect and could be repealed in the second Bill. If on the other hand the TUC said that unless they had an assurance that no Bill containing penal clauses would be introduced that they would not continue negotiations, the government clearly could not accept such an ultimatum and would have to go ahead with the Bill in any case.

The model rules would be in the second Bill and the penal clauses on cold storage in the interim legislation. 'Mr Feather might be able to carry his people on this', suggested Wilson. But Jenkins wondered 'if the TUC proved to be adamant and would not budge an inch from their present position on cold storage, he wondered whether the present proposals would be approved by cabinet and he also wondered what the PLP reaction would be'. Wilson said that he 'was not entirely happy about the Chief Whip's position on this', because he had 'strong feelings himself on this issue and his report might not be uninfluenced by his own opinion'. He added that the 'main question now was, if the talks were going on with the TUC reappraising paragraph 42 and including the possible substitution of model rules for the penal clauses, what would be the chance of getting a Bill containing penal clauses in cold storage through the House'.

Mrs Castle said her officials believed that the TUC 'would be mad' to accept the model rules proposal because it 'was so draconian'.

> At the present time most union rules had no reference to unconstitutional strikes. Some militant unions preferred unofficial to official strikes as they viewed them as commando force operations which paid dividends. This was why Mr Scanlon was so reluctant to surrender authority to the TUC. It therefore became important to turn the 'may' in paragraph 42 to 'must'. In her view if the model rules approach was used to do this it would not be as flexible an instrument as the original proposal of the conciliation pause because it would not leave the same degree of discretion to the Secretary of State.

Wilson disagreed, suggesting that the model rules clause could be drafted to give discretion to the Secretary of State and not the Registrar. He still believed that 'the Labour movement generally was fully in support of the government's proposals and he had been surprised at the good reception he had from workers and from Labour party members' on a visit the previous weekend to the north and Yorkshire. Wilson concluded that the government was operating in a highly political situation and in dealing with Mr Feather they were dealing with 'a very political animal. No firm decisions could be taken at this meeting nor the cabinet tomorrow until the TUC reaction to the proposals the committee had discussed had become clear. It was obviously important that the TUC were not provoked at the meeting tomorrow.'

Wilson, Castle and her senior advisers met the TUC general council on 9 June. Feather led off for the TUC, explaining that the Croydon congress had backed by a ten to one majority the TUC's own programme for action, and there was 'no difference between the government and the trade union movement about the aim, which was to minimise strikes. Their differences were about means.'[19] Feather assured Wilson that the TUC's own proposals to deal with unconstitutional strikes

> had the necessary authority and would be backed by the necessary sanctions to make them effective. But no-one could guarantee success in every case. Nor was it possible to say in advance what particular sanctions would or should be imposed in various circumstances to ensure compliance with a recommendation or award. The TUC did not envisage taking over any part of the present conciliation work of the DEP but wished their existing links with that department to continue and to become closer if possible. This continuing liaison, however, must be dependent on the government dropping the 'penal clauses' since the TUC could not cooperate or appear to be co-operating with arrangements which might lead to penal sanctions.

Wilson tried to be conciliatory in tone, praising the TUC for the progress that had been made, particularly in dealing with inter-union disputes. 'In this field, the government regarded the TUC proposals as effective because an award by the TUC would be binding on the unions and the unions had voluntarily accepted this provision', the prime minister told them, but he added that their response to measures to deal with unconstitutional conflicts was still unsatisfactory.

> It did not spell out sufficiently clearly and positively the actions which unions should take in order to secure compliance with a TUC recommendation or award; nor did it provide any means by which the general council could enforce the 'requirement' in the first sentence

which did not seem to amount in practice to more than an 'expectation'. No human agency could devise perfect proposals but paragraph 42 required strengthening to ensure that the unions did in fact take all action available to them to secure compliance of their members.

Wilson wondered whether there was some way in which the government could 'back the authority of the TUC in implementing the proposals in paragraph 42, perhaps by changes in the law or by adopting some recommendations' in the Donovan Report. If both sides could find an agreed alternative to deal with unconstitutional strikes as a substitute for the so-called 'penal clauses', that would be satisfactory. But Feather emphasised the TUC proposals could 'not be strengthened' and 'would be fully effective' as they were already spelt out.

> Affiliated unions would be reviewing their rules so as to ensure that they had the necessary powers to secure the compliance of their members with a TUC recommendation or award. But the union executives themselves would determine in each particular case what sanctions should be applied in order to secure compliance.

Wilson would not accept this, arguing that the TUC's paragraph 42 would have to be strengthened under agreement with the government. Fred Hayday of the GMW tried to reassure him that placing the TUC general council's authority behind any imposition of sanctions by unions on their members would strengthen the position.

> Hitherto union executives had sometimes feared that if they attempted to discipline their members, the latter would transfer to another union with laxer discipline. This fear would now be removed. The trade union movement were fully convinced that legal sanctions would do nothing to solve industrial disputes but would indeed make matters worse.

Wilson made it clear that the talking should continue. Even if agreement could not be reached before the introduction of the first Bill, action could be taken in the second Bill in the next parliamentary session to remove the so-called 'penal clauses'.

After meeting Feather and Hayday on 9 June, Castle and Wilson agreed that negotiations should continue with an inner group from the TUC that would include Feather but also Scanlon and Jones. The prime minister gained the impression that Feather and Hayday were 'very cool' about acceptance of the 'model rules' formula. Wilson told the management committee that 'he believed that they were so concerned they were prepared to discuss anything which gave them a way out. His view remained, however that Mr Feather might take a very different view when he received legal advice.' Wilson added that he had repeated to the general council that the government was prepared to drop the penal clauses if they could make paragraph 42 more acceptable, and he also indicated in general terms that in default of any breakthrough in the negotiations the following week, the government would then introduce a Bill containing penal clauses in cold storage, but that the clauses could be repealed before the second Bill came into effect. All this has been indicated in general terms and without committing the cabinet in any way.[20]

It is apparent from the public records that Feather was seeking – independently of his general council colleagues – to find a way forward that would prevent a split between the TUC and the government. 'Mr Feather is in a very exposed public position himself in relation to his constituents', Wilson admitted to the management committee. The prime minister convinced himself that the TUC would give 'grudging, reluctant acquiescence' to the appearance of a Bill containing penal clauses in cold storage and the Croydon decision could be interpreted in that way. Healey wondered if Feather could be persuaded to get the September congress to agree to the implementation of the TUC proposals while the Act containing the penal clauses in cold storage remained in operation. Wilson replied that 'his impression was that the TUC did not feel themselves bound not to go ahead in these circumstances and in any case the government might get agreement with them on an alternative to penal clauses before the September conference'. He added that he wanted to keep the government's proposals in reserve for the moment until the TUC had established its small seven-strong negotiating committee, and when this was done, he and Mrs Castle 'could then decide as a matter of tactics when to say the government would be going ahead with the Bill containing the penal clauses in cold storage'.

Wilson was convinced that

> if the government did not continue to press on with the Bill, Messrs Jones and Scanlon would in fact not surrender sovereignty to the TUC even though they supported the Croydon decisions. The basic difficulty with the TUC was that they were bound not to accept fines on unions and workers. The government could offer them that no

penal clauses would in any case be in effect until well into next year but they had made clear that they did not wish to see penal clauses on the statute book even in reserve, and again they had returned to the argument that in 1966 after they had voluntarily introduced a Prices and Incomes policy themselves the government had nevertheless taken and used their reserve powers.

Healey admitted at the meeting that 'if he had realised the impact the proposed Bill would have on party morale he would not on balance have supported it in the first place'. Wilson also admitted he had not been 'at first' in favour of a short Bill in the present session but he 'had then been persuaded and convinced this was right'. 'The party was already in a poor state in any case at the time the decision was taken. He was sure that if the Bill had been left over until next year it would never in any event have been introduced.'

But support in the cabinet for Wilson and Castle was ebbing away. Many ministers were impressed by Feather's efforts to reach a compromise settlement that would prevent a dangerous division of opinion between the TUC and the government, as the 17 June Cabinet Minutes indicated.[21] As they argued:

> The government had already procured a very substantial advance by the TUC from their original position; and if they could now reach agreement on the sole outstanding issue they would be seen to have secured, in a few months, a more significant reform of trade union organisation than had been achieved in many years. It would be foolish to put this potential achievement at risk for the sake of a difference of presentation which would, in any event, be of little practical importance.

But Wilson and Castle continued to agree that the TUC must be required to accept an amendment to their own rules to deal with unofficial disputes that would have some teeth. They told the cabinet that both Scanlon and Jones were opposed to this because they did not want the TUC to acquire the power to order workers back to work in an unofficial strike. Neither said they were impressed by the TUC offer to circulate a letter making its obligations clear. As they reasoned:

> It was clear the more intransigent elements in the general council hoped, by blurring both the precise nature of the TUC's obligations and the means by which they would be discharged to reduce those

obligations or to evade them altogether. The essence of the problem was their refusal to be made publicly answerable for the effective implementation of the principles to which they themselves purported to have subscribed in the TUC's own document Programme for Action.

Wilson and Castle acknowledged that Feather had told them the TUC would withdraw its own proposals if the government pressed on with 'penal' legislation, but they believed the TUC instead would in practice modify that position, especially if it became clear that penal clauses would not take effect for a defined period. But if the government backed down and accepted the TUC promises because of 'their fear they would be unable to carry legislation which was against the wishes of the TUC and the parliamentary Labour party, in that event they would forfeit all respect and authority both at home and abroad'. Many cabinet ministers were unimpressed by such arguments and took comfort from the TUC's position. As they reasoned:

> The gap between the positions of the government and the TUC was now so narrow that it would be politically unwise to confer the privilege of martyrdom on the more recalcitrant unions by introducing legislation which public opinion would regard as directed largely against them. The government's position would be far more defensible if they took their stand on the solid achievements already secured in the course of negotiations with the TUC and did not jeopardise all the ground they had won for the sake of one exposed salient which was in fact untenable.

Wilson and Castle argued that the cabinet must stand firm and require rule 11 to be toughened up, believing that to do otherwise would mean caving into the TUC militants like Jones and Scanlon.

The final meeting took place at 12.30 p.m. on 18 June at Downing Street.[22] The TUC side was made up of John Newton, the TUC's chairman, Feather, Hayday, Allen, Greene, Scanlon and Jones. Feather told Wilson and Castle that the general council did not object to the wording of the draft amendment to rule 11 which the government had proposed. The question was whether it should be made an amendment to the rule or issued as a circular to affiliate unions on how they proposed to operate in future over unofficial disputes. He said he favoured a circular rather than a rule change, and was backed up in this by Hayday who thought a 'solemn undertaking by the general council' would be 'more binding' on unions than amending rule 11. Wilson told them that the

> government would not introduce penal clauses in any legislation introduced in the present Parliament if a satisfactory agreement could now be reached with the general council, with the provision that this must be subject to review if the TUC Congress in September failed satisfactorily to endorse the agreement. The government was insisting on a change in the rules because it was necessary, if legislative sanctions were to be abandoned, to demonstrate that the TUC itself had 'legislated'.

But Alf Allen from USDAW, the Shopworkers' union, said that any undertaking on the lines of the draft amendment given by the TUC to the government would be an unprecedented commitment.

> The government should recognise the very great difficulty which the general council would have in securing the agreement of union members to a change of rule which had been dictated by the government. The undertaking offered which would have the unanimous support of the general council would be far more valuable than an offer to seek an amendment to the rules; it was indeed doubtful whether the proposed amendment to rule 11 could be carried. The government's proposal was simply not a runner.

Jones added that the general council could give no undertaking that an amendment on the lines the government wanted would get through congress in September. He pointed out that the TUC's promised 'firm undertaking' would have all the force of a rule change. The Bridlington provisions that regulated inter-union conduct may not appear in the TUC rule book, but they were clearly rules. 'In substance and in public presdentation, the undertaking which they were offering was as binding and important as an amendment to the rules', he added. But it was Hugh Scanlon's intervention that proved to be the decisive moment that ended the crisis. He told the prime minister that his union's National Committee had only agreed by a narrow majority to back the TUC's 'programme for action', and then only on the basis that 'no further sovereignty would be surrendered by the TUC'. If the government insisted on an amendment to rule 11 he would have to bring back his union's National Committee, and 'he could not predict the outcome'. But on the other hand, it would not be necessary to recall the National

Committee to authorise him to support the general council's proposed undertakings on dealing with unofficial disputes. Sid Greene of the NUR added that it was really a 'mere technicality' whether the TUC made a solemn declaration or amended its rules, but there was a 'very real risk that all the ground gained' at Croydon would be lost if a rule change was attempted at September's congress. Wilson was unconvinced, even at this late hour. A change in rule 11 was vital, he told them, if agreement was to be reached and the government was to drop any legislation with penal provisions for the rest of the parliament in exchange for 'clear and binding procedures' by the TUC to deal 'effectively' with unofficial strikes.

In fact, the breakthrough came after a short recess with Scanlon's suggestion that the TUC would accept a 'solemn and binding' commitment on the lines of the Bridlington rules to deal with inter-union disputes and unconstitutional strikes. This was treated as a face-saving compromise that enabled the government to back down, but it was a better outcome than had seemed possible only hours before.

Wilson reported back to the cabinet that the TUC had promised to give a 'solemn and binding undertaking' which would be 'the virtual equivalent of the more stringent formulation of rule 11 proposed by the government at an earlier stage'. Moreover, it would have the 'same binding force as the TUC's Bridlington principles and regulations'. In return, the prime minister agreed to abandon the government's intention to introduce interim legislation, and there would be no 'penal clauses' in any future Bill in the present parliament unless the TUC failed to ratify its undertaking at September's congress. Wilson concluded that the deal would never have been achieved unless the TUC had 'been allowed to understand very clearly that the only alternative was legislation incorporating "penal clauses"'. 'In the event, however, good sense had prevailed', Wilson told the cabinet. 'The final outcome could be regarded as a very significant advance in industrial relations. It was essential that it should be so presented to public opinion and that neither side should claim that its views had prevailed over those of the other.'[23]

The final settlement of the TUC's gravest crisis since the 1926 General Strike owed much to Feather's indefatigable energies and negotiating skills. As Barbara Castle conceded, he 'kept the TUC's part of the bargain, intervening as an intrepid fire-fighter of unconstitutional disputes and he undoubtedly helped us to avoid several strikes'.[24] Jones noted that 'A victory had been scored in defence of the right to strike without fear of legal sanctions but the TUC took aboard some big new responsibilities.'[25]

Castle was convinced that the TUC had done itself great harm as a result of its hands-off attitude and would a pay a price for its behaviour from a future Conservative government. The crisis over 'In Place of Strife' has been seen ever since as a lost opportunity in the modernisation of the trade union movement. But it did not really seem like it at the time. The TUC had agreed to a highly proactive strategy for itself, designed to reform industrial relations. What it represented was a significant step forward by the unions towards greater self-coordination. During the following twelve months up to the June 1970 general election, the TUC under Feather became an energetic focus of trade union activity. But as Wilson noted: 'Strikes did not diminish in number, scale or duration after 18 June 1969. All the spectacular strikes in which the TUC failed were disputes where our legislation directed mainly against unofficial strikes would have been ineffective.'[26]

Indeed, growing rank and file militancy was rapidly undermining the position of union leaderships, let alone newly acquired TUC authority. Moreover, speaking at his first congress as general secretary, Feather reassured delegates that the TUC would not be seeking to acquire power at the expense of affiliate unions. 'The TUC never has been and never will be something separated and apart from the unions, sitting in judgement on them', he said. 'I never talk of TUC authority or union discipline or chain of command. Unions are independent voluntary organisations and the TUC is their federal body. We move by discussion, persuasion and argument.'[27] In the new militant atmosphere evident at congress in the shape of Jones and Scanlon as heads of the two largest unions, there was little desire to build constructively on the June 1969 settlement. Indeed, the industrial scene was worsening. By the early months of 1970 unrest was growing in the docks, in the car industry, and above all in the public services sector among low-paid manual workers. The industrial relations legacy bequeathed to Edward Heath and the Conservatives after their surprise June 1970 general election victory was hardly an enviable one.

Working with the Conservatives

Feather was not personally hostile to Heath. On the contrary, the two men had grown to like each other when Heath had been Minister of Labour under Harold Macmillan. After Heath left the Ministry in July 1960, Feather wrote to him saying he was sorry to see him go because he had 'so quickly won the respect and confidence of the unions'.[28] 'Vic Feather was a delightful man in many ways but my dealings with him were often frustrating', Heath later admitted. 'Time and time again he was obliged to be inflexible in the face of perfectly straightforward problems because of the fundamental weaknesses of his position.'[29] In Heath's opinion, Feather 'must go down in history as a victim of circumstances, for the early 1970s could not easily accommodate such a reasonable and inherently decent man in the position of TUC general secretary'.

At his first private meeting with Feather after he became Prime Minister on 1 September 1970, Heath made it clear that he was keen 'to resume the cordial and constructive relationship' they had enjoyed a decade earlier. 'Although I knew that Vic was close to Harold Wilson, I was determined that the TUC should never be able to accuse me of being aloof or hostile towards them.' Heath suggested that Feather agreed with him that 'we had to stop the economic cat chasing its own tail through wage inflation and even indicated that the TUC might help with a policy of wage restraint'. 'He did not believe that he and his colleagues could at this stage at least sign up to such an agreement publicly', Heath wrote in his memoirs. 'The meeting was an amicable one but although I had always liked Vic I knew that he was not really in a position to deliver: the general secretary of the TUC has no troops.'[30] Perhaps Feather flattered in order to deceive. It is hard to believe he gave Heath the impression that the TUC was in any mood to talk about wage restraint in the autumn of 1970. If Feather had found it increasingly difficult for the TUC to hold back wage expectations in the last months of the Wilson government, it is unclear how he could have expected to exercise any similar moderation with the Conservatives in office, with a election mandate to reform the trade unions through the use of comprehensive legislation.

However, Feather continued to hold regular private meetings with Heath unbeknown to the TUC general council or his Congress House colleagues. He tried to convince the prime minister that his proposed industrial relations legislation would not work because most companies would simply not use its provisions against the unions. It was Feather in April 1971 who suggested talks over incomes policy of a voluntary kind to break the inflation cycle. Feather told Heath that Jones and Scanlon wanted 'the kudos of militancy without really desiring to achieve the results for which they are fighting. They are in a way relieved when they find themselves out-voted by the moderates.' Heath believed Feather 'privately agreed with what we were trying to achieve'.[31] He informed the prime minister in June 1971 'there was widespread realisation among leaders of the trade unions that it is not possible to continue with the present rate of wage and price increases'. But Feather was looking to the CBI rather than the government for a closer understanding on how both sides of industry could cooperate. Nevertheless, he informed Heath on 15 February 1972 that 'the TUC would always be ready to cooperate if they were properly consulted and agreed in advance about the basis for cooperation'.[32] However, if Feather was determined to keep informal channels of communication open between the TUC and the government, in public Congress House was clearly set on a collision course with Heath and his cabinet. The TUC general council was dismayed in the autumn of 1970 at the refusal of Robert Carr, the employment secretary, to negotiate on the details of the proposed comprehensive industrial relations legislation the Conservatives had prepared while in opposition. Their meeting with him on 13 October confirmed the view of more militant union leaders that the government had no genuine wish to consult with the TUC and were hell-bent on pushing through their proposals on to the statute book, even if it meant risking a confrontation with organised labour. The atmosphere was not improved by the growing industrial unrest, particularly in the public sector with strikes by local government manual workers and electricity power workers. In addition, the TUC was opposed to what it saw as Heath's disengagement of the state from industry with suggestions that lame duck enterprises should not be saved by government subsidies. Rising unemployment added to a sense of a crisis. The TUC found itself with little direct influence over government policy while the increase in rank and file militancy, reflected in the growth of the Communist-dominated Liaison Committee for the Defence of Trade Unions, was unsettling Congress House.

The TUC general council was united in its opposition to the Industrial Relations Act from the beginning but it was not certain how to combat the legislation effectively. The measure was highly complex and enormous in scope with 163 clauses, 8 schedules and 97 amendments. Even Carr admitted he did not understand all of it. But its aims were clear enough – to reform industrial relations by bringing trade unions within a new framework of law and giving workers new rights and responsibilities. Its very intricacies ensured that it was a flawed piece of legislation. The TUC, helped by Bill Wedderburn, the eminent law professor at the London School of Economics, were able to work out an effective method of rendering the more important parts of the legislation inoperable. The measure accepted that trade unions should decide for themselves whether or not they should stay on the existing register and by doing so ensure they did not become vulnerable to crippling financial damages in the event of their involvement in unlawful disputes. The act of deregistration by a union was a clear and legal option it could take to defy the new law quite legitimately. Carr and Heath were anxious not to force the unions into doing what they did not want to do, confident that they would see the advantages open to them of staying on the register. A late amendment to the Act, however, sought to trap the unions on the register by indicating they would be transferred automatically to the new permanent register unless they took the positive step of requesting their removal. But there was another weakness that the TUC quickly saw in the Act. The government decided that trade unions and employers should not be compelled to sign collective agreements that were legally enforceable if they did not wish to do so. In practice, employers made it clear they did not want to invoke the Act except in a last resort, preferring to reach voluntary deals with unions. It is possible that Feather gave the wrong impression to Heath that once the Act was on the statute book the unions would come round to accepting it despite their public hostility. As Brendan Sewell, special adviser, confessed: 'In opposition, private talks with trade union leaders had led us to believe that, while the unions would be bound publicly to oppose the introduction of legislation on industrial relations, once the law was passed it would be accepted. Where we (and probably they also) went wrong was in not realising that such a head of opposition would be built up that it would become impossible for the law to operate properly.'[33]

From the start, Jones and Scanlon sought to mobilise resistance on the general council among those who wanted nothing to do with the measure. They believed the TUC would need to 'instruct' affiliate unions to deregister and then boycott the National Industrial Relations Court as well as the other bodies designed to administer the Act. Such an absolutist and pure position was, however, difficult to sustain in practice. Nobody could doubt the TUC's strong and united opposition to the measure. As many as 140,000 trade unionists attended the TUC protest rally in London's Trafalgar Square on 21 February 1971. It was the biggest event of its kind the TUC had ever organised. It is true that public opinion in general was more sympathetic to the legislation in so far as they understood it. But the TUC's reasoned opposition was based on a trade union perspective. Feather was as convinced as the general council that the measure was both unnecessary and dangerous. At a special congress the TUC held at Croydon in March 1971 it was agreed that the unions should seek to nullify the Act and they were 'strongly advised' not to remain on the register or serve on the new statutory bodies.

Unions were also promised financial indemnification against damages by the TUC in 'exceptional circumstances' that were not spelt out if they found themselves forced before the new court to defend themselves.[34] However, the TUC rejected by 5,055,000 votes to 4,284,000 against an attempt by left-wing affiliates to 'instruct' all unions to deregister under the threat of the ultimate sanction of expulsion from the TUC if they refused to do so. As Congress House argued: 'To impose on unions such a general condition of affiliation would impose on the TUC the obligation to support unconditionally an affiliated union which put itself in jeopardy by one of its members – by an action that would not have been in contravention of the Act if the union had been registered. The general council could not commit its affiliates to accept such an automatic obligation to each and every member concerned.'

Feather was anxious to preserve the maximum unity of action among affiliate unions. But the moderate stance adopted by the TUC at Croydon proved difficult to sustain during the summer of 1971. On the eve of the September Congress the general council noted that:

> Many unions were interpreting the Croydon registration decision as passive and had not endeavoured to implement it. Six months after Croydon members were still sitting on the fence and as a result there was disarray. Very soon, if the policy was tightened up a large number of unions which intended to carry out the Croydon registration request would reconsider their position.[35]

Indeed, a week later Feather found himself out-voted when congress backed a motion moved by Scanlon that instructed affiliates to deregister, with 5,625,000 votes in favour and 4,500,000 against. 'A single scratch can lead to gangrene', warned the AUEW president. 'Whatever the motives a single step forward towards an implicit cooperation with the Act by any section of our Movement might give temporary relief but it the long run it would be disastrous to all.'[36] This was generally interpreted at the time as a serious defeat for the TUC Establishment but it was hardly the final word on the matter. The passage of a militant-sounded resolution in the heated atmosphere of congress was one thing, but its automatic acceptance in practice by every affiliated TUC union was quite another matter. Many union leaders were extremely reluctant to take any action that involved them either in breaking the law of the land or placing their union's financial assets in jeopardy. The TUC made its position quite clear on that point in the spring of 1972. It was agreed by its finance and general purposes committee that: 'It would be wrong for the TUC to deliberately to court actions by putting itself in a position where it was clearly contravening the law just as it would be wrong for the TUC deliberately to encourage unions to break the law.'[37] The issue of legality came to head inside the TUC with the formal request from the Transport and General Workers to others unions for advice on what it should do when it was fined £55,000 for contempt of court in refusing to attend the National Industrial Relations Court or obeying its order to stop unofficial picketing and blacking by its dock members of goods being transported to the new container terminals by Heatons, a road haulage company on Merseyside. In the face of an imminent threat to the sequestration of all its assets the TGWU asked the TUC for support. The TUC Finance and General Purposes Committee told Jones his union would have to pay the fines. 'The whole movement could not be expected to meet fines arising from an unofficial action which was also in defiance of specific advice from the union', it reasoned.

Two months later the committee went even further and warned that 'trade unions existed to protect the interests of their members and this implied they should defend themselves against attacks in the bodies established by the Industrial Relations Act'.[38] Feather was particularly concerned that affiliate unions should not take their hostility to the legislation so far as to defy the law. He told the general council at its April 1972 meeting that 'there was a danger unions would not be lame ducks but sitting ducks. He expected the great majority of trade unionists would expect trade unions in certain circumstances to defend themselves before the new courts.'[39] Feather's efforts to dampen down emotions alarmed Scanlon who warned the general council that it was 'on a slippery slope which would lead to cooperation with the NIRC, injunctions and involvement of the Act into the trade union movement'. But Fred Hayday from the moderate General and Muncipal Workers' Union, suggested the unions 'must move away from a situation of defying the institutions of the Act and facing endless fines which unions could not meet. It would be better to reconsider and reassess the situation at this juncture rather than have a reconsideration forced on them later by force of circumstances.' An attempt at that meeting to have a recall congress to reassess strategy was defeated by 15 votes to 11.

It was becoming clear that a majority of the general council was not prepared to confront the government through an uncompromising resistance to the Act in practice. The whole edifice of TUC opposition seemed in danger of collapse by the early summer of 1972. At the end of June as many as 38 affiliate trade unions had still not deregistered from the provisional register. These included large unions like USDAW, the

EETPU, ASTMS and the ISTC, the steelworkers' union. Their behaviour angered the left on the general council who believed they were threatening to undermine the tough stance adopted at the 1971 Congress. Scanlon urged the TUC to start disciplinary action against the errant unions. However, if those unions had remained on the register in defiance of a threat of expulsion from the TUC, it is hard to see how the facade of unity established by Congress House could have remained intact for very long.

Unforeseen events, however, came to the TUC's rescue. They were saved by the London dockers. The TGWU had gone to the National Industrial Relations Court arguing they lacked the power to stop their docker members from picketing a container terminal in east London in what was an unofficial strike. When it failed it took the case to the Court of Appeal which then unexpectedly decided that indeed the union was not liable for the behaviour of its shop stewards. This transformed the situation. As a result five dockers' leaders were committed to Pentonville prison for contempt of court over a case involving unofficial blacking and picketing of Midland Cold Storage. The spectacle of trade unionists being sent to prison in such circumstances threatened to provoke widespread national sympathy strikes. A triumphant Scanlon told a shocked TUC general council that, while he 'did not want to see confrontation, revolution or a general strike', the unions could 'not permit the imprisonment of five dockers however misguided they may be'.[40] The crisis ended with the unlikely intervention of the Official Solicitor who had the dockers leaders freed. But it dealt a fatal blow to the credibility of the Industrial Relations Act. Key unions like USDAW and the EETPU now decided to deregister as a mark of their disapproval at the imprisonment of the dockers. Their decision ensured the vast majority of TUC affiliates would remain united in their resistance to the Act as non-registered organisations. But such an outcome had by no means been inevitable. The TUC's strategy had succeeded but it was a close-run thing.

However, there were already clear signs that Feather's desire for negotiations with the government on a broad policy agenda was coming to fruition. By the early months of 1972 the government was in retreat. In the face of the work-in at Upper Clyde Shipbuilders its industrial policy was falling to pieces. Unemployment was threatening to rise above the politically dangerous figure of 1 million. Above all, the first national miners' dispute since 1926 threatened to bring the government to its knees. The TUC took a backseat in these events. Its influence over the mineworkers' union had been limited since 1926 and it was not asked to intervene. But the outcome strengthened Feather's bargaining position. The famous Heath U-turn provided the TUC with the opportunity to try and help bring an end to the politics of industrial confrontation.

The return of relative industrial calm by the late summer of 1972 after the trauma of defeat at the hands of the miners also enabled Heath to bring the TUC and the CBI into serious discussions on the creation of a new national consensus for managing the economy. The breadth of the lengthy tripartite discussions that lasted until the beginning of November was astonishing. It seemed that Feather's faith in the willingness of Heath to negotiate with the TUC had been vindicated. After being frozen out for nearly two years, the TUC found itself being actively encouraged by the prime minister to abandon its public intransigence to the government and accept an active and positive role in the public policy-making. At first the going proved difficult. Union leaders were in no mood to either forget or forgive the turbulent industrial events since June 1970. It took all Feather's guile and finesse to keep the discussions on course, and it was only after the September 1972 Congress that a serious and protracted effort was made to reach a common agreement between the TUC, the CBI and the government.

Jack Jones was impressed by what he saw as a serious attempt by Heath to negotiate a deal with the TUC. 'No Prime Minister either before or since could compare with Ted Heath in the efforts he made to establish a spirit of camaraderie with trade union leaders and to offer an attractive package which might satisfy large numbers of work people', he wrote in his memoirs.[41] The more conciliatory Heath was in evidence when he met senior TUC leaders on 9 March 1972 and offered them 'wide-ranging discussions without any limitations on the subjects concerned'.[42] At their meeting at Chequers on 27 September, the prime minister told Feather and his colleagues that he was ready to commit himself to a 5 per cent growth rate for the next year in return for voluntary wage and price restraint. He was prepared to create an independent body to help the low paid and introduce threshold payments to protect workers from inflation, something the TUC had been demanding.[43] Heath also made a gesture to Jones by offering a better deal for old age pensioners. He sought, in his own words, a 'new era of cooperation'. But the TUC drew up a massive shopping list of its own demands which seemed to grow longer with each meeting. These included a prices and rent freeze, a wealth tax, a surcharge on capital gains, a huge rise in family allowances, and above all the repeal, if not suspension, of the Industrial Relations Act. The tripartite discussions dragged on through the autumn but it is doubtful they could have proved successful. Whatever Feather might have wanted, most of the general council had no desire to reach a deal with Heath that might ensure him a second term in office. Indeed, the TUC was developing a much closer relationship with the Labour Party through the newly formed Liaison Committee. Leaders like Jones and Scanlon were not going to rescue a Conservative government in such circumstances.

And yet it is clear that the TUC was being offered an unprecedented package of measures which would have guaranteed it a more prominent institutional role in the political economy than it had ever enjoyed before. Even after the end of the tripartite talks in November 1972 and the imposition of a statutory prices and incomes policy, Heath believed that the TUC should be given the opportunity to participate in key areas of policy. He pursued a conciliatory and activist employment policy which assumed close future TUC involvement. The Manpower Services Commission was formed after extensive consultation with the TUC and its nominees were given equal representation with the CBI in its development. A similar approach was made with the creation of the Health and Safety at Work Commission where TUC nominees were to have a key role to play. There seems little doubt that if Heath had won a second term in February 1974 he would have developed other such bodies to cover conciliation, sex and race discrimination and even worker participation. In fact, some of Labour's Social Contract agenda after February 1974 was already being developed by the Conservatives in their final months of office. It had never been Heath's intention to ignore or marginalise the TUC.

Feather retired as TUC general secretary in September 1973. Heath was saddened by his departure. He stayed in touch with him. 'In January 1974 I had a chat with Vic Feather about how things might be after the next election', he wrote in his memoirs. 'I recall saying to Vic that "your people are always complaining about some aspect of the Industrial Relations Act but when I give you the opportunity to raise it in discussion you never utter a word." "Look Ted", he said. "If you win the next election we will discuss it all with you and it will be there for ever. But if you lose the next election the whole thing will be wiped out in the first week." Feather never said a truer word.'[44]

For most of his time Feather had been involved very much in a high-profile fire-fighting role – working against 'In Place of Strife' in 1969 and the Industrial Relations Act after 1971. But his years at the top of Congress House were not entirely negative. Feather enhanced the stature and influence of the organisation through the sheer force of his flamboyant personality, his boundless energy and never-ending bonhomie. His long experience in the backroom of the organisation department had enabled him to establish an unparalleled network of friends and contacts which he had often been able to use to good effect. In many ways Feather was the man who could have given a human face either to the Social Contract or a One Nation arrangement with the Conservatives. He may have lacked Woodcock's brains, but he was probably better equipped to jolly along the TUC general council in turbulent times. Never a deep thinker, he was perhaps more what the TUC needed when faced with the dangers of a confrontation with the state.

Moreover, he did preside over two pieces of internal reform that very much reflected his experiences as a TUC organiser. In 1973 a TUC report recommended the formation of regional councils to replace the advisory committees that had been established during the Second World War to perform liaison work. They were to provide a more consistent institutional presence for the TUC in the regions. Feather's other change was the introduction of more industrial committees, designed to improve policy coordination and common action between unions in the same industry and perhaps to smooth the path to further union mergers and amalgamations. He was also keen to press for more and better TUC services in areas like union education and training, legal advice, press and publicity. During his time as TUC general secretary Feather took a steadfast pro-European Community position, even if congress vacillated from one side to the other over the argument about UK membership. In 1973 he was made president of the newly formed European Trade Union Confederation (ETUC), a body which included members from countries outside the European Community. He also raised the increasingly important issue of industrial democracy. No doubt, in quieter times much of Feather's behind-the-scenes efforts to reform the unions would have received recognition. But this was not to be the case.

Both Wilson and Heath had reasons to thank him for his constant efforts to seek compromise and conciliation between the TUC and their governments. Feather and the TUC are often criticised because they failed to achieve a reform of the trade unions in the way the impatient critics wanted. However, the TUC offered perhaps more sensible and moderate alternatives. There is no doubt that Feather rescued Wilson and Castle from disaster in June 1969 with his TUC programme to intervene in inter-union and unofficial disputes. This may well have proved impossible to sustain in the face of rising rank and file militancy, even if Labour had won the 1970 general election. Again, Feather rightly detected, when his general council colleagues did not, that the TUC would eventually be able to do business with Heath despite set-piece public confrontations over public sector wage restraint and the Industrial Relations Act.

It is most unlikely that Feather would have made any difference to the final days of the Heath government with its second confrontation with the National Union of Mineworkers in only two years if he had remained TUC general secretary. Heath may have regarded Len Murray, his successor, wrongly as a more politically partisan figure, but the main difference was that he missed Feather's endless efforts to conciliate and cajole behind the scenes. Would it have really made much difference to the outcome? There was perhaps one missed opportunity to settle the mining dispute without any resort to a general election. On 9 January 1974 at the regular monthly meeting of the National Economic Development Council, Sid Greene as chairman of the TUC economic committee told Chancellor Tony Barber that the general council would give the government an 'assurance' that other unions would 'not use as an argument in negotiations with their own pay settlements' what would be used to resolve the miners' pay claim.[45] This was not perhaps what it seems. It is unlikely that the electricity power workers and other groups with muscle would have heeded such TUC advice, no matter what Congress House pressure there might be. Heath noted in his memoirs that the TUC could not give him the firm guarantees he required. Perhaps Feather might have found a way out of the crisis, but probably not.

6
Jack Jones and the Social Contract: Myths and Realities, 1970–1977

I have never been an Emperor. I have never been a king. All I have ever been is a soldier in the great army of Labour and I will remain that until my death.

Jack Jones[1]

The union I lead and myself personally have never supported the idea that trade unionism is a licence for any group to look after themselves and to hell with the rest. Our policy is to use our general strength and influence to promote social justice.

Jack Jones[2]

He was a rod on my back right from the beginning.

Len Murray on Jack Jones[3]

No period of the TUC's history has suffered more from distortion and caricature than that covering its Social Contract with the Labour Party during the 1970s. Conservatives have condemned those years, alleging they were a time when the trade unions became over-powerful and destructive forces in the economy, even a dangerous threat to the future of representative democracy itself. Many on the left have denounced the TUC for its Social Contract with Labour, seeing it as a corporatist arrangement that frustrated the militancy of a self-confident and aggressive shopfloor, intent on much more radical change. But the Social

Contract also aroused widespread criticism from many members of the Labour cabinet of the time. 'Of course any government must work closely with the TUC but apart from the pressures that flowed naturally from our historic relationship with the trade unions, we went much further in the way we cooperated under the terms of the quaintly titled social contract supposedly enshrining a new relationship between government and unions', recalled Joel Barnett, chief secretary to the Treasury during those years.[4] 'To my mind the only give and take in the contract was that the government gave and the unions took.' Such a view was to become the conventional wisdom and it was to shape TUC–New Labour government relations after May 1997. The time is long overdue for a reasoned and balanced reassessment of the social contract, to look at its formation, development and sad conclusion stripped of the hysteria and hyperbole that has too often shaped our understanding of what happened to British industrial politics during the 1970s.

It was Jack Jones, general secretary of the Transport and General Workers Union, more than any other trade union leader of his generation, who was the real architect of the Social Contract. He was a towering figure in the trade union movement, perhaps its most formidable, intellectually fertile and effective leader since Ernest Bevin. 'Though, in a sense, he represented the rejection of much which Bevin had stood for as the creator of his union, he was one of the few union leaders I have met who shared something of Bevin's political vision', wrote Denis Healey, Labour's Chancellor of the Exchequer.[5] During the crisis years of 1974–77, in particular, he became the austere Cromwellian embodiment of the Social Contract in the face of frightening economic conditions and deep political antagonisms. It was Jones who provided the necessary initiative and dynamism required to enable the TUC to shoulder a thankless but crucial responsibility in helping to save the economy from inflationary disaster by agreeing to voluntary wage restraint.

But Jones's role as custodian of the Social Contract seemed to run counter to his fundamental beliefs about the nature of free trade unionism. Jones was never really a true believer in the virtues of a corporate state, of centralised collective agreements being negotiated on high between the TUC and government or employer associations in the supposed national interest. On the contrary, he was often to be the rather uncritical and romantic champion of workplace trade unionism. Indeed, he came to personify the rise of shopfloor power at a time when it seemed that industrial democracy would become more than just a well-meaning slogan but a way of advancing working-class interests in an economy dominated by class inequalities. Jones was often suspicious of, if not downright hostile to, full-time trade union bureaucrats, even in his own union. It was the senior convenors and shop stewards in the country's larger manufacturing establishments who were Jones's role models for the future of trade unionism. On the other hand, in his leadership of the TGWU, Jones turned out to be a domineering figure in the autocratic Bevin–Deakin–Cousins mould. His forceful personality was stamped on the organisation at all levels. It was always clear that despite his personal belief in the virtues of workplace union activism, Jones did not intend to relinquish or decentralise his own exercise of power if it threatened to fragment his union's authority or weaken collective bargaining structures. On the contrary, during the Jones years, almost to the end, nobody was left in much doubt who ruled Transport House. But he was never a blustering, narrow-minded union boss. Jones set out a far-reaching and imaginative agenda for action, most of which was translated into Labour Party policy during the 1970s, and much was even to outlast Thatcherism.

Formative years

Jack Larkin Jones was born in York Street, Garston in south Liverpool in 1913, the son of a docker.[6] After leaving school at 15 he worked for seven years on the docks. A precocious youngster, he imbibed left-wing Socialist politics from an early age, becoming secretary of his ward Labour Party at 15. He was elected as a Labour member of Liverpool city council at 23. Jones – like other idealists in the Labour Movement in the 1930s – believed in international solidarity. He fought at the battle of the Ebro in the Spanish Civil War as a political commissar with the Major Attlee company of the International Brigade. His Spanish experiences were a formative inspiration in his early life and they helped to shape his particular brand of left-wing politics for the rest of his life as a trade union leader. Many have insisted that he was a member of the Communist Party, at least in that period, but he always denied this, though admitting his wife Evelyn had once been a member. The most formative influence on Jones's approach to industrial relations came during his years as full-time TGWU district secretary in Coventry, the West Midlands car and then munitions town, between 1939 and 1948. It was during that period that he came to appreciate the potentialities of workplace power as he provided the inspirational drive for union organisation and recognition in the burgeoning manufacturing plants and encouraged the training of a cadre of shop stewards to be the

TGWU's true officer class at the head of an industrial army.[7] As Jones wrote in his memoirs:

> The early 1940s in the Coventry area saw a remarkable transformation in attitudes on the shop floor ... Step by step we inched forward until it became commonplace for shop stewards to be elected at shop-floor meetings, to hold committee meetings during working hours, and to report back, after meetings with management or the works committee, to members on the shop floor. This encroachment on managerial control over the workplace had considerable repercussions over the years. In my experience it prevented many disputes and strengthened trade union participation in the war effort.[8]

Jones's belief in shopfloor power was strengthened by his personal involvement in the creation of the joint production committees, made up of elected trade union representatives, that emerged across much of the war industries after the spring of 1942. 'It was the first time the principle of consultative rights on matters relating to planning and organising production had been conceded to workers', Jones recalled.

> On the whole the trade union response to this new opportunity was constructive and effective. Ideas emerging from the shop floor started to be taken into account in quite a new way, even if the successes were not spectacular. The system laid the basis for a new era of trade unionism and to my mind provided strong reasons for the expansion of industrial democracy.[9]

Jones was the man mainly responsible for the development of the system of piecework and incentive bargaining in Coventry's engineering plants after the 1940 tool-room agreement. It was under his able leadership after the war that manual workers in the town won a five-day working week and a fortnight's holiday with pay, starting at the Standard Motor Company. Jones – even then – was never a negative force but a positive and constant source of practical ideas. His local activities may have angered Arthur Deakin, his autocratic boss of the TGWU who believed in a top-down system of union control through full-time officials, but they went with the current of the time in a post-war labour market experiencing full employment and inflationary pressures. As his union's regional secretary for the West Midlands in Birmingham, Jones was also instrumental in pressing for the negotiation of security of employment agreements for workers displaced by the arrival of automation. 'Many men would accept industrial change, even in middle life, if they felt they were not going to be pushed down to an unskilled occupation or out of the industry in which they have spent most of their working lives. People should be able to change their jobs and acquire new skills elsewhere', he argued. In an interview in 1963 at the time when appointed the union's assistant executive secretary in London, Jones raised his concern about the arbitrary power of employers over individual dismissals. During his period on the Labour Party's national executive committee, he chaired a party inquiry into industrial democracy. Over those years his reputation as a reasoned but principled militant grew across the trade union movement. There was never any doubt that he would be Frank Cousins's successor as general secretary in 1969. In fact, he won a landslide victory – securing as many as 334,125 votes or 64.4 per cent of those participating in a 40 per cent turnout in a branch ballot.

All power to the stewards

Jones believed his triumph reflected rank and file approval for his brand of workplace unionism. In a speech to the union's 1969 biennial delegate conference as general secretary-elect he voiced his commitment to shop steward power. He told the conference:

> Industrial democracy is a development of the role of the trade union representative. It can, in our view, only be founded upon the trade union movement. It means giving more information and power to the shop stewards or the office representative. It means the challenging of authority in industry. Never has this concept been so badly needed as it is today, for we see day after day the concentration of power into the hands of fewer and fewer faceless men at the top of industry.[10]

'We demand an extension of industrial democracy so that we can share in the decisions and protect our own future as workers and extend the right to participate in industrial progress', Jones explained to the delegates.

> The overlords of propaganda often accuse workers of being Luddites. There is an easy answer to that one – do not make it necessary for us to be Luddites, bring us in on decision making – make use of our intelligence, our knowledge and skills so we can make industrial change the ally of the working man and not his enemy. In this union

we say 'trust the commonsense and intelligence of our people'. That is why we are decentralising authority itself within the union.

Jones envisaged the creation of 'joint control' between management and shop stewards over issues such as overtime working, manpower planning, hiring and firing, health and safety; even the appointment of managers. 'We must talk more about management/worker philosophies. We want the right to talk about investment because this means our future as well.' Jones believed that shop stewards needed to know all about a company's production strategies, its turnover, unit costs and future planning, and this meant a greater openness. 'Trade unionism with a human face', was his slogan. 'Why can't we bring the stewards and workers' representatives into the planning of work and make sure they get the information they need to discuss and report to their members at the places of work?', he questioned.

Jones carried his industrial democracy message to the 1969 conference of the Institute of Personnel Management. His address to the managers laid down an articulate and coherent vision of a new kind of trade unionism in tune with the times. As he told his audience:

> The centre of attention in modern trades unionism is increasingly becoming the place of work. The developments at the grass roots of our movement have been of great significance; what remains now is to translate these into change throughout the whole of the trade union and industrial structure.[11]

This meant that there would have to be a devolution of power to every worker. 'We have got to get our agreements down to the point where the workers themselves are involved in the negotiations – and want to keep the agreements because they have had a decisive hand in making them and therefore understand them.'

Jones argued that the change would transform the role of full-time trade union officials, who would become more the coordinators, the encouragers; the men and women called into the workplace only when a problem could not be resolved without them. He insisted there was no place any longer for the centralising union leader in industrial relations. 'I am not a boss and don't want to be one', he explained.

> I am working for a system where not a few trade union officials control the situation but a dedicated, well-trained and intelligent body of trade union members is represented by hundreds of thousands of lay

representatives – every one of whom is capable of helping to resolve industrial problems and assist in collective bargaining. The union must not be the boss of its members. It must be responsive to the needs of ordinary people.

His early years as general secretary appeared to do little to diminish his faith in the shop stewards.

The average modern-minded manager knows that without such men and women industry would indeed be undermined. For (and this is perhaps the major factor affecting industry from the late fifties onwards) workers today just won't accept being ordered mindlessly about. They expect to get a better living standard out of their jobs and they require more and more to be treated as adults when they are at work. The great contribution of the shop steward is to articulate those feelings and come to agreements that reflect them. The key is, of course, that they do come to an agreement, in almost every case.

Jones saw himself as the champion of the 'great and largely peaceful revolution achieved in British industry' during the 1960s. As he explained:

Massive industrial changes in methods, machines and labour practices are being brought about without strikes. Disputes procedures are being shortened, thus reducing the main cause of strikes (ie sheer frustration arising out of the long-drawn-out nature of resolving a dispute). Agreements are being localised, simplified in their wording and above all being made accountable to the workers themselves. The old situation, whereby a very limited agreement was made in isolation by a few union officials, and then announced to those who would have to operate it, is fortunately growing more and more rare.

Jones insisted that the role of the steward was not to foment industrial conflict but to bring an end to needless strife by seeking negotiated agreements close as possible to the point of production. In an article in defence of the shop stewards published by the *Spectator* magazine, he called for 'a new high-level, mutually respected conciliation service', also for shortening disputes procedures and pressing on with worker partic-ipation and democracy.[12]

Jones remained implacably opposed to any form of state regulated incomes policy. He even described the Labour government's voluntary approach to pay restraint in 1965 as 'just a bloody gimmick'.[13] During the 1969 'In Place of Strife' crisis he was seen by Wilson and Barbara Castle as their next most dangerous foe after Hugh Scanlon. A left-wing delegate at that year's Labour Party conference told Castle: 'I yearn for the day when you and Jack Jones will be fighting side by side.' 'So do I but it will only come when Jack is ready to discriminate. It won't come as long as he says that every demand from every worker – well paid docker as well as underpaid dustman – is sacrosanct', she commented in her diary.[14] And yet even at the height of his popular reputation as a trade union militant, Jones was, at least in private, willing to display a much more cautious view of the development of workplace trade unionism. On 15 May 1969 Castle disclosed having dinner with him. Afterwards she described him as a

> genuine responsible social democrat. He certainly gave me the impression he wanted to avoid a disastrous breach with the government ... He assured me he was no supporter of unofficial strikes and when I asked how he saw the shop stewards fitting in, say to Ford's machinery, he was quite clear they should not be negotiating but that there should be effective arrangements for consulting them before final decisions were reached – a rather less disturbing approach than I once anticipated. It seems clear he doesn't want to undermine the unions' authority.[15]

In his first report as TGWU leader to the union's general executive council, Jones set out the outlines of his constructive agenda for industrial change. He was determined he told them to press for the creation of a 'high wages/high efficiency system based upon an adequate minimum below which no worker should be allowed to fall'. But above all, he emphasised the need to ensure greater lay participation for shop stewards and other activists in existing bodies like the industry-based little national economic development councils. Jones added:

> Whilst the general secretary has a strong influence (on making the union more effective) major reliance must be on active members with decisions increasingly being taken directly by the membership. The operation of practical democracy will prove, in my opinion, to be our basic strength.[16]

Making the Social Contract

Labour's surprise general election defeat in June 1970 provided Jones with the opportunity to launch a ferocious attack on politicians and

Britain's 'sham democracy' at the party conference. He even spoke somewhat wildly of 'shop stewards in the streets'.[17] But such bellicose rhetoric was coupled with a clear determination on his part to rebuild a close relationship between the TUC and the Labour Party after the divisive conflict of 1969. Jones launched his personal initiative for the establishment of a new accord in the Labour Movement in the improbable setting of a Fabian Society tea meeting at the 1971 Labour conference. He called for the creation of a liaison committee which would bring together the TUC and the Labour Party and help them to work out a common programme for action if Labour won the next general election. Jones spelt out in more detail what he had in mind to the conference itself:

> There is no reason at all why a joint policy cannot be worked out. But let us have the closest possible liaison. Let us put an end to the stress and strain between the trade union and intellectual wings of the party. This is not just a matter of brainstorming in the back rooms of Congress House and Transport House just before the next election. In the past we have not had the dialogue necessary. The unions and the party leadership perhaps have both been unsure of their own ground but we can market this policy into a great campaign to open up the approach to genuine industrial democracy based on the unions.[18]

Labour leaders and the TUC quickly fell in behind Jones's initiative. The resulting Liaison Committee met for the first time on 23 January 1972. It grew rapidly into an important policy-making forum and an effective counterweight to the party's national executive committee. The new body was composed of six members each from Labour's shadow cabinet, the party's national executive committee and the TUC general council. From the start, Jones envisaged the Liaison Committee as a necessary and permanent way of ensuring there would be regular consultation for the trade unions through the TUC with any future Labour government. He insisted, despite left-wing objections, that shadow cabinet members should be sitting on the Liaison Committee as of right. 'To most of us at the TUC it would have been a waste of time if the MPs had not been there. We wanted commitments, especially for the repeal of the Industrial Relations Act and only the leaders of the party could deliver these', he explained.[19] The TUC's direct involvement in the Liaison Committee was to guarantee that it enjoyed close and formalised links with the Labour Party for the first time since the National Council of Labour was revived after the 1931 crisis.

The new committee's initial agenda was certainly dominated by issues of primary concern to Jones and the TUC – a better deal for pensioners, rehabilitation of the health service, a massive new housing programme, public control of investment, measures to eradicate low pay, support for industrial democracy, and above all a repeal of the hated Industrial Relations Act. Within six months of its existence the Liaison Committee produced its first joint statement calling for the abolition of the Act and the formation of an independent conciliation and arbitration service made up of union and employer representatives as well as independents. The document also proposed an extension of the right of a worker to belong to a union and enjoy legal protection against unfair dismissal, as well as shorter qualifying periods of employment for receiving minimum notice and longer periods of notice from employers. Trade unions were to be given the legal power to take employers before a new independent arbitration committee if they refused to provide union recognition when their workers requested it or refused to disclose company information for collective bargaining purposes. The Liaison Committee also called for a commitment to binding awards on employers over individual employment contracts. All these ideas came from the TUC.

But if Jones and other TUC leaders were ready to discuss a far-ranging programme of workplace and social reform on behalf of working people to be introduced by Labour when it came into government again, they were not prepared to countenance even a discussion with party leaders about having another incomes policy. 'It would be disastrous if any word went out from this meeting that we had been discussing prices and incomes policy', he told one Liaison Committee meeting.[20] 'So bruised and sensitive were the trade unions that any mention even of a voluntary policy was taboo', noted Barbara Castle. The furthest the TUC seemed prepared to go was to accept there was a need to keep prices down and establish a fairer economic climate to which the unions could be expected to respond positively. In February 1973 the Liaison Committee published a policy document on 'Economic Policy and the Cost of Living'. It said this involved a new approach, that involved securing a 'strong feeling of mutual confidence which alone would make it possible to reach the wide-ranging agreement necessary to control inflation and achieve sustained growth in the standard of living'. Harold Wilson suggested that this 'was widely interpreted as a voluntary agreement to accept restraint in pay demands as part of a wider social agreement'.[21] But Jones and the TUC did not really see it that way at all. The 1973 Liaison Committee document was little more than a shopping list of TUC demands. It called for state control of food prices with subsidies for essentials and public transport, 'a large scale' redistribution of wealth and income and a phasing out of social service charges. Pride of place went to a commitment to improve the position of the old age pensioners, a cause always dear to Jones's heart. But the highest priority was for a rapid repeal of the hated Industrial Relations Act.

Despite his clear opposition to any suggestion of an incomes policy, Labour left-wingers like Tony Benn believed Jones had abandoned his left-wing beliefs by the summer of 1973. 'Far from being a left-wing radical he has settled down into a central position which could best be described at the moment as the Healey stance', Tony Benn noted in his diary on 12 June.[22] For his part, Jones criticised Bennism as 'airy fairy stuff' and urged Benn to make speeches about pensions and prices. 'There is no doubt that Jack Jones has completely abandoned his serious left-wing position', Benn wrote in his diary on 26 September.[23]

> He is quite crudely against the adoption of the socialist programme because he is for sticking to the bread and butter issues – pensions, food subsidies, repealing the Industrial Relations Act and so on. I think the incident in the summer of 1972 when the dockers broke into his office, threw an ashtray at him and abused him was a deep shock.

It was certainly true that the incident referred to by Benn had shaken Jones. As Jones noted coolly in his memoirs:

> It was clear that most [of the militants] had little idea of the Jones/Aldington committee agreements [bringing an end to casualised dockwork] and some of the men at least began to realise the measure of our efforts. Others went out muttering abuse. I had spent over two hours in rough argument. It might not have been necessary if only more of the rank and file members had participated in union activities.[24]

By the autumn of 1973 the Liaison Committee was regarded by Labour leaders as an alternative rather than a complement to the party's increasingly left-wing national executive. The TUC was providing a badly needed policy balance for Wilson in the face of Benn and his supporters. However, the lack of any formal commitment to an incomes policy with the TUC continued to trouble the party leaders in the run-up to the February 1974 general election. Shadow Chancellor Denis Healey did not want a pact or norm, but he certainly sought some sign from the TUC that it would respond positively so as to ensure his economic growth strategy could succeed. But a discussion held over the wages question at the 4 January 1974 Liaison Committee proved inconclusive. TUC general secretary Len Murray made it clear to Wilson and Healey that no TUC statement would be forthcoming that committed the unions to an incomes policy. He argued that fixing norms meant that many workers would expect automatic wage rises, nor was it self-evident such a policy would improve the balance of payments. 'We have said to this government time and again that if it would do so and so, the TUC would respond. God help us we cannot go beyond that.'[25] 'The greatest disservice the TUC could do to a Labour government was to pretend it could deliver more than it could; the disillusion resulting from failure would be far more damging than the refusal to make impossible promises in the first place.' Wilson concluded that what they needed was 'more the creation of a mood than a compact'. 'We were footsying weren't we?', Murray recalled in an interview on the eve of his retirement in 1984. 'But what sort of campaign slogan is it to say – Vote Labour and have your pay frozen?'[26]

Facing the crisis

In the months after Labour's narrow election victory in February 1974 Jones was the crucial and influential trade union figure in the TUC who sought to help Wilson's minority government through what were the worst economic conditions faced by an incoming administration since the Second World War. He was to exercise a considerable impact. It was Jones who insisted that Michael Foot must be appointed as employment secretary instead of the right-wing Reg Prentice who had held the shadow portfolio when Labour had been in opposition. As John Elliott, *Financial Times* labour editor noted: 'The priorities in Labour's programme, the rent freeze, repealing the Industrial Relations Act and raising pensions, are directly in line with Mr Jones's own personal priorities.'[27] But Jones accepted that stage three of Edward Heath's incomes policy must last its full course into the summer of 1974. It was a recognition by him of political and eocnomic realities. But the TUC called for restraint and an 'orderly' return to voluntary collective bargaining in the summer of 1974. 'Over the coming year negotiators generally should recognise that the scope for real increases in consumption are limited and a central negotiating objective in this period will be to ensure that real incomes are maintained.'[28] Barbara Castle wrote in her diary of the 'gargantuan efforts' made by Murray, Jones and others to turn the Social Contract into a constructive reality.[29]

At the 24 June 1974 Liaison Committee meeting Mrs Castle described Jones as 'brooding with his usual stern intensity', but also expressing his disapproval of 'exaggerated pay claims like [those of] the miners and engineers'. 'We are genuinely trying to make a contribution to the reduction of tension', he told the meeting. But Jones was still opposed to any suggestion that the TUC might introduce pay monitoring machinery at the end of the incomes policy. Instead he called for flexibility and insisted the government must judge each case for a wage increase on its merits.

However, two days later, at the TUC general council's 26 June meeting, Jones threw his formidable weight behind the cause of voluntary wage restraint with an impassioned defence of the government's record. He pointed out that Labour in only a few months of office had 'already gone a long way in carrying out their obligations'. It had frozen rent increases, started to deal with prices, subsidised milk and bread and given a priority to old age pensions. The government had also abolished the Pay Board and repealed the Industrial Relations Act in close cooperation with the TUC. 'The aim must be to keep the Labour government in office and when the election came to get them returned with a majority', explained Jones.[30] He did want to see the government being consumed by union claims for wage rises of 10, 15 or even 20 per cent in response to soaring living costs. But the shopfloor mood of 1974 was not favourable to such calls for voluntary pay restraint, whether made by Jones or anybody else in the trade union movement. 'We were running loose. There was a feeling of liberation. People felt they had to make up for lost time but they knew it could not go on', recalled Murray.[31] But he did believe the TUC would have been able to restrain the shopfloor upsurge at that time if it had attempted to do so. 'Market forces were working in favour of big pay deals. We would have simply been ignored by the shop stewards if we had tried to stop it.'

At the 1974 Congress Jim Callaghan, as Labour's fraternal delegate, announced that the government's Social Contract with the TUC had become a 'means of achieving nothing less than the social and economic reconstruction of the country'.[32] Certainly the TUC could claim that 'since taking office the government had demonstrated their commitment to implementing the general approach of the social contract'.[33] But Jones, for one, took the TUC's obligations under the Social Contract seriously. He told an election meeting at Ipswich on 2 October 1974 that this meant that trade unions would have to exercise 'voluntary self-discipline' in ensuring that real incomes were maintained. 'Free collective bargaining will avoid the anomalies, the frustrations and the unfair dictates of the Tory Pay Board which led to a decline in the living standards of many workers', he added.[34] 'The main purpose of the social contract is to keep prices and costs down', he told an audience in Braintree. The Labour government in its first seven months had sought to replace a free-for-all with a fair for all.[35] As Jones explained:

> The TUC general council has acted as a general staff of the trade union movement, not as a dictator but rather as an adviser on the policies to be applied. I believe its advice will be heeded by the mass membership ... A major aspect of the social contract is to seek to develop and restore rest for collective bargaining but if deadlock or difficulty arises to make available an alternative to the use of the strike weapon.

But Jones was dismissive of the suggestion that he was a boss or a bogeyman. 'The fact is we have no authority or influence except that derived democratically from our members. It is simply not true that we control the Labour party.'

In Motherwell in October 1974 he told his union's Scottish conference:

> The main objective in the fight against inflation should be to increase the value of the pay packet not necessarily the amount of paper in it ... The TUC general council is a very different body from the old days and is genuinely seeking to act in the best interests of all trade unionists. The collective bargaining advice which has been offered is the considered view of a leadership no longer divorced from the membership. We hope our members will respect the advice given.[36]

But concern was growing at the spiralling level of wage claims and settlements as the winter months passed by. During the TUC general council discussions on its own voluntary pay guidelines on November 20 1974, Jones warned that he 'did not think the general council could afford the luxury of a major measure of disunity between the trade union movement and the government, especially since it had only recently been elected and care was needed to avoid a situation in which it could be brought down'.[37] He told his colleagues that 'it was essential to reduce competitive claims and have regard to TUC guidelines, as had been done in several recent settlements'. 'There would always be difficult situations and the miners faced exceptional circumstances in their industry but unions should always be careful to explain why the TUC guidelines were needed and should bring home the gravity of our very difficult situation', added Jones. The TUC circular – *Collective Bargaining and the Social Contract* – set down voluntary guidelines for affiliate unions which emphasised the need to ensure there would be no fall in living standards for their members. It accepted that 'the scope for real increases in consumption at present was limited and a central negotiating objective in the coming period would therefore be to ensure that real incomes were maintained'.[38] 'This entails claiming compensation for the rise in the cost of living since the last settlement, taking into account the fact that threshold agreements, where they apply, will already have given some compensation for current price increases.' The TUC also pointed out that there was no need for unions to seek to break the twelve-month interval between pay deals to anticipate and avoid a wage freeze or reimposition of statutory controls over collective bargaining was unnecessary because Wilson and other ministers had given specific assurances that there would be no such state intervention.

But Jones was not unaware of what was happening in the pay round as settlements began to surge ever upwards. Barbara Castle noticed his change of mood at the January 1975 Liaison Committee meeting. Jones, whom her Department of Employment officials had once seen as the 'archetypal trade union official who had in fact been arid and negative then', was becoming 'an almost gentle and certainly benign influence'. 'I believe he is the greatest voice in the trade union movement today in favour of what I have always wanted to see – the trade union movement being made socialist.'[39] Healey found support from the TUC in its concern over excessive wage settlements. Jones declared: 'We must disabuse the people of the idea that the government is trying to force the unions to go further. We must implement the guidelines and above all we must go forward together in understanding and unity.' Although he disliked much of Healey's 1975 budget, Jones informed the TUC general council on April 23 that 'the important thing was to keep a Labour government in power and hope that they could produce a situation where the economic balance of the country could be changed as a result of the production of North Sea oil supplies'.[40] He added that the TUC

should have another look at the social contract but the central issue remained that of maintaining living standards within the context of free collective bargaining. Prices had been a weakness in his view and a lot more could be done to check them at the shop level. But if the TUC wrote off the social contract on account of the budget they would in effect be writing off the Labour government.

In early May Jones finally took the initiative in the face of wage-push inflation by calling on the TUC to propose a voluntary flat rate pay policy for all and urged the government to impose a price freeze. But it was an uncertain and hard-pressed moment. 'Saw JJ as lone, valiant and almost tragic symbol of the defenders of the social contract', noted Castle.[41] 'We are anxious to help you.' 'If we are going to win over working men and women we have got to explain a little more the nature of our policies. We must talk to workers in the language they understand. Civil servants can't draft speeches.' At the May meeting of the TUC general council Jones argued passionately for his proposed flat rate pay policy.

> He thought the TUC should be prepared to seek agreement with the CBI but should avoid a return to tripartite discussions. The weakness in the social contract had been the failure to control prices at shop level and this needed to be examined. If the TUC could reach agreement about wages they would be in a strong position to talk to the government about prices and also about pensions.[42]

The crucial debate over the introduction of a flat rate £6 pay increase policy took place at the general council's June meeting where Jones threw his support behind Len Murray. His contribution was a formidable intervention. As the TUC Minutes record, Jones laid out in stark terms the magnitude of the crisis facing the country. As he argued with his colleagues:

> Because of high inflation, there was the threat of a withdrawal of funds from Britain by outside investors and resistance to the massive borrowing which was needed to maintain essential services. They could avoid the real arguments and say that they should go for socialist policies but that was not feasible because they were not in a position to do so. Unless trade unions assisted the government, there was a strong probability of another general election and of the fall of the government. There were people in the cabinet who would be prepared to move towards a coalition government. If the TUC said that they would not cooperate in finding a basis for a voluntary policy they were inviting the return of a government of the right. This could cause very severe damage to the Labour party and lead to the possibility that Labour would not be in power for generations. A statutory wages policy would be introduced, the aim of which would be not just to freeze wages but to secure massive reductions in real

wages. The answer the general council had to find in the economic circumstances facing the Labour government was what was best for the working people of this country.[43]

Jones told his general council colleagues that the key to the problem was to reduce the rising level of unemployment. 'Rising unemployment – which was even worse than statutory wages policy – put enormous pressure on wages anyway', he warned them. 'Prices were rising every week in the shops and ordinary people did not know where to turn and were beginning to doubt everybody.' The government was ready to ensure some measure of price stabilisation, but action would only be possible if the unions responded with restraint and thus ensured that living standards could be maintained. Jones insisted that he was not against wage differentials, but 'present circumstances called for exceptional solutions without which they could be faced with a situation similar to 1931. In his view this called for unity in the movement on the principle of reasonable equality of sacrifice.'

> A figure for pay, related to the achievement of the price target, would be set and unions would be expected to settle on the basis of that figure in the form of a flat-rate money increase to be universally appplied for twelve months at the end of which there would be restoration to normal free collective bargaining in which differentials could be argued.

Jones said he believed a flat rate pay rate 'would enable unions to avoid accusations of letting each other down and leap frogging. On such a basis they would be able to insist that the CBI made sure that price levels came down. The minutes record that Jones

> believed the gravity of the situation was known to their members and that they would respond. He did not think they should consider figures at this stage but the principle whether they were prepared subject to assurances from the government and the CBI about a determination to reduce price levels, to base their claims on the position next year rather than on the past. If there were arguments about special circumstances, arbitration might be used to look at such cases.

Hugh Scanlon, president of the Engineers' Union and ever the gloomy realist, disagreed with Jones. He said that he did not believe the TUC could or would deliver on pay restraint, and that there was no alternative to 'very unpleasant fiscal and political decisions'. Scanlon added: 'It was more honest and straightforward to face up to that than to commit themselves to policies they could not deliver because they were victims of their own differences and contradictions and more important were the servants of those they represented and who determined the policies they had to operate.'

But Jones's words were echoed by those of Murray. He made it clear that the TUC 'could not allow even their very intimate relationship with the government to lead them into the sort of impossible position which had been created in 1947–51 by too ready an acceptance of government influence'. But he added that the TUC economic committee had worked on the assumption that the general council wanted to keep a Labour government in office. Murray complained that some 'trade unionists said they wanted socialist policies to operate', but were 'acting and speaking in ways which would not help to keep a Labour government in power'. The TUC general secretary put his shrewd finger on the real issue: 'Some ministers had grave doubts about the credibility of the TUC and its ability to deliver its side of an agreement.' This was the crux of the position – whether the general council considered there was anything they could offer to the government which would be acceptable to the government and which would not lead to failure and totally discredit the TUC. 'The unions wanted to protect living standards and employment', said Murray, but there was 'no simple solution'. 'It was a matter of finding the least dangerous solution in a dangerous situation.' Going for wage rises of 30 per cent or more was one option, with the spreading belief that this was becoming the going rate. But this would lead to ever higher prices and unemployment. Then they could persist with the guidelines, with percentage increases based on cost of living increases, but the basic defect of this was that it led to comparability claims, and this would also lead to ever rising settlements. Alternatively, the TUC could simply leave it to the government and 'wash their hands of the whole business'. As Murray argued:

if that happened he did not believe the present PM and most of his colleagues would introduce a statutory policy involving penal sanctions on unions. What was more likely would be massive cuts in public expenditure and letting unemployment float upwards – not, as had been emphasised to ministers, that that would solve the problem anyway.

Murray called for a package around a flat rate increase linked to a price target with subsidies and measures to prevent unemployment.

> The TUC had failed to establish in the minds of the membership the connection between their own actions and the overall policy of Congress but he believed that trade unionists recognised the reality of the situation – that it was fatal to proceed on the basis of 30 per cent plus wage increases. The unions and the members were looking for a lead from the general council and he believed what was now emerging provided a basis for that lead. If the TUC was to be attacked, it should be for trying to win support for a feasible policy not for backing away and saying to the government they washed their hands of the whole matter.

The compelling arguments by Jones and Murray carried the day by twenty-one votes to only six against.

Murray for one was in no doubt that Jones was crucial for the introduction of the £6 flat rate pay policy. 'Anybody with up to two million votes in the TUC is a force to be reckoned with', he said. 'If he wanted those hands up around the general council table then that was it.' Murray did not defend all the practices that ensured Jones's success, but he commended his 'intellect, drive, persistence, stickability'.[44]

Jones again showed his mettle at his own union's 1975 biennial conference in arguing the case for the flat rate pay policy. The verbatim account of his speech, locked away in the head office archives, conveys the high emotions of that occasion. His was a simple but highly effective appeal for unity with a Labour government facing desperate economic problems. 'There is no other way', he told them to loud applause from the delegates. 'We simply must help to keep this Labour government in office and stand by it during this terrible economic crisis.' Jones spelt out the nature of what this meant:

> The simple issue is that this country is in a very bad state; it needs to borrow heavily from abroad to maintain the essential services we need to have. Inflation increases our problem and, if it cannot be contained, the cost of borrowing from abroad will be increased and our public services curtailed and prices continue to rise. It would mean massive cuts in public expenditure – and that leads to massive unemployment. Of course, wages are not the main cause of inflation, as so many delegates have said in the course of this debate. One of the principal causes was, indeed the oil crisis, but wages do react to higher prices

and feed inflation. We expect the government to act to restrict the growth of unemployment. We, in turn, must make our contribution. For a time it means moderating wage claims and moderating wage settlements. We have done this in part but not enough. The government, particularly in the field of price control, has done a great deal but not enough. We both need to tighten up. If we act together we can win through. That is the meaning of the social contract. We have to make it not just a workers charter but a housewives charter. Getting prices down and increasing the value of the pound in the pay packet was and is a major objective of the social contract. We simply have to break the vicious circle of increasing prices.[45]

'We know you cannot have free collective bargaining in a situation of massive unemployment', he explained. Jones said that it was true that the Social Contract was never just about wages. He pointed to the many changes the government had made to help workers and the unions, such as the extension of public ownership to the aircraft and shipbuilding industries, as well as British Leyland; the repeal of the hated Industrial Relations Act and the arrival of employment protection legislation with union recognition provisions, as well as an increase in the social wage by a third to average workers, and the introduction of food subsidies. But Jones also argued that the unions needed to act on pay in order to ensure that the Labour government survived until the oil revenues began to flow in from the North Sea. With only an overall Commons majority of one, the government was going to find it difficult to hang on. But Jones told the TGWU conference that if the unions launched an offensive against the government by rejecting pay restraint, it would not bring a shift to the left but 'strengthen reaction'.

It would mean years of misery and a real decline in living standards. Capitalism, friends, is not the issue today. There will be a lot of general elections yet before you can finally determine that capitalism is abolished. The executive firmly believed however that a progressive distribution of wealth and power is more likely to be brought about under a voluntary social contract with a Labour government than under statutory wage control imposed by a Tory government or some sort of coalition. Which do we choose? Which side are we on?

Jones insisted that his views on pay had not changed fundamentally. 'I do not believe in wage restraint as a normal policy', he said.

Neither do I believe in controlled bargaining. We all want to get back to the normal and effective functioning of the trade unions and that is the intention of the social contract. I do believe, however in a Labour government and we would be fools or pygmies to let this government collapse. In all history there have been times to advance and times to stand still, even to retreat a little in order to advance later on. That time is now. The dangers are very great indeed. The circumstances, including the betrayal of 1931 could happen again. Do we want it to happen? The MacDonalds, the Snowdens, the Jimmy Thomas's are lurking around. Their names do not have to be spelt out. Some of them, including a few in very high places, are ready to stick a dagger into the heart of the Labour government. Shall we leave the field to them or shall we keep Labour in office? Shall we help the Labour government in crisis and sustain it until the oil flows in from the North Sea and our economy and trade improves?

Jones pointed out that the economists believed the UK would prosper in the 1980s and that was what the trade unions should recognise, to ensure that Labour was still in office so that the wealth would flow to the people and not to a few millionaires. 'Bring down the Labour government now and I tell you that we sacrifice the prospect of another Labour government for generations. The coalitionists would jump in – and make no mistake – would use every means, including so-called electoral reform to prevent Labour ever returning to power. It is on the cards.'

Jones argued that the £6 flat rate pay policy was a means to ensure that the living standards of the low paid were maintained, with high-income earners making over £8,500 a year expected to have no rise at all – and even a reduction to set an example to the rest.

We believe that this approach is one that can succeed. It will be seen to be socially just and morally right and it can be applied effectively. This is not a question of trying to replace a trade union board to control workers. It means trying to ensure that we return to free collective bargaining as soon as the country is effective and strong again.

In his final peroration Jones spelt out what was at stake. As he explained to the delegates:

Think seriously about what is the best course for the working class as a whole. To stand for unity between the trade union movement and the Labour government or separate ourselves, weaken ourselves, divide our forces and allow this movement to be cast asunder. I cannot believe that our conference will allow that to happen. The social contract represents a great aim, a great dream, a great ambition – in some part suspended by a temporary setback caused by world events. In this period of set-back our stand must be equality of sacrifice not destruction of the Labour government.

He concluded:

I do not question the honesty of purpose of any delegate in this room. But we must make our decisions in terms of that which will help the majority of workers and people of this country. We are in an hour of crisis, we have got to ride the storm, and in due time sail into more peaceful and prosperous waters. Until we do, our platform must remain – each for all and all for each. On that platform we will win a better future for the people that we represent.

But it was not easy for Jones to secure unity on the TUC general council. His flat rate pay strategy only secured 19 votes in favour to 13 against at its special 9 July meeting to endorse it. Jones again spoke forcefully in support. He told his colleagues that the decision they faced 'was one of the most difficult' in the general council's history. 'Incomes policies and controlled wages are repugnant to us and emphasis has been laid in the discussions on preventing the inclusion of sanctions on workers and trade unions', he said.

The fact is that the country is facing a major economic collapse and there is no doubt about the threat of intervention from the IMF. The Labour government is weak in terms of parliamentary influence but it has to act; if they do not they will be out of office. If the TUC does not give assistance there would be a division in the cabinet and in the party and many of the measures the movement wanted to see achieved would be lost. The question is how far the TUC can cooperate in this setting without having legal sanctions or a freeze – which would happen if the government fell and was replaced by a Conservative government ... If the TUC was to preserve its role of collective leadership, notwithstanding the strains that would be put upon it, the general council should give their maximum support to the government and endorse the document that was before them; not to do so would defeat the interests of the government and the trade union movement.[46]

But a formidable array of union leaders were lined up to oppose him – Scanlon; Ken Gill, the tough Communist general secretary of TASS, the technicians' section of the Engineers; Clive Jenkins, the gadfly leader of ASTMS, the white-collar union; Alan Fisher, NUPE's never-satisfied general secretary, and Geoffrey Drain from the white-collar local government union, NALGO. 'Sometimes I despair but no one who attends these liaison meetings can be in any doubt how far Jack and Len have gone or that Hughie and people like Alf Allen who voted against the policy on technical points, are willing to be silent co-operators in it', reflected Barbara Castle in her diary on 21 July 1975.[47] 'Ted Heath would envy us the collaboration we have achieved.' But without Jones's formidable role in the events of that summer, it seems unlikely that the TUC would have been able to endorse any pay policy.

Rise and fall of pay restraint

Over the next twelve months Jones fought hard to ensure pay restraint was a success with his 'Cromwellian New Model Army authority'.[48] But it was never going to be easy. The minutes of the TUC general council do not reveal a picture of complacent and arrogant union leaders, but rather bewildered, concerned and uncertain men and women facing the real prospect of hyper-inflation. Jones – by his firm defence of pay restraint – also found himself the target of vicious attacks from the Communist Party and in particular from Bert Ramelson, its industrial organiser. In two highly influential pamphlets published by the Liaison Committee for the defence of trade unions, Ramelson dubbed the Social Contract the 'social con trick', and denounced union leaders for betraying free collective bargaining and their commitment to the so-called Alternative Economic Strategy based on import controls, nationalisation of industry and the creation of an autarchic economy. Jones publicly warned Ramelson on one occasion to keep out of his union. But such Communist influence among union activists, not least in the TGWU, was to grow stronger with the passing months.

By the end of 1975 the TUC's direct influence on the government was much less than it had been and members of the general council began to question its economic strategy as unemployment continued to climb. At the December general council meeting, Murray warned that the TUC 'must avoid becoming mere apologists for the Labour government or trying to defend the indefensible. Neither would the general council want to appear as professional critics of the government.'[49] In the early months of 1976 the TUC pressed the government for action to stop rising unemployment while emphasising that it did not want to abandon the achievements of the previous 18 months. Jones told the January general council meeting that the TUC had pressed Chancellor Healey for selective import controls, assistance to the construction industry, state assistance for training, higher pensions with a £6 a week increase and further help for the unemployed. Scanlon warned that 'continued support of the trade union movement would be jeopardised' unless the TUC's measures were adopted.[50] However, Barbara Castle recorded that the February 1976 Liaison Committee meeting revealed that

> the union attack was far more muted than the ragings of the Tribune group might have led one to expect. There is no doubt they are worried men and angry at not having been consulted beforehand about the cuts ... But they have no patience with irresponsible talk about bringing the government down.[51]

Murray said they would accept responsibility for the things on which they had agreed. But Jones warned: 'We hope you will reconsider an end of food subsidies. If you imply this is a change of strategy or philosophy on the lines of Margaret Thatcher we are finished ... there are some things this party must defend or we go down eventually.' Scanlon added that 'if the budget doesn't ensure that industry does get the investment [it needs], you are going to make our position almost impossible'.

But a few days later Jones urged the TUC general council to

> take account of the tremendous progress that had been made and recognise the movement's enormous indebtedness to the government ... if the Tories had been in power there would now be 2m unemployed. Means of government intervention in industry had been established which had resulted in the saving of various companies and acquisition of substantial state control. Legislation such as the Employment Protection Act with all its advantages to trade unions was now on the statute book. These achievements were an essential part of the social contract.[52]

By that stage protracted negotiations were underway between the TUC and the government for a second year of incomes policy, with the Treasury keen to ensure a more flexible approach linking tax cuts to lower pay increases. At the April TUC general council meeting Jones said that he did not think union members would want them to act in a way that would force the government to withdraw its tax adjustments, even though they were looking for a floor below which wage increases would not fall for the low paid.[53] Jones told his colleagues, at the special TUC general council meeting in May to endorse the new policy, that the negotiators had been 'working against the constraint of the falling pound and there had been a considerable degree of discussion to reach the proposed agreement'. Higher figures in terms of the pay policy had been pressed but that would have led to a substantial reduction in the amount of the tax concessions and they had wanted to avoid that. The price code would be retained in spite of opposition from the CBI, and there were some limited concessions on public spending. 'In general the government accepted that the trade union contribution would eventually lead to a halving of the inflation rate.' He pointed out that those workers earning £50 or less a week would get £2.50, and those on £60 a week would get a full 5 per cent increase in earnings, with a £4 limit for all those earning more than £80 a week. It was important to keep in mind that the position of the pound was a continual constraint, and he hoped that there would be no further pressure from the trade union movement should the agreement be accepted, since the situation would continue to be highly sensitive. At a later stage it would be necessary to go more deeply into the question of future policy. But at this stage he recommended acceptance of the present proposals as the best that could possibly be obtained while keeping full conditional tax concessions. 'I felt terribly dissatisfied because I knew the figures were inadequate', Jones admitted in his memoirs. 'But in the end I felt we should not take the risk of a catastrophic run on the pound and a general election.'[54]

Winding up the debate, Murray warned that unless the general council backed stage two by a large majority the government could be forced from office. 'Of course there could be a price too high for the trade union movement to pay for a Labour government', he added. 'But this was an honourable agreement and one they must ensure was honoured. The bargaining had shown the government that they could not take the TUC for granted.' Murray accepted that the government's economic policies were too orthodox and said that the TUC would continue to argue for their objectives. But the general council endorsed the second year of wage restraint by twenty-five votes to only five against.

But it was already apparent that the TUC would not be able to persist with pay restraint beyond the summer of 1977. Jones told the general council at its 23 June 1976 meeting:

At the end of the policy which had been approved by Congress last week there should be an orderly return to free collective bargaining which would necessitate a degree of planning. The Chancellor had welcomed that point of view in parliament and that was the position that would be held. It was known there were strains in industry that had to be dealt with – problems of productivity and efficiency – but it would be wrong to go into that kind of detail in a document dealing with major social objectives.[55]

The restraints of the pay policy did not mean an end to Jones's wider trade union ambitions. He remained a firm industrial democrat. In a lecture at Birkbeck College, London University, on 2 December 1975, he talked of a 'new civilisation' that would require that all involved in acceptance of decisions in industry should be given the opportunity to take part in the determination of policy. Jones argued that the unions and Labour wanted a 'fundamental change in property relationships and in the derivation of authority'. He held his own union up as the example.

In many places of work a healthy respect for each other between union and man led to both an expansion of collective bargaining to all areas of policy and a much clearer understanding of the interdependence of all involved in industry – public or private. This is no phoney paternalism nor is it a reflection of managerial weakness.[56]

Jones was a forceful member of the Bullock Committee on industrial democracy, established by the government in 1976 to examine the TUC's proposals to empower trade union activists in private company decision-making. He believed that a new law was needed that would provide them with statutory rights to practise industrial democracy. The majority of the committee backed a complex formula called '2x plus y', made up of equal numbers of managers and union representatives and a few independents to hold the balance on unitary company boards. Although it failed to win widespread union support and aroused hostility among most employers, Jones remained convinced that this would have been a sensible way forward in the transformation of industrial relations.

His high-profile role in the running of the Social Contract made Jones almost a household name. In January 1977 a Gallup survey discovered 53 per cent of people polled believed that he wielded more power and influence in the country compared with only 25 per cent for the Labour prime minister. But in that same month he wrote an article in his union's journal that revealed his own different perception of his role as general secretary. As he explained to the members:

> There is a constant need to be on guard against the union becoming bureaucratic and soulless and thus losing the confidence of the members. Anyone attempting to exercise dictatorial powers endangers the very spirit of trade unionism and indeed workers may require protection against officials who become too dictatorial. A general secretary, in my opinion, must be a guide and a teacher, helping to make policy but never seeking to become the master of the members. He must be the servant of the members in the collective sense whilst preserving the right to put an opinion and to offer guidance. The trade union leader worth his salt must, from the beginning, forget about his own importance and avoid pomposities at all cost. In our thinking, above all, we need to make members trade union conscious and seek to inspire a feeling that the union belongs to the members and that it is their own instrument.[57]

But it was also at that very moment that Jones was becoming painfully aware that he would find it almost impossible to convince his union activists of the need for any more negotiated pay arrangements between the TUC and the government for a third round. On the other hand, he accepted that the immediate economic outlook remained perilous. He tried to explain this to his general executive council.

> High unemployment, rising costs, low investment, a balance of payments deficit – these factors don't vanish at the return of 'free collective bargaining'. To lead our members into a situation which resulted in more closures, more redundancies and even worse inflation would discredit trade unionism and undermine our credibility. In the orderly return to collective bargaining we must not do it in a fashion which will split the movement and weaken our efforts to defend, in particular, the low paid and the pensioners.

He went on to warn his executive council:

> It is an illusion to think that by a sudden change of policy we can get big incomes in real wages for the majority of our members. Any union negotiator knows of the harm done by encouraging false expectations. The real economic facts of life which are providing a rise in living standards are not going to disappear before any words of rhetoric ...

This country is living on borrowed time and borrowed money and no one should forget it. The Public Sector Borrowing Requirement and the loans negotiated to cover our current deficits and sterling balances are necessary – but they are a costly and inflationary pressure on our productive resources. Everything possible must be done to reduce those debts and the associated high rates of interest as quickly as possible. This means we must have regard to the value of the pound. All of this strategy depends upon our ability to pay our way with competitive goods and services so our wages policies to reduce unemployment and increase productive capacity should be geared to these requirements.[58]

At that stage Jones may have hoped he could gain enough flexibility to at least ensure the TUC could adopt a 'responsible' attitude to pay. He acknowledged that there would have to adjustments to deal with anomalies and differentials and the linking of output bonuses and other incentive schemes, as well as protection for the most vulnerable workers. Jones was concerned above all that the orderly return must 'maintain the essential solidarity of trade union purpose'. He then laid down his position to his executive council.

The big question is can we effect a return in a manner that will strengthen the trade union movement, not weaken it? Voluntary collective bargaining is both necessary to our movement and essential to the health of industry but it never has been 'free' in the sense that we can do what the hell we like, regardless of the effects on our basic ability to protect our members. Any sudden uncontrolled move to normal bargaining would expel large groups of union members to defeat in terms of wages and conditions and weaken every union in the country.

But at the Scottish TUC in Rothesay in April, Jones was turned over by his own union delegates when they refused to abstain and voted for a belligerent motion from the miners, calling for an end to any more wage restraint. It was a harbinger of things to come. The 1977 TGWU biennial conference turned out to be Jones's nemesis. Indeed, it signalled the beginning of the end for Labour's Social Contract with the TUC. Anybody present on that memorable day in Douglas, the Isle of Man, cannot but have been moved by his brave but ultimately doomed attempt to hold back the tide of organised opposition coming ironically from those very shop steward delegates whose freedoms he had championed all his trade union life. Afterwards Jones confessed that his heroic task had been impossible, 'like trying to make a river flow up hill'.[59] However, the verbatim account of what he said that day deserves to be remembered. It was perhaps Jones's most impressive and poignant speech as TGWU general secretary and highly prophetic with his pessimistic fears for the future of the unions. He was not arguing, whatever many delegates may have believed, for a phase three of a nationally imposed pay policy.

> All we are saying to conference is: do not let us throw the baby out with the bath water and destroy the unity between the trade union movement and the government. We still can work together and if we disagree occasionally we can close ranks to remove the real injustices in our society.[60]

Jones argued that negotiations between the TUC and the government were still essential to improve real incomes and reduce the wage differentials between rich and poor. These problems could not be solved through collective bargaining. He urged delegates to recognise the need for priorities in pay negotiations and a cut in the working week.

> The cry – and it has been made recently – every man for himself goes out when the ship is sinking. I say that we should not allow the ship to sink. Our policy is to keep it afloat and not to allow it to go down. Surely it is right to remind ourselves, to have regard to the social and economic consequences of whatever we do, we should be determined to maintain a Labour government, warts and all, and certainly no action of ours should bring about the fall of that government.

Jones warned that calls for unfettered wage bargaining would increase the danger of bringing the government down. He was unapologetic for what had happened over the previous two years. As he explained to the delegates:

> Whatever our critics say, it was absolutely right to provide for flat rate increases at the time of the biggest economic crisis which has faced this country since the 1930s. This was not just another pay policy. It was a reaction to circumstances over which the government had no control. When we experienced real crises in the past – for example in time of war – we have accepted rationing. The trade union reaction on this occasion in the depth of this severe economic crisis was to

decide to ration wages and any rationing must be on an egalitarian basis. We tried by collective decision and collective goodwill to act together on pay and we succeeded part of the way. If we did not succeed all the way, no one should blame us for trying.

Jones believed that the unions would have to 'exercise some collective responsibility' towards their fellow members. 'To ignore their interests is not trade unionism and to smash down the 12 months real settlements under phase two will only increase conflict. It can create industrial chaos and cause dissension in our ranks.' Douglas was the scene of Jones's first and last defeat at the hands of his union. But it was full of a sad irony. The shop stewards from the docks, the car industry and road haulage, whom he had encouraged and championed all his life, had rejected him.

At their 13 July 1977 meeting, a few days later, Callaghan was left in no doubt by the TUC that it could not and would not deliver a third year of wage restraint. All the government could hope for was an 'orderly return to collective bargaining' based on a commitment to a twelve-month interval between pay deals. Healey explained: 'The unions have too much responsibility and too little power with their members.'[61] But Callaghan was not completely disheartened by what he had heard from union leaders. He believed that the government 'could count on understanding for its policy' from the TUC, if not 'positive agreement'. Just so long as the government showed itself to be 'sensitive to trade unions' attempts to remove the distortions that pay policy had brought about'.[62]

In fact, as long as he remained TGWU general secretary, Jones refused to pursue 'unfettered' collective bargaining. On the contrary, he held firm to the TUC line on the need for the twelve-month interval between wage settlements. As he told his executive council in September 1977:

With a return to voluntary collective bargaining a great responsibility falls upon our officers and shop stewards. The union's standing and reputation will be related to their efforts. My appeal to them is to prepare the submission of claims with care and detail and ensure maximum consultation with the membership in the process. Now more than ever we must act in such a way as to demonstrate a full sense of responsibility and encouraging the membership to take a greater part in branch and works meetings is very much part of this. We are not a 'business union', we are essentially a 'member's union' and it is necessary to listen closely to what the members have to say. This approach breeds confidence and as it grows increasing numbers of non-unionists are attracted to our ranks and the union moves forward ever stronger. An enlightened, participating membership is the safeguard of our union's decency and the guarantee of progress.[63]

The role of the industrial department of the Communist Party inside the trade unions during the period of the Social Contract cannot be ignored in any assessment of its rise and fall. 'We have more influence now on the Labour movement than at any time in the life of our party', Bert Ramelson, its industrial organiser, claimed in December 1973.[64] 'We can float an idea early in the year and it can become official Labour policy by the autumn. A few years ago we were on our own but not anymore.' The permeation of the cadres of full-time trade union officials and shop stewards by Communist strategy was important in ensuring a strong, broad left. 'Where the struggle is, there are where Communists are', said Ken Gill, general secretary of the TASS section of the Engineering union. He was elected to the TUC general council in September 1974 where he stayed until his retirement in 1990. A tough and able Communist, Gill provided leadership to the broad left group organised on the general council. They used to meet regularly in the head offices of the ACCT cinematograph union in Soho Square, London, before TUC general council monthly meetings to plan their strategy and decide how they should vote on key issues on the TUC agenda. Gill recalls that this brought some order and discipline to the broad left, who may have remained small in number but punched above their number by giving a sense of direction to the general council. Ramelson was a close friend of Gill and although he did not attend those broad left meetings he was certainly a key influence on their deliberations. Certainly TUC leaders believed that the Communist Party's industrial activities had been very important in the collapse of the Social Contract. They argued it was less a genuine revolt by rank and file members and more an uprising by the shop stewards under broad left influence.

Len Murray is scornful of those who believed the TUC exercised great power and influence during the period of the Social Contract. 'It is sheer myth', he asserted. 'I believe the Confederation of British Industry got more out of the Labour government than we did. We made very little impact on its economic policy and we achieved no industrial democracy.' Nor in retrospect was he grateful for the repeal of the Industrial Relations Act.

It died the death outside the gates of Pentonville prison before Labour came to power. Most of what we got in industrial relations law was to help non-unionists and not unions. It is true we got union recognition provisions but this was dust and ashes, useless, indeed dangerous to us.[65]

John Monks, future TUC general secretary, also agreed that the gains made by the unions during the Social Contract period were more modest than many recognised. 'Only in two areas – unfair dismissal and the maternity provisions – was really new ground broken and employers generally pressed to make advances in the interests of their employees', he argued.[66]

There are those who argue that the Labour governments of the 1970s called on the TUC to take on responsibilities it lacked the power or authority to shoulder. The Social Contract was in practice a much more modest arrangement than many realised, but much of its rhetoric left many with the mistaken impression that the TUC was somehow equal to the government in the running of the country. In fact, the TUC did not establish any greater collective strength during those years over its affiliate member unions than it had done before. Professor William Brown is highly critical of the damaging legacy left by the myth of the Social Contract.

Unions are reactive, bargaining organisations, ill-prepared for writing the agenda for government … In attempting to placate, for tactical economic reasons a largely unprepared trade union movement, the government did the movement lasting damage. It perpetuated the myth of the centrality of trade unions to the British inflationary process … but as the CBI itself was aware, a fragmented bargaining structure was a major contributor. By placing unions so centrally on the political stage, it prepared the way for the devastating Conservative reaction.[67]

However, it is also possible to see the Social Contract as a lost opportunity in establishing a consensual approach to public policy-making similar to that adopted by other and more successful European social market economies in the 1970s. Jack Jones was probably the most far-sighted and imaginative of post-war trade union leaders. Certainly he held a romantic view of shop stewards and his faith in workplace bargaining tended to heighten the acquisitive and competitive sectionalism between work groups that did so much damage to industrial relations. But during the 1970s – through the TUC – he was also developing a coherent and progressive strategy that was practical and credible in its attempt to modernise collective bargaining and prepare the means for achieving a more efficient and competitive economy, but one also based on social justice. Jones set the pace inside the TUC for radical change. His tragedy was that he was unable to take his shop stewards with him. Instead, he became the victim of the contradictions that lay at the heart of his philosophy of democratic workplace trade unionism.

7
Into the Wilderness:
The TUC under Len Murray and
Norman Willis, 1978–1993

The TUC will find its way to influence – just like a stream when blocked finds a new channel.

Len Murray[1]

It will be said of us here that we did our best, and if we do it together it will be said we did our best and it was good enough.

Norman Willis[2]

Len Murray was elected TUC general secretary in September 1973 at a time when the organisation appeared to be at the height of its national influence. On the eve of his election he was clear about what he intended to do. 'I want trade union activists to realise the TUC's potential', he explained. 'We must be the generaliser of good labour practices – the pusher out and puller in of ideas and information. The TUC is not just a platform of people who meet once a year by the seaside nor is it merely a name at the top of official headed notepaper.'[3] His self-proclaimed objective was to 'give everybody a share in the action'.

Murray was born on 2 August 1922, the son of a Shropshire farm labourer. His Border country burr remained one of his most recognisable features. After leaving the local grammar school he spent a year reading English literature at London University before leaving in disgust because of the degree's concentration on Anglo-Saxon. This was followed by an unhappy period as a school-teacher who could not keep order in the classroom. Murray served with the Shropshire regiment in the Second World War. A lieutenant, he took part in the Normandy landings in June 1944. He was struck down in action. For a short time afterwards he worked as an assistant store-keeper in Wolverhampton when he also joined the Communist Party for a short spell or what he called a 'relatively brief flirtation', leaving because he disliked its disciplines. But he never regretted it. 'The Communists taught me the importance of effective organisation, hard work and dedication to a cause', he reflected.[4] Murray went back to university, to New College, Oxford, where he graduated with a second class degree in politics, philosophy and economics after only two years of study. This was followed by a training course with Reeces, the Liverpool catering firm. It was then that he applied for a post in the TUC's economic department. At his job interview Murray impressed general secretary George Woodcock by his cynical but realistic observation that trade unions bargained best where an employer enjoyed a monopoly so that wage increases could be passed on in price rises. By 1956 he was head of the TUC economic department and he stayed in that position until becoming Vic Feather's deputy in April 1969.

In his first five and a half years as TUC general secretary Murray often seemed to be little more than the self-effacing, earnest custodian of the general council's collective decisions. Although quietly sceptical of the more ambitious objectives of the Social Contract and worried that the TUC might be asked to shoulder too many responsibilities, he was nevertheless an articulate and effective voice for Congress House in the outside world. His quiet, studied calm suggested that he was a man who could absorb the intolerable pressures imposed by the crises of the 1970s. But Murray was faced with an increasingly hostile public opinion, convinced that trade unions had become over-powerful and arrogant. This ensured an understandably wary outlook to a bleak outside world, which wrongly saw the Social Contract as an undemocratic attempt to provide the trade unions with a stranglehold over government and the economy.

Murray had to perform a variety of bewildering roles as TUC general secretary. He was the grave industrial statesman arguing with government for TUC policies. He was the publicist for the trade unions in the media. He was the conciliator seeking to prevent or limit inter-union rivalries and conflict. He was on occasions the bargainer trying to resolve tricky disputes. He was the apparatchik smoothing out the wrinkles on a divided general council. Murray's crowded diary took him from dinners at 10 Downing Street with the prime minister and chancellor, to trades council gatherings in draughty halls in the industrial north. High office did not make Murray either pompous or vain. Unlike many trade union leaders he was not over-impressed by the seductions of public life. He was made a privy councillor in April 1976 – the least controversial of Sir Harold Wilson's resignation honours list. On his retirement he accepted a peerage and took the Labour whip in the House of Lords.

Murray sought to make the TUC a more open, relaxed organisation, less hidebound by convention and rules but still respectful of the procedures of yesteryear. He made no attempt to surround himself with cronies from the general council. Murray walked with everyone but consequently he was very much alone. Perhaps in the beginning he was too painfully aware of the limitations of his office. The TUC general secretary – even at the height of trade union influence – never had any big battalions at his instant command. He had to cajole and persuade through logic, wisdom, common sense. Murray was very much a consensus man, who always disliked vote-taking on the general council and wanted a TUC collective view to emerge from debate. This gave the mistaken impression that he did not believe passionately about anything. In fact, Murray was always keen to defend and further the TUC ethos of public policy-making in the trade union interest. His keen intelligence as well as an ability to get to the guts of a complex issue and explain it to others in a cogent no-nonsense manner was usually appreciated around the general council chamber. But for most of the time until 1983 he did not take the initiative, moving at the pace of the slowest.

However, Murray – a Methodist lay preacher – held strong and ethical opinions about the role of trade unions in a free society. He certainly believed there was a genuine conflict of interest in the workplace. 'I believe there are two sides in industry', he once explained. 'I believe there are those who own the industry and the assets and the people who are employed, who work in industry. I believe their interests are different, that they are in conflict, that they are opposed a lot of the time or some of the time.' Of course, Murray accepted there were things that both could agree on such as improving productivity, the use of manpower, making workplaces better to work in. But when it came to deciding who got what out of the proceeds of industry, then there was a clear difference. 'We have to recognise this and live with it.'[5]

He was always sensitive to any suggestion that the TUC should become a corporatist partner with the state. Murray emphasised the freedom and autonomy of trade unions. He liked to quote the words of Frederick Rogers, general secretary of the Bookbinders' union: 'We shall enlarge the frontiers of the state and control so far as the government can control, the power of the capitalist over the labourer more and more. But there must be an independent life within the state to prevent government becoming tyranny and the trade unions will be chief among those who shall call that independent life into being.' As Murray explained in a 1970 lecture:

> Unions look to the state to facilitate the performance of trade union functions, to provide assistance in securing the peaceful settlement of disputes which arise between groups and to provide minimum standards for groups of workers where union organisation is not sufficiently strong to secure them, they insist that these are complementary, not alternative, to the exercise by unions of their proper functions.

He believed that the relationship between the TUC and the state should be based on bargaining and not seeking out favours. 'Trade unions are disposed to question the absolute sovereignty of the state and to regard it at least for some important purposes as a federal society in regulating the affairs of which the government has an important but not necessarily an overriding authority.' Murray was keen to avoid absolutes and concentrate on the room for manoeuvre 'to accommodate the shifts and fluctuations of industrial activity'. He believed the use of the law or executive order was not the best way of achieving success for a government in seeking agreement with trade unions. While favourable to the 'closest collaboration' between the TUC and the state, he was also determined to ensure the trade unions protected their independence and were not asked to shoulder responsibilities in the political economy which were beyond their powers to make effective. Murray believed the TUC was asked to do too much by the Attlee government after the Second World War. 'The TUC leadership in most of the period of the first post-war Labour government accepted demands laid on them by the government that strained almost to breaking point their relations with the membership', he argued. The reasons for that loyalty were understandable – memories of the inter-war depression, the commitment to full employment, the genuine advances to a welfare state. But Murray added that asking the TUC to uphold wage restraint 'could do no more than temporarily dam forces within the trade union movement that eventually burst out'. While he accepted that the state wanted trade union cooperation and there was no inconsistency between trade union independence and voluntary agreements with the state, each side needed to recognise the legitimacy of the other if the relationship was to be of mutual benefit. However, as Murray perceptively noted in 1970, the 'essential' interests of trade unions were narrower and more specific than those of the state, easier to identify and to that extent therefore more defensible.

Filling the vacuum

The departure of Jones and Scanlon soon after each other proved to be a severe blow to the TUC's stability as resistance to further wage restraint grew more intense among the shop stewards. Murray needed to try and fill the power vacuum. Neither Moss Evans, Jones's successor at the TGWU, nor Terry Duffy, AUEW president after Scanlon, were able to establish the authority of the once 'terrible twins' who had grown into responsible custodians of the Social Contract. Callaghan, for one, believed the two men had formed a strong partnership within the TUC through an 'amalgam of gritty integrity, strength and subtlety'.[6] But the TUC general council was not in any mood to continue having a close relationship with the Labour government if it included yet further annual understandings on incomes. The new more hostile mood was evident in the anguished debate on the general council in 1977 over the firefighters' dispute. The Fire Brigade Union wanted the TUC to launch a public campaign against the government's 10 per cent pay limit and the twelve-month interval between wage settlements. Evans threw the TGWU's full weight behind the demand, and the opposition nearly carried the day on the general council when it came to the vote.

During most of 1978 the TUC and the government were moving inexorably apart. Callaghan and Healey still yearned for a broad agreement with the TUC that would ensure that the maximum level of earnings increases were kept compatible with keeping down inflation. Murray told ministers to trust the unions to behave responsibly and not try to interfere in collective bargaining. The TUC issued a statement on pay policy in July 1978 arguing that unions had 'no wish to return to the inflationary difficulties of 1974–75 nor to see the results of their past self-restraint and sacrifices frittered away'. 'It has been on the achievement of higher levels of growth, productivity and real pay that stability in overseas countries has been based not on policies which concentrate on restricting pay.'[7] 'We warned Callaghan that he would have industrial trouble if he tried to impose a 5 per cent wages policy', said Murray. 'He was over-impressed by the quality of the Treasury printout and started thinking with his head rather than his stomach.'[8] Callaghan, in his memoirs, recalled that Murray and his colleagues were 'conciliatory and helpful' when he met them during the summer of 1978 to discuss the government's counter-inflation programme.[9] The TUC general secretary told him that they all 'shared the same objectives and acknowledged that without the efforts the government had made unemployment and inflation would have been higher', adding that the unions 'were anxious to avoid a wages explosion but employers were increasingly blaming the government for their failure to pay higher wages with the result that beating the norm was becoming a challenge'.[10]

Most union leaders assumed Callaghan would call a general election in the autumn of 1978 and would not soldier on through the winter or insist that the government's 5 per cent pay policy should be taken seriously. 'We urged him to go to the polls and not wait', said Murray. 'But he had this image of himself as the tough guy who would take no nonsense from the unions and steal the Tories' clothes.'[11] In retrospect, Murray insisted that the TUC might have been able to hold down pay deals in the 1978–79 wage round to 8 or 9 per cent. 'Ministers thought they knew better than the general council what trade unionists wanted', he argued. At the 1978 Congress delegates voted overwhelmingly against any more wage restraint. A resolution from NALGO, the local government union, calling for the introduction of a coordinated approach to wage bargaining on the West German model, suffered a heavy defeat. Murray urged the need for 'sufficient flexibility' if trade unions and employers were 'to sort out difficult problems and anomalies and to take account of profitability without splash headlines about defeats or surrenders or nonsense of that sort'.[12] He said he was sure that union negotiators would 'be influenced to adopt a prudent attitude to pay negotiations' because of the 'deep and cautionary effects' on their thinking after the hyper-inflation threat of 1974–75. But the Labour Party conference hardened attitudes still further when a motion from the Liverpool Wavertree constituency was passed by a huge majority that not only rejected any form of wage restraint but also suggested that the planning of pay would only be acceptable when prices, profits and investment were also planned within the framework of a socialist economy.

In the aftermath of the conference a renewed attempt was made by the government and the TUC to try and find at least a *modus vivendi* which might go some way to prevent widespread industrial conflict against the 5 per cent pay policy. The TUC wanted a concentration on dealing with prices. If action could be taken by the government to control them, then union negotiators might be more sensible in their wage claims. The 14 November general council meeting was presented with a document – *TUC Guidance to Negotiators* – that had won cabinet approval. This made it clear the TUC would not vet claims or 'act as watchdogs in the process of negotiations or scrutinise settlements'. But it was suggested that union bargainers should have a regard to the effect their claims would have on prices. 'Unions should seek the maximum efficiency in the use of resources and have regard to the need to produce a balanced allocation of benefits between workers, investment and the consumer', the document declared.[13] It also committed both sides to keep the annual inflation rate down to its current level in 1978–79. The joint TUC–government statement suggested that measures would be needed to promote growth, cut unemployment and improve real living standards, and this meant 'policies affecting costs, incomes, investment, the exchange rate and fiscal and monetary developments'. Murray made it clear to the general council that the statement did not commit the TUC to a 5 per cent pay policy or any variant of it. 'The aim which general council members considered they had achieved was to begin to lever the government away from its present inflexible approach and to open up more scope for collective bargaining', he argued. Murray also added that the proposals were not incompatible with TUC policy 'which itself had emphasised that trade unionists were still concerned to avoid a return to the 1974–1975 situation of escalating wages and prices'.[14] He pressed the case in a soberly realistic way: 'While the statement was far from perfect, it could open up possibilities for negotiators which could in practice become increasingly more advantageous as the situation developed and unfolded.' But in the end the general council had a tied vote on acceptance of 14 to 14. As chairman Tom Jackson of the Post Office workers' declared, the statement had not been carried. It was the end of the road. Murray was relieved at the outcome. He believed a narrow victory would have proved useless. The deal had needed a broad base of general council support, and this it clearly lacked.

At their meeting at the Treasury on 19 December 1978, Murray and the TUC general council argued that they remained

firmly committed to voluntary collective bargaining. They believed the government's pay policy was an over-reaction to circumstances, that 5 per cent had become a symbol and that the government had created a climate in which every legitimate dispute was seen as a challenge to their authority, and which prevented negotiators from carrying out their essential role of resolving problems in a constructive way. The TUC understood the need to maintain the fight against inflation but the government's current stance was in danger of creating the maximum of industrial problems with the minimum of effective results.

But the minutes added:

> The TUC recognised the government's concern to avoid a sudden lurch from a restrictive to a free pay situation but the government should recognise the need at least to move steadily and by agreement in the direction of giving more scope for meaningful negotiations on particular problems in the public and the private sector. In particular negotiators should have the right to determine what methods they deemed appropriate to help to resolve their pay difficulties, including, where appropriate, comparability arrangements.[15]

Healey pointed out to the TUC that UK growth was now the fastest in Europe, unemployment at 5.4 per cent was lower than in many other countries, the current account was broadly in balance, the pound was holding against other currencies and the inflation rate had been 'cut more dramatically than in any other part of the world'. As a result the government had been able to cut tax and increase benefits and the average increase in real living standards at 7.5 per cent was greater than in any single year since the war. If unit labour costs were kept at around the international level and a 'sensible level of pay settlements' was maintained, the government could maintain economic progress. But this meant keeping pay deals to around 5 per cent given that slippage and drift and special case increases would result in a higher level of average earnings.

> The government had attempted last year to run a flexible pay policy requiring settlements to average 10 per cent bu there had been no volunteers for settlements below the average and the government had been compelled to treat the 5 per cent figure as a limit. The government would welcome any policy which would produce a rate of increase in earnings in the current round consistent with single figure inflation without a rigid pay limit but they had to be convinced that such a policy was possible and would work in practice. Unless the rise in average earnings was less than 10 per cent then the inflation rate would not be kept in single figures.

In response the TUC argued that the current industrial unrest was

> largely a result of the attempt by the government to rigidly apply the 5 per cent policy which was indeed acting to suppress production rather than trying to create a situation on the pay front to which they felt the economy would respond while the TUC felt strongly that the need was to create the economic and industrial climate to which pay negotiators could respond.

At their meeting at Downing Street, Callaghan sought the 'active cooperation of the trade union movement' because the 'government alone' could not achieve its economic objectives. 'The government and the TUC had to live together', he told the general council.

> Another government might feel otherwise and attempt alternative action on the lines of balancing the budget, cutting public expenditure and using the law to shackle trade unions. The government and the TUC had a joint responsibility to ensure such an outcome did not occur. There was just time to stop the rot, provided there was a positive attempt on the part of all concerned, including the public service unions who would have more to lose than any other group if the Conservatives won the next general election.

Callaghan also told the TUC that 'no one should condone or under-estimate the damage done' through the waves of industrial disruption. He warned that 'it could lead to an attempt at legislation which could set back the trade union movement for a decade'. This meant that 'action had to be urgent; there were only a few weeks in which to recapture lost ground'. He accepted that a pay freeze was impossible but 'there had to be a statement which covered such issues as leapfrogging, the maintenance of essential services and the relationship between public and private sector incomes'. The prime minister accepted that they could have plenty of discussion about medium- and longer-term strategy, but people would expect them to address current problems. He was hopeful that there was now 'a real chance of a successful outcome'.

Murray assured him on behalf of the TUC general council that they wished 'to restore the basis of understanding with the government, which they believed to be in line with the interests of trade unions and working people'. The TUC recognised the extreme difficulties of the present situation economically and politically and were convinced a complex industrial society could only run on the basis of agreement and intelligent working arrangements between the government and the TUC. They recognised an understanding would materially assist the Labour government in winning the election; this was as valid an aspect of Congress policy as any other. They also accepted an agreement had to stand up in the face of public opinion. However, the government should understand that the TUC would not and should not promise more than it could deliver.

Murray informed Callaghan that the TUC 'was not prepared to enter into an agreement based on a variation or renegotiation of a pay norm; this was neither desirable nor practicable. While the TUC recognised the urgency of the present industrial situation, the issues should be kept in perspective and the general council would not allow themselves to be pushed into indefensible areas by reacting in a panic-stricken way.

Murray and his TUC staff did the best they could to lessen the ferocity of the so-called 'winter of discontent' But the upsurge of bitterness reflected first in the lorry drivers' dispute, and later in January 1979 with the low-paid workers' public sector offensive, inflicted severe moral damage on the trade union movement. It is true that there was considerable media exaggeration in the reporting of those events. But enough happened to undermine what had been seen as the special relationship between the TUC and the government. At times the prime minister and his colleagues seemed to be paralysed by the brutality of the conflict. Callaghan was later to regret that he had failed to introduce a state of emergency. His 5 per cent wages policy was in tatters, but the upsurge in the level of pay settlements above an annual rate three times that figure did not suggest either employers or union negotiators were practising responsible collective bargaining. In the acquisitive scramble after two years of supposed restraint, the TUC seemed powerless to moderate expectations.

At his meeting with the TUC general council on 5 February 1979 Callaghan suggested that his government 'should be given credit for resisting pressures for a legal approach to industrial relations – even to the point of being accused of complacency – because of their belief in a voluntary approach'. 'Cooperation on the part of the unions involved in industrial disputes has helped the government to fend off this pressure', he told them. 'He welcomed the decision to examine issues of good trade union practice.' The Minutes record that the prime minister understood what had been said about the TUC not promising more than it could deliver and not wishing to renegotiate a norm, though he had to say that if everybody negotiated 15 per cent, no one would be any better off than if they had all negotiated 5 per cent. The country would not understand if the government were simply to say 'get on with it' and ignore settlements of 20 per cent or even 30 per cent. The government wished to stick as closely as they could to 5 per cent, which they thought was in the best interests of the country, though they accepted there were particular problems, especially in the public services where a phased comparability approach might be needed, embracing the principle of comparable pay for comparable work and effort. What the country needed at the moment was a period of industrial calm encouraged by the trade union movement against the background of a voluntary code of practice on industrial relations, together with a general statement of intent on the reduction of inflation to below 5 per cent by the spring of 1982 and on the policies required to bring this about.[16]

Strenuous negotiations were held over the following seven days between the TUC and the government to try and reach some wider understanding that came to be known as the concordat. The TUC general council was called to Downing Street on 14 February to meet the prime minister, who told them the cabinet was prepared to endorse the negotiated statement if they accepted it. Murray urged his colleagues to support it. He told them:

> It had to be acknowledged that it was not without its limitations. Nor did it comprise an immediate and detailed answer to all current problems. However, it did set down the means by which some of the answers might be found. Given the initial differences, it represented the best that could be done in the present circumstances and he hoped the general council would endorse the statement as a basis for continued cooperation with the government.[17]

Strong opposition was voiced to much of what had been agreed. Harry Urwin, as chairman of the employment policy committee, sought to reassure them that the voluntary codes of conduct for unions in disputes were not 'a guide to be adhered to irrespective of circumstances' and there was no suggestion they would involve any legal intervention. But the TUC had suggested that unions should limit the number of pickets deployed in a strike and ought to consult their members through secret ballots before calling them into dispute. Some union leaders also feared that the accompanying economic statement did not give enough attention to the TUC's own agenda of planning agreements in industry with unions, the introduction of selective import controls and the control of profits and dividends. It was suggested that there was

> too much emphasis in the statement on incomes in the context of inflation and too little in the context of redistribution. The frequent references to incomes carried with them the implication of a future attempt at central pay determination and this, together with the proposal for an annual economic assessment, could be construed as a step towards the corporate state.

Some general council members even wondered whether there was too much emphasis on low pay and comparability in the public sector, giving the impression that the TUC and the government were 'ignoring the plight' of those employed in the private sector who suffered from the same problems. As the TUC's own minutes explain:

> There was no question of the statement implying an acceptance of pay norms or envisaging TUC advice to unions on how to frame specific claims. At the same time, however, the statement did recognise and set down some of the basic facts of the present situation in an attempt to create a climate of opinion in which responsible collective bargaining could take place. Whilst questions of pay claims and settlements were ultimately matters for the union membership to decide, it was surely right for the TUC to draw attention to general considerations, including the need to negotiate on the merits of particular situations rather than blindly adopt, or seek to better, the 'going rate'.

In the end both sides endorsed the documents. However, the prime minister refused to excise words in the concordat that indicated the government would take 'possible future monetary and fiscal action'. It was accepted that agreement 'would not be possible' on words in every paragraph that 'would please everyone on both sides', but 'the statement should be seen as a useful starting point to joint discussions over the coming months', the value of which would be tested by events. It was all too little, too late. As Healey admitted in his memoirs: the winter of discontent 'destroyed the nation's confidence in the Labour party's ability to work with the unions'. Without an overall Commons majority,

Callaghan's government was defeated by one vote in a confidence motion in March after inconclusive devolution ballots in Scotland and Wales, and lost the resulting general election.

Towards new realism

The arrival of Margaret Thatcher and the Conservatives at 10 Downing Street after Labour's defeat in May 1979 did not immediately seem to worry the TUC too much. 'We simply did not believe what she said she would do and we didn't believe most Conservatives did either', Murray explained.[18] Union leaders convinced themselves that sooner rather than later, the new prime minister would recognise the error of her ways, perform a U-turn and call in the TUC to help her out with a face-saving deal. 'We completely misread history', admitted Murray. The TUC held one meeting with Mrs Thatcher before she came to power. Their exchange, in Murray's opinion, was 'one of mutual incomprehension'. 'We were horrified', he recalled. 'Conservative leaders have always been able to recognise a vested interest when they saw one. But she did not seem keen on institutions, whether it be the TUC, the CBI, Whitehall or even the City of London.' The general council was to hold one further formal session at 10 Downing Street on 15 June. But there was never any prospect of a meeting of minds. She lectured them on the need for free market economics. Although cautious to begin with and ready to accept the emollient One Nation Tory Jim Prior as her Employment secretary, Mrs Thatcher did not disguise her visceral dislike of trade unions and the collectivist values they claimed to stand for. She agreed with the forthright attacks delivered on them by her friend and colleague Sir Keith Joseph who had suggested that the trade unions were a key part of the British problem of low productivity and profitability.

Murray believed that his greatest failure was 'not recognising when Mrs Thatcher won the 1979 general election that she had tapped into some profound changes in thinking and attitudes among British people, including trade unionists and believing she was a passing breeze which would blow itself out'. As a result, he thought the TUC 'delayed far too long in making some changes that were patently necessary and got stuck in a rut of opposition'.

In the autumn of 1979 TUC general council decided to launch a campaign for 'economic and social advance' aimed at mobilising public opinion against the Thatcher government. 'It should be made clear it was not conceived as an attempt to force a general election', suggested the general council Minutes.[19]

It was emphasised that the general council should act as a whole, along the lines set out in the motion [on the planned offensive]. Action must not split or isolate different groups or be divisive in any way. In 1976 the trade unions had not been totally unified in their manner of opposition to spending cuts and this should not be repeated.

Murray warned his colleagues that 'it would be unrealistic to proceed on the assumption that the position could be rapidly changed. It would be a major task to explain and win support for the TUC's strategy and criticism of government policy.' The proposed industrial relations legislation to limit picketing, enforce periodic reviews of existing closed shop agreements and urge holding postal ballots before strikes and for the election of union leaders with an inducement of state aid. Urwin told the general council that Prior was

attempting to manoeuvre the general council into a negotiating position whereby some parts of the government's proposals would be accepted but the others would not. This approach had to be rejected. The committee would be seeking to deflect the government from its proposals on industrial relations legislation and emphasising that the best way of dealing with these matters was by voluntary action.

In September 1981 the right-wing Norman Tebbit replaced Prior as Employment Secretary and the TUC found itself facing a formidable opponent. 'He was a rough sod but very able', said Murray. 'He would put his knee in your stomach just to attract your attention with a smile on his face. But he was the sort of fellow you could do a deal with. He would drive a hard bargain but you knew he would deliver.'[20] The 1982 Employment Act delivered a body blow to the unions by removing their legal immunities from civil actions for damages in unlawful disputes. It was the key change in all of the Thatcherite industrial relations legislation, and the TUC general secretary realised this. An attempt was made by the TUC to mobilise opposition to the new measure. A special fund was created to help unions in trouble from any employers who decided to use the Act. At a one-day TUC conference in Wembley in the spring of 1982, union leaders lined up to show their solidarity with a non-cooperation strategy. It seemed – to some – like a repeat performance of 1972 when the TUC had defeated the Industrial Relations Act. But it was all rather unreal. On this occasion the government was not going to back down in the face of TUC opposition. The set-piece national strikes, from the steelworkers in 1980 to the miners in 1984–85, reflected Mrs Thatcher's determination not to bow the knee to what she saw as irresponsible trade union power.

Murray believed that union leaders grew more and more out of touch with the views of their ordinary rank and file members and were over-sensitive to the attitudes of their minority of activists. 'We thought if we pressed the right button our members would come alive. The scales would fall from their eyes and they would realise that they had been misled by the Conservatives.' But as Murray moved from one march to another, 'days of action' and mass demonstrations, he received a 'great shock'.

I came to realise I was meeting the same people wherever I went. They were old pal's reunions. My worst experience was at a Hyde Park meeting on Jobs for Youth. Only a handful turned up. We didn't have the youngsters and above all we didn't have their parents.

'I started questioning in my own mind whether we were on the right track', he said. 'I was told we needed to print a million more leaflets for one campaign we had launched but where were they all going? I thought they were being used to prop up a three-legged table in a union office in the west midlands.' Murray questioned:

How representative were those who came on our marches of people in the factories and offices? There was a certain arrogance about union officials and stewards who said they knew what their members wanted and if they didn't know they had to be told. I was brought up to believe that you can only do what your members will let you.

But in a 1980 lecture on the 'democratic bargain' Murray expressed his abiding conviction that trade unions had a legitimate role to play in a free society and this meant involving people as workers.[21] But he was also well aware from experience that trade unions had the power to impede change, to say no and to stop things happening. 'This power cannot be removed by turning back the clock nor can attitudes be changed by changing the law', he explained. 'The real issue is how we can get trade unionists to use their industrial power wisely, at the minimum to take account of their own longer-term interests.' Murray did not doubt that governments were elected to govern; that neither the TUC nor any trade union had the right or the wish to usurp the powers of the state. However, he also believed that 'effective' government acknowledged the 'pluralist basis of our democacy, accepting there is a variety of legitimate interests in our society and finding means of reconciling these different interests'. He saw the TUC as a bargainer with governments in establishing areas of agreement. 'Governments which treat unions as responsible organisations are entitled in return to expect unions to act responsibly', he argued. However, if the state refused to treat unions as worthy of sharing or accepting responsibility, then it must expect unions to go on the defensive and exercise 'their traditional functions of defending their basic rights'. In 1980 Murray had been convinced that Mrs Thatcher would recognise that she would have to bargain with the TUC. 'Set-piece battles are no way to solve the problems which face Britain', he argued. 'I do not believe the present government or any other can continue indefinitely to withstand the inevitable progress of the democratic forces which are at work in industry and in every other part of society.'

It was not until the aftermath of Labour's catastrophic performance in the May 1983 general election that Murray decided that the time had come for the TUC to reassess its entire strategy towards the government. His speech to Congress that September spelt out what came to be called briefly the 'New Realism'. After years of self-imposed caution and defensiveness Murray tried to take the initiative. 'We cannot talk as if the trade union movement is some sort of alternative government. Brother Bonnie Prince Charlie waiting to be summoned back from exile', he told delegates.[22] 'We are representative organisations and being representative organisations and respecting what our members want and expect from their unions – not the government's unions, not the Labour party's unions, not even our unions but the members' unions.' Murray insisted that the TUC's task was now to win back the lost ground that it had 'assumed was safe for ever'. A Conservative government had been re-elected for the first time since 1945 that did not regard the maintenance of full employment as a 'dominant' policy objective, nor the welfare state as a 'binding force' in British society. Murray's outspoken comments were not warmly received by some union leaders. But they were seen by many in Congress House as long overdue. On the eve of his retirement he conceded that he had not always taken the lead in such an unequivocal manner.

> It is a fair criticism that I have not led from the front. I have not gone round the country with my heart on my sleeve. It is only in exceptional circumstances when you have to declare like Martin Luther – 'Here I stand, I can do no other'. Running about in public was not my style temperamentally. At the end of the day it was my job to carry out what the general council decided collectively.[23]

Within weeks of his New Realism speech, however, Murray and the TUC were confronted with a bitter dispute between the National Graphical Association and the *Stockport Messenger* newspaper. Under pressure, he decided that the TUC was going to do nothing that involved breaking the law. The unthinking TUC posturing of 1982 was at an end. The TUC might not like the new employment legislation, but it was not defying the courts and opening its funds to sequestration as a result. Murray's refusal to give any backing to the NGA that might be deemed unlawful aroused strong criticism from the broad left on the general council, especially from Clive Jenkins, general secretary of ASTMS, the white-collar union, who appeared to be plotting for Murray's dismissal. But Murray insisted on standing firm and he gained a majority on the general council for his position. The NGA was going to receive no TUC approval for defying the courts. Murray took a kind of grim satisfaction at the fact that the TUC was the fall-guy for unions in trouble.

> Many union leaders wanted to be told what to do. I had national officers sitting in my room saying send me back to my executive so I can tell them the TUC is cudgelling me. There was a bit of masochism in the job. You got excoriated in public but so what?

He believed that the NGA wanted to be let off the hook over the *Stockport Messenger* dispute, 'if truth be told. They knew they could not win.'

But if Congress House believed that the TUC's refusal to join in the *Stockport Messenger* dispute would ensure an appreciative response from the prime minister, they were to be quickly disabused. Within weeks she had decided to ban staff trade unionism from the government's intelligence communications headquarters in Cheltenham. In doing so she dealt a fatal body blow to Murray's pragmatism. The TUC made strenuous efforts to convince Mrs Thatcher to change her mind, even offering a no-strike agreement as the price for continuing union recognition. Mrs Thatcher would have none of it.

Murray said:

> We thought we were carefully putting something together that would establish a more civilised relationship. Then just like that – bang – without a second thought she made the GCHQ decision. She either knew nothing about the discussions we were having with government departments or they meant nothing at all to her.

At an emergency meeting on 19 March 1984 the TUC general council reassessed its relationship with the government. Murray argued strongly against those union leaders who wanted the TUC to withdraw from the National Economic Development Council and the little NEDDYs in protest at the government's behaviour over GCHQ. 'It would be very hard to explain to the membership why the TUC was withdrawing from NEDC but still seeking meetings with ministers in order to make representations', he argued. Even the TUC's suspension of attending NEDC meetings could put that tripartite organisation at risk. Congress House was reluctant to encourage a TUC pull-out from the innumerable public bodies where it still had representation. 'This government has not displayed any eagerness to meet the TUC to discuss issues which the TUC regards as important; on the other hand the TUC can table such issues for discussion at the NEDC and secure valuable publicity for its views', it argued.[24] 'To rely on seeking bilateral meetings with government as opposed to meeting the government at NEDC would be to meet the government on its own terms.' The TUC warned that to permanently suspend involvement in the NEDC and the EDCs

would reverse the direction of TUC economic and industrial representations which has been followed over the past 22 years. Suspension of TUC membership would in fact damage the TUC and the unions and their members far more than it would damage the government. Indeed, it could be secretly welcomed by the Prime Minister and those government ministers who disliked meeting trade unionists and having to listen to their arguments.

However, it was really the national miners' strike that brought New Realism to at least a temporary standstill. For most of the time after it began in March 1984 the TUC was not directly involved in any way in its dramatic developments. Memories of 1926 and the sense of betrayal nurtured by many miners for generations was perhaps one obvious reason why neither side sought a close relationship. Mineworkers' union president Arthur Scargill was right to believe that if he allowed the TUC into the conflict he would lose control because the general council would have been far more amenable to seeking a compromise and an early settlement of the dispute. As in 1972 and 1974, relations between Congress House and the NUM remained tenuous and suspicious much of the time. Murray would ring up the NUM's general secretary, Peter Heathfield, before monthly general council meetings to find out whether the miners wanted any TUC help, and be told it was not necessary.

However, Murray could hardly disguise his contempt and irritation with the excesses of Scargillism as the strike dragged on through the summer. He was fiercely opposed to any suggestion that the TUC should turn itself into a purist revolutionary organisation that engaged in a class struggle with Mrs Thatcher's government. 'We are problem solvers', he explained. 'Any attempt to split the TUC from the left or the right will be resisted by the overwhelming majority.'

Some concern was expressed on the TUC general council on 23 May at the 'present impression of a divide'[25] between the TUC and the NUM, but it was pointed out that the Finance and General Purposes Committee were maintaining contacts and the unions were prepared to give assistance if asked to do so. Murray and others were irritated by the NUM's efforts to involve other unions in the strike outside the TUC's own framework. But most agreed that it was up to the NUM to decide for itself whether or when to approach the TUC. As the general council minutes argued:

> There had been many major disputes in this country where the union concerned had not approached the TUC and it should not be thought that TUC involvement should be a normal act by a union in dispute. The general council should be content to wish the NUM well in their struggle and leave it at that unless the NUM made a special request.

But it was already apparent that the mining dispute threatened to divide the unions. Bill Sirs of the Iron and Steel Trades Confederation said that the NUM could not expect British Steel workers not to cross NUM picket lines when these were placed in front of steel plants, because it was essential that coal was provided to them to keep the blastfurnaces in optimum condition. General council chairman Ray Buckton warned that the longer the debate went on, the more likely it would be that they would open up divisions about the tactics being pursued in the dispute.

Murray's departure at the September 1984 Congress was a sad affair for him. In his last twelve months he had made genuine attempts to refocus the TUC to adopt a more realistic approach to its dealings with the government, but had found insufficient support to ensure this change of strategy could expect much chance of instant success. But at that time he was pleased with the 'sheer professionalism' of the TUC. His astute recruitment policy had produced a small and able cadre in Congress House. In unsung areas like union education, reform of the general council to make it more representative and less dominated by the large unions through their use of patronage, and extending TUC decision-making and accountability through conferences of union officers, Murray made quiet but solid progress. He may have lacked a grand design, but with limited resources he maintained respect in difficult times for the TUC secretariat in Whitehall departments. 'Mrs Thatcher might have come along and tried to lop us down to the roots but we will grow stronger again. I have no fears for the future of trade unionism in this country', he told me in September 1984.[26] But Murray was also emphatic about what had happened in the early 1980s.

The members did not walk away from the unions. But they walked away from taking instant industrial action when asked to do so by union leaders and they no longer voted automatically for the Labour party. We have got to become much more conscious of that. We are building on strength in the 1980s and not trying to recuperate from a deteriorating weakness.

But Murray by that time seemed like a forlorn and despairing figure from another age whose anguished greyness seemed far from the histrionics of the miners' strike. However, he was always a champion of reasoned argument and common sense, a much more substantial figure than perhaps he often seemed to be to the outside world at the time.

The wilderness years

Under his amiable successor Norman Willis, the TUC sank into inexorable decline. But Willis faced a formidable legacy as newly elected TUC general secretary. During his first weeks in office Willis sought as best he could to resolve the miners' strike. He was left in little doubt about the nature of the problem with Scargill's intransigence. But Willis showed a willingness to face up to the threats to TUC unity posed by the dispute. In a speech before angry striking miners at Aberavon in south Wales, he condemned the violence on the picket lines and the refusal of the NUM leadership to repudiate it. A noose was lowered in front of him in a clear act of intimidation. But Willis did not bend the knee to such tactics. Indeed, he made strenuous efforts to try and help to broker a deal between the NUM and the Coal Board. This involved drawing in government ministers including Mrs Thatcher herself, but any moves to a settlement failed to win Scargill's approval. However, Willis was able to ensure that the TUC would not become a scapegoat for the NUM. He had displayed enough willingness to try and ensure an honourable outcome of what turned out to be a seminal event in modern labour history. Certainly Willis and Congress House could not be criticised for the way they behaved in the final weeks of the miners' dispute as they sought a way out for the miners.

In fact, it is hard to believe that anyone other than Willis would really have made much difference to what happened to the TUC after 1984. The defeat of the NUM, the shock troops of the Labour Movement, paved the way for a self-confident and aggressive strategy by the government as Congress House found itself fighting a rearguard action as Mrs Thatcher rolled back many of the gains made by the TUC under the post-war social settlement. However, the long-term consequence of Scargillism's humiliation was to help the TUC to recover some initiative to launch a modernising agenda that repudiated the use of industrial muscle in the pursuit of its objectives. However, the advantage to the TUC was not so apparent in 1985, nor appreciated.

Willis – who only came to work for the TUC in 1973 after many years running the TGWU's research department, where he had worked closely with both Frank Cousins and Jack Jones, as deputy general secretary – was a jolly man with a seemingly endless series of jokes. But to the outside world he often seemed to be a strangely unserious and inarticulate figure. He was supported loyally for nine years by Congress House staff who recognised his wealth of knowledge in the minutiae of trade union organisation, his impressive range of contacts and his absence of personal malice. He survived a number of futile attempts to unseat him. But perhaps none of this really mattered. Slowly but surely the TUC was being marginalised by a hostile state for the first time in the twentieth century.

The TUC did not help itself either by trying to put pressure on the government through threatening to pull out of the tripartite public organisations on which it sat. The National Economic Development Council was a particular object of Conservative derision. The body formed under Macmillan in 1962 with Woodcock's blessing had become an anachronism to many ministers. After her June 1987 election victory, Thatcher reduced its monthly meetings to four a year. Tebbit could hardly hide his delight. 'I scarcely saw the union leaders at all except at meetings of the NEDC', he recalled in his memoirs. 'Somehow that old corporatist tripartite forum escaped the axe, much to my personal irritation as I detested wasting a morning in an agony of boredom when I had better things to do.'[27] The NEDC was finally abolished altogether by the Major government in the autumn of 1992. The TUC itself helped in its own demise as a member of the tripartite Training Commission. Even during the early 1980s the TUC had been able to retain an important role in influencing the government's training and employment strategies and enjoyed a good relationship with Lord Young, Mrs Thatcher's favourite minister, when he was Employment Secretary. The TUC's involvement was seen as essential for the working of the Youth Training Scheme to assist unemployed youth. But in September 1988 Congress decided to boycott further commission meetings in protest at the government's refusal to increase the allowances for those participating in the scheme. As a result, no time was lost in the government's decision to close down the entire Manpower Services Commission and transfer its functions back to the Department of Employment.

However, the Willis years were not completely barren of achievement. It was under his leadership that the TUC's policy was changed towards the European Union in 1988. As president of the European Trade Union Confederation where he won the respect of other union leaders, Willis displayed a consistent support for the European cause. He also showed his courage in an open backing for the cause of the Polish Solidarity movement and in public criticism for the more repressive actions towards workers displayed by the Soviet Union in the final years of Leonid Brezhnev. Willis was particularly well liked in Washington where AFL-CIO president Lane Kirkland was a close personal friend. A kind and humorous man, he was welcome across the international Labour Movement. Certainly in his relations with the US unions, he was able to repair much of the damage done between the TUC and the AFL–CIO during the later years of the Cold War.

Willis was helped in his efforts to refocus the TUC on European affairs by David Lea, assistant general secretary, who played a particularly vital role in the TUC's move to a more positive pro-EU position. Lea was impressed by EU president Jacques Delors' speech at the 1988 Stockholm congress of the European trade union movement and won the support of Willis and Ron Todd, the TGWU general secretary, who invited him to that autumn's congress in Bournemouth. The EU president's address to delegates was a defining moment for the TUC in what had been an often tortuous journey from one side to the other on the European argument for over 30 years. 'Your movement has a major role to play. Europe needs you', he declared. The creation of an EU single market would be incomplete without the establishment of a platform of guaranteed social rights.

He told the delegates:

While we are trying to pool our efforts, it would be unacceptable for unfair practices to distort the interplay of economic forces. It would be unacceptable for Europe to become a source of social regression, while we are trying to rediscover together the road to prosperity and employment. Social dialogue and collective bargaining are essential pillars of our democratic society and social progress.[28]

After Delors' visionary evocation of a social Europe, an ecstatic TUC turned itself into one of the most pro-EU institutions in Britain, opening its own office in Brussels in 1993.

Willis was also important in developing a much warmer relationship for the TUC with Neil Kinnock's Labour Party. His wife worked for Kinnock as secretary, ensuring that the two men were close and on amicable terms. By the mid-1980s the TUC believed it would have to develop a common strategy with Labour in the face of remorseless opposition from the Thatcher government. At the 1987 general election, and to a lesser extent in 1992, the Willis–Kinnock alliance developed a new agenda for the trade unions. Willis made it clear that the trade unions could not expect a wholesale return to the employment laws of the 1970s. There was no enthusiasm in the Labour Party for any move that would have resulted in a revival of legislation that would tolerate flying or secondary mass picketing. Moreover, Willis insisted the mandatory use of strike ballots and ballots for the election of union officials introduced after 1984 would not be abolished in the event of the return of a Labour government. It was also under his direction that the TUC began to examine the concept of social partnership between unions and employers and an extension of individual worker rights. In addition, there was an acceptance there could be no return to the use of the closed shop to enforce trade unionism in the workplace.

Although Willis was often criticised for lack of direction and coherence, he did act effectively to prevent a deep split in the TUC that might have destroyed its ability to function. The expulsion of the EETPU electricians' union from congress in 1988 came only after strenuous efforts by Willis to avoid such a development, and other unions did not follow. His memories of the miners' strike had made him well aware of the dangers of an ideological civil war breaking out between the unions that would have inflicted enormous damage on the cause of TUC unity. In his sensitive relations with the AUEW engineering union, for instance, Willis battled to limit the self-destructive, introspective tendency that gripped parts of the trade union movement in the late 1980s.

It is true that the TUC's own efforts to replicate the campaigning activities of the American labour movement in the search for new members failed to make any headway in the early 1990s. The TUC's 'Union Yes' offensive launched in London's East End and the Trafford Park industrial estate in Manchester made little headway. But at least Willis showed that he was not resistant to new ideas and determined to try and refocus the TUC on positive ways of responding to falling membership and a government hostile to the trade union cause.

For most of the period that Willis was general secretary, however, the TUC found itself forced on to the fringes of industrial politics, a seemingly unloved and unwanted institution. Membership density declined rapidly, and Conservative governments as well as employers did little to encourage closer relations with the TUC. 'Unions individually and collectively through the TUC have not had a scintilla of influence over government policies', complained the CPSA civil service union in 1994. 'In no other country in Europe have unions had to face such hostility from their government. Uniquely Britain also remains the one country where the role of trade unions in national life is still questioned.'[29] Inevitably the organisation became increasingly introspective, concerned primarily with inter-union relations that worsened with the competitive struggle for union members in a shrinking organised labour market. It was very much the TUC's age of stagnation. Sporadic efforts to modernise made little progress. Congress House found itself drifting. This was not entirely Willis's fault. Indeed, his bon viveur style probably went some way to defusing serious conflicts between union leaders that could have led to a fundamental split in the TUC. Certainly there were those in Congress House who believed that his hearty and jokey style helped to diminish the tensions. But inevitably Willis was seen as the fall-guy for the trend of failure and irrelevance that seemed to immobilise the TUC after 1992. Ever since the 1920s, even hostile governments had always believed it made sense to at least develop some kind of public policy relationship with the TUC. Now ministers saw little purpose in doing so at all. In the new world of deregulation and liberalisation, trade unions and the TUC in particular seemed to have lost any meaningful role. This trend was not confined to Britain but it was more pronounced than elsewhere in the western industrialised world. By September 1993 the TUC seemed to have lost any clear sense of purpose. But this was an exaggerated picture of decline. The TUC still played an important role in surviving tripartite bodies like the Advisory, Conciliation and Arbitration Service; the Health and Safety Commission; the Equal Opportunities Commission and the Commission for Racial Equality. Its nominees remained on the Monopolies and Mergers Commission, the British Overseas Trade Board and a further 48 different government committees and outside bodies. While this amounted to a much more limited TUC presence than in the 1970s, it was better than nothing. Willis decided to take early retirement in September 1993. His departure provided the opportunity for a TUC revival. From the high-water mark of early 1979 to the nadir of the early 1990s, the TUC suffered a protracted period in the political wilderness. This all came as a great shock to the TUC general council. In fact, it was the most traumatic reversal of fortunes the trade union movement had suffered since the early 1920s. For nearly 40 years after 1939 the TUC had developed as a recognised Estate of the Realm, courted by governments of all parties. It may never have grown in the way that Citrine had really wanted, but its opinions and advice were sought by ministers across the public policy agenda. Indeed, many union leaders had come to believe they were indispensable for the successful management of the political economy; some even believing no government could run the country without their consent. But under Margaret Thatcher they were being cut down ruthlessly. There was little that Willis could have done to prevent this, particularly after his strategic alliance with Kinnock failed to secure any political advantages. On the other hand, in areas like employment law, union membership campaigns and Europe, the first seeds of TUC recovery were planted by Willis. There was more continuity with the New Unionism of his successor John Monks than is often appreciated. The object of cruel jokes and personal abuse, Willis kept his dignity and tolerance. In unprecedented times for the TUC, he ensured the organisation remained intact, preparing for better days. This may not have been seen as a great achievement in the early 1990s, but it was appreciated later. For all his manifest weaknesses and follies, Willis deserves to be remembered for holding the TUC together and pointing the way out of its impasse, caused mainly by events outside its own control.

8
John Monks and New Unionism

> The time is ripe for a resurgence of trade unionism in Britain and the TUC is gearing itself to help engender that resurgence.
>
> John Monks[1]

John Monks, the TUC's general secretary from September 1993 was a man for whom nobody seemed to have a bad word. Even the anti-union policy advisers at 10 Downing Street found it hard to criticise him. Labour Prime Minister Tony Blair learnt to treat him with wary respect. The trouble for them was that Monks failed to live up to New Labour's caricature of a trade union official – reactionary, bureaucratic, pompous and opinionated. When Blair denounced the old discredited culture of the Labour Movement with its trade union block vote bullies, male-dominated cliques and punch-ups by the seaside, it was hard to identify Monks with such unseemly spectacles. Monks was – like Blair – an arch moderniser, and perhaps a much more substantial one. His New Unionism was not a spin-doctor's sound bite but a vital strategy designed to save the TUC and with it British trade unionism from oblivion. From the moment of his election, Monks in a thoughtful and credible way sought to restore the self-respect, authority and legitimacy of the organisation which had been drifting, unloved and irrelevant to the flow of events. But he had to do so against many of the currents of a world that was growing more hostile and less favourable to the attraction of organised labour.

Monks and the TUC were not alone in trying to reposition and modernise trade unionism during the 1990s in what was becoming in the western world an increasingly post-industrial society. In the United States the AFL-CIO under John Sweeney, for example, looked like it was battling to avoid extinction with less than 9 per cent of workers employed in the private sector unionised. Elsewhere trade union membership decline may have been less dramatic, but in many democratic countries the ranks of organised labour fell, even though – unlike in the UK – their national trade union centres continued to negotiate social dialogues and pacts with governments and employer associations. The reasons for the contraction of the unions are well known – deindustrialisation, the rise of individualism among younger workers, the decline of collectivist values and public policies designed to support trade unions, the passing away of mass production in much of manufacturing in large plants with the increase in small enterprises and the emergence of non-standardised forms of work like part-time, temporary and contract employment. Rising unemployment also clearly weakened trade union organisation. But Monks knew that the decline of organised labour was particularly dramatic in Britain between 1980 and 1997 with the rundown of former union strongholds like coal, shipbuilding, steel-making and textiles. Above all, it was the TUC's deliberate, if gradual, exclusion from much of public policy-making by the Conservatives after May 1979 and the resulting hostile anti-union climate in the workplace that had done more than anything else to weaken many trade unions and force them into retreat. Monks's formidable task in 1993 was to try and reverse that ominous trend, to restore confidence and hope to a battered trade union movement and create a new positive and realistic agenda for the TUC to pursue in an almost totally different world from that of the 1970s.

He was the right man at the right time to take on the job of TUC general secretary. Monks was born on 5 August 1945 in Manchester, the son of a district parks superviser. He took a degree at Nottingham University and was then a management trainee with Plessey for two years. But he felt he was not cut out to be a manager and, seeing a job vacancy advertisement in the *New Statesman* magazine, he applied for a post with the TUC. He joined Congress House in September 1969, initially to cover production management techniques. But he soon found himself spending most of his time working on labour law under the canny Ken Graham in the TUC's organisation department during the days of the Industrial Relations Act and the Social Contract. The talent-spotters talked of him even then in the early 1970s as 'pure gold'.

In that turbulent decade Monks was the young, moustachioed, prudent and discreet trade union diplomat with the task of trying to calm union tempers, helping to devise TUC strategies on trade union legislation and nudging the hot-heads on the general council in sensible and pragmatic directions. It was not surprising that he made a political enemy out of the Communist Ken Gill who saw the industrial conflicts of the period as part of the endless class struggle. Monks must have needed the patience and self-restraint of Job to deal with some of the intractable inter-union disputes of those years. One of his particular disappointments was to see the rejection by print workers of his reform proposals in 1977 to modernise national newspaper working practices, even though he succeeded in winning the backing of their national leaders. Rupert Murdoch's eventual move of his News International printing operations to Wapping and the resulting demise of print union power in 1985–86 was to be the sad but perhaps inevitable consequence that flowed from the defeat of Monks's practical programme to ease the pain of transition for workers in an industry experiencing profound technological change.

Behind the scenes Monks was always a force for common sense and realism. He was instrumental in drawing up the 1979 codes of conduct for the unions in the TUC's concordat with the Labour government, recognising the public damage being inflicted on the unions by the aggressive bitterness displayed on the picket lines during the 'winter of discontent'. As a member of the governing body of the Advisory, Conciliation and Arbitration Service he won widespread admiration among officials and employers for his focused contributions. It was no surprise when he became deputy general secretary under Willis in September 1987. But unlike other number twos at Congress House over the years, Monks was given a real job to do. He displayed a remarkable loyalty to Willis during his five years in the post. But then Monks's style is never confrontational. He sought agreement and consensus, but not in any easy-going manner. He is a practical and constructive realist. But he is ready to take the initiative, set the agenda and push the general council in the direction he wants it to go.

Monks launched his New Unionism at the 1996 Congress. As he told delegates: 'For seventeen years trade unions have been painted as part of Britain's problems. Our challenge is to prove we are part of the solution.' 'Trade unionism is at the crossroads', he declared. 'Unless public policy changes and above all unless we change we shall be forced down the road marked Retreat.'[2] At that time the TUC faced the threat of yet more hostile industrial relations legislation designed to weaken trade unions still further if the Conservatives were to win their fifth general election victory. But Monks drew comfort from the poll evidence that the centre-left was on the verge of a great general election victory, and the Labour Party, under its new dynamic leader Tony Blair, was committed to a new fairer balance in the world of work, with the promise of new rights for workers and effective means for unions to organise themselves and gain recognition to bargain from employers.

Monks emphasised the need for the creation of a new organising culture inside the trade unions, enabling the launch of successful recruitment drives; especially among young workers who were becoming increasingly unsympathetic to the idea of becoming union members. A TUC organising academy was created to train eager and able young people on how to go out and convert workers to trade unionism, following the model of the American Federation of Labor and Congress of Industrial Organisations (AFL-CIO) in the 1990s. Monks also sought to reach out to employers in his 1996 New Unionism launch. 'Without successful companies, we know for sure there is no security, no growth and no prospects', he warned, pointing out that the TUC was already promoting minimum standards agreements with employers. Monks called on unions to negotiate deals with companies on workplace innovation in their mutual interest.

Even in 1996 he revealed his unrepentant admiration for European social market models. He believed that the countries of mainland western Europe had proved the effectiveness of the social partnership approach to industrial relations over the past 40 years. As early as 1992 he was arguing that the creation of a fairer balance between employers and employees and unions was what characterised the successful economies of western Europe based on social dialogues, accords and pacts that recognised that trade unions had a legitimate and active role to play in public policy and macro-economic policy coordination. 'Elsewhere in Europe social protections for individual workers and measures to promote worker and trade union consultation rights in individual enterprises are an integral part of their industrial cultures', he argued. 'Indeed, they are a central first step for their strategy for growth. Only in Britain, it seems, is there this apparently ideological hostility to the very concept of social partners.'[3] Monks was also a firm believer in UK membership of Economic and Monetary union and the common currency. He led the TUC into a more pro-Euro position than any national institution; often to the irritation of Mr Blair's New Labour government after May 1997, which adopted a much more cautious attitude in the face of a high level of scepticism among the general public. Monks wanted the government to take the lead in the battle to convert people to UK entry into the Euro. This was an issue on which he showed no readiness to waver or tone down the TUC's position. His strong belief in UK Euro membership reflected a deep conviction that the country and the trade unions should look more and more to the social regulations of the EU to humanise and civilise the UK workplace, and in doing so help to lessen the impact of the macho individualistic approach of the US model, lauded by Gordon Brown, New Labour's Chancellor of the Exchequer. Monks believed that the battleground of British politics in the twenty-first century would be whether the UK would become Americanised or grow more like the European continent in the extent of its workplace regulations. There was no doubting on which side of the argument Monks stood.

As he told the Unions 21 conference in March 2000, the TUC and its member unions must embrace a revived Social Democracy. 'The need to ensure orderly change, tame the excesses of the market, reduce inequality, provide protection for people at work and a strong welfare state all provide the foundation for any modern left of centre politics.' Monks added: 'It is the unregulated market that gets people working longer and longer hours, that stops people getting a sensible balance between work and home, that puts people out of work overnight when mega-mergers driven by stock market sentiment take place.'[4] The TUC's modernising agenda was not anti-business or dogmatic, but aimed to save business from itself and assert democratic priorities over market forces.

In another important shift of direction for the TUC, Monks also sought to transform the mainland European concept of social partnership into a radical new strategy to drive on the cause of workplace modernisation. He aimed to convince employers that the business case for cooperating with the unions on such an idea was an overwhelming one; that firms who were prepared to negotiate partnership deals with unions and workers enjoyed higher profitability and greater productivity than those who did not. In a 1997 Congress speech, Monks called for a new settlement in the workplace based on his concept of partnership. He defined it as meaning 'a determination to maximise areas of agreement, a common desire to work to the very highest standards and the opportunity to negotiate the best terms and conditions and lay down outside the workplace the best social framework'.[5]

Partnership means breaking the old-style approach, the employer who says 'I will pay the smallest wage possible', yes and the employee in return who says 'I will do as little as I can get away with'. Partnership means promoting employment security and new skills for all; it means recognising that change is the only constant but that with respect at work goes the willingness to change.

'The days when trade unions provided an adversarial opposition force are past in industry', said Monks in an interview with the author. 'We have to admit that one of the reasons for the UK's inadequate post-war economic record has been bad industrial relations and trade unions must take some of the blame.'[6]

The positive language used by Monks in support of workplace partnerships revealed a clear change in the TUC's attitude, undoubtedly helped by the election in May 1997 of a Labour government. But the TUC was well aware that there would be no return to the kind of relationship it had enjoyed with Labour in office during the 1970s. Tony Blair insisted that he would not tolerate a revival of what he characterised as the bad old ways of trade unionism. In his early years in government he did not seem to visualise the TUC playing any active or important part in the development of the political economy, and he continued to reveal a scepticism about whether the unions had really modernised. Perhaps at any moment the union mask would be ripped off and the TUC would start making impossible demands on the government.

Blair made his views known on that matter in his first speech to Congress as Labour Party leader in 1995 when he sought to define what the relationship should be between the trade unions and a Labour government. As he told delegates:

We have an obligation as a government to listen, as we do to employers. You have the right to persuade, as they do, but the decisions, however, as you know must rest with us. We will be the government and we will govern for the whole nation, not any vested interest within it. That will be the distinction between ourselves and the present Conservative government.[7]

Blair warned the TUC then that Labour in power would not be going back to the old battles.

There is not going to be a repeal of all Tory trade union laws. It is not what the members want, it is not what the country wants. Ballots before strikes are here to stay. No mass or flying pickets. All those ghosts of time past – I am glad there is a round of applause for that.

He wanted nothing less than a cultural revolution in the TUC, an end to block vote fixing and negative attitudes that had characterised many past congresses.

Instead of being a negative force, the unions led by the TUC would develop a modernisation agenda, seeking to replace the adversarial attitudes and policies of the past with a partnership model which aimed to help companies compete more effectively through workplace reorganisation, much more training in new skills, and union cooperation in increasing the added value of the enterprise. Monks began to develop a more positive relationship with the Confederation of British Industry on areas of common interest like training and equal opportunities. The degree of TUC modernisation was revealed to the prime minister on 7 September 1998 when the TUC gave him a personal presentation on what progress the unions had made with their partnership agenda. As he wrote in a foreword to the TUC's seminal April 1999 document on partnerships:

> I endorse the clear message of the TUC that Britain works best when unions and employers work together. This important new initiative exemplifies the willingness of modern trade unions to seek common ground with employers to cooperate to solve shared problems and to improve the lives of the people.[8]

The prime minister's speech to a special TUC conference in March 1999 on such partnerships was seen as his personal support for Monks's New Unionism strategy. Most of the large affiliate unions accepted the partnership approach, despite some reservations about whether it might lead to destructive competitiveness between them in the search for more members and whether it might strengthen the power of employers by encouraging them to sign up with those unions more compliant than others in meeting the demands of business.

The TUC's attitude to the New Labour government was complicated. There was less sentimentality about traditional ties. Monks and his colleagues were able to meet and lobby ministers, including Mr Blair, but this was not a special relationship. Indeed, the prime minister appeared to give more of his time to wooing big business tycoons like Rupert Murdoch of News International. Some union leaders and officials were given peerages, other honours, places on public inquiries and working parties. But the patronage for them was never on the scale of the 1970s. In comparison, business was well rewarded under New Labour, taking on most of the advisory jobs offered by the government. Only the independent Low Pay Commission reflected the traditional representative approach of tripartism, which is perhaps why the introduction of the national minimum wage turned out to be much more successful than the government's bilateral methods of dealing with other workplace issues such as the implementation of the working time and part-time worker regulations.

But on the other hand, Monks and the TUC were pleased by the impressive range of new legal rights acquired by workers and unions after 1997. The introduction of the statutory minimum wage and the £4 billion Welfare to Work programme for the long-term unemployed were both welcome to the TUC. It is true there was a protracted and tense round of negotiations through 1997 and 1998 over the exact provisions of the fairness at work legislation. Under pressure from employer associations, the government introduced tough clauses into the Bill on union recognition, requiring unions to secure affirmative support from at least 40 per cent of workers in an agreed bargaining unit in order to secure recognition. However, unions were to have automatic recognition if they were able to recruit half the workforce. Blair had argued that even after the range of legal rights were introduced, Britain would have one of the most 'lightly regulated' labour markets in the western world, but for the time being the TUC seemed relieved to have gained as much as it had. No doubt Monks made substantial progress behind the scenes in holding the line and not allowing the government to ignore TUC pressures.

Nonetheless, Monks's irritation with the more unsympathetic attitude of some New Labour enthusiasts towards union leaders was occasionally made public. He displeased Downing Street when he likened their official attitudes towards the TUC to those of 'embarrassed elderly relatives' at a family reunion. In June 1998 at the TUC's Fairness at Work conference Monks compared the 'kid glove' approach to employers with the hostile attitude towards the unions. 'We are cast in the role of stooge – to be used as a contrast to New Labour – not modern, not new or fashionable, old, in decline, in hock to sectarian politics which resonate with only a tiny proportion of the British people', Monks complained. 'There is little public acknowledgement of change in trade unions or of the positive partnership role of unions in raising standards of performance as well as terms and conditions of work.'[9]

In a lecture to the Manchester Statistical Society in February 1999 on the future of trade unionism, Monks sought to widen the perspective of organised labour.

Our job is to raise standards, not just of pay and conditions, not just in treatment but the way people do things, the way they relate to each other, the quality of their relationships – we want a sense of mutual respect, of mutual dependency, of teamwork at its best, to encourage managers to keep the standards that the best seem to set themselves and not just take the easy relationships of trust.

'I did my stint as a class-warrior once upon a time', Monks told his audience. But he added that the TUC had carried out a survey in 1987 that had showed that workers wanted most of all a feeling of security, but after this they wanted to be held in high regard by the person for whom they worked. 'Obvious when you think about it. Nobody likes to work for somebody who thinks they are a clown', he added. 'Everybody wants to have that sense of respect.'[10] This is an important element in Monks's New Unionism.

But of course at the beginning of a new century there is also a wider appreciation of the importance of the TUC and trade unionism. As Monks explained in Manchester in 1999, following the collapse of Soviet Communism as a political ideology both nationally and internationally,

we now live in a world where, for want of a better word, capitalism reigns supreme. There is nowhere it cannot reach. Russia resembles a cross between McDonald's and the Mafia in terms of values. China too has made historic compromises.

The TUC general secretary believes that in the war of the models today in the UK between the neo-liberal US and the social markets of western Europe, the organisation he leads must identify and campaign for the latter. As Monks explained, the European way has

a sense of mutual reliance, the sense of working together, the sense of seeking to eliminate poverty, to have civilised cities, to ensure the rich do not get too far out of reach, that wealth is not too conspicuous and that consumption is not too far over the top. These are values which European countries have developed with some pretty good economic growth rates. The model in which trade unions will live and breathe is the European one, not that of North America, and the sense of values which we have for the future are European ones, not from North America. It may not be a huge difference when compared to the divide between the old Soviet Union and the United States, yet it is a crucial one. It is the difference, I think, of having the room to breathe and to develop the union perspective for the future.

It was appropriate that Monks set down such thoughts publicly in 1999 in Manchester, the TUC's birthplace. After a century of successes and failures, but of overall undoubted achievement in making Britain a fairer, more decent and civilised country in which to live, the TUC's future is bound up with the wider political economy of Europe. With signs of union growth once again and a more sympathetic public policy climate for trade unions, the TUC under Monks may be at the beginning of a lasting revival in the new world of e-commerce and information technology. This seems unlikely to take the TUC back to the kind of public role it played in the golden age of Social Democracy in the 30 years after the end of the Second World War. But it could restore the TUC as a necessary and effective national institution in facing the challenge of the new world of work.

'We are in the best position for decades to start to grow once again', Monks told the Unions 21 conference in March 2000. 'But it won't happen if we go on as we are.'[11] However, while Low's lovable old carthorse may have been transmogrified into a leaner and sleeker beast suitable for the modern age, the fundamental values of the TUC and the trade union movement it seeks to represent remain as relevant today as they were a hundred years ago. The TUC's New Unionism emerged from a rich and diverse historical tradition. During the twentieth century, from Citrine to Monks, the TUC sought in often difficult circumstances to become an Estate of the Realm. In the years between May 1940 and May 1979 the TUC established itself as an indispensable institution with a coherent and credible participation in the public life of the country. It neither claimed nor achieved the position of a full-blown corporatist partner in the running of the democratic state, whatever its enemies suggested. The TUC remained – for all its undoubted increase in national influence and authority – a body beholden to the often divided and inchoate views and attitudes of its affiliate trade union members.

Now, under Monks, the TUC is growing again. Its general secretary is developing an ambitious agenda for modernisation based on social Europe, partnership with industry and an assertion of workplace rights. Whether or not he has strong allies to support him on the general council is perhaps more problematic. But there is really no other way forward for the TUC. As Britain increasingly comes to resemble a mainland European society, the growth of social rights, social partnership and social dialogues will need a stronger and more decisive

TUC. There can be no going back to what is now the lost world of labourism. Monks knows this. He believes that most union members agree with him. In the never-ending quest for more security and self-esteem for workers under global capitalism, the TUC has found an exciting new role for itself in the twenty-first century.

Notes

Preface

1. W. Citrine, 'The Problem of Trade Union Leadership', *Labour* magazine, March 1926, p. 487.

Introduction

1. Queen Elizabeth II speech to the TUC, 5 June 1968, TUC Library.
2. Quoted in R. Taylor, *The Fifth Estate*, London, 1978, p. 37.
3. For the TUC's origins see A. E. Musson, *The Congress of 1868*, London, 1955; W. J. Davis, *British Trades Union Congress: History and Recollections*, two volumes, London, 1968; E. Frow and M. Katanka, *1868: Year of The Unions*, London, 1968; B. C. Roberts, *The Trades Union Congress 1868–1921*, London, 1958.
4. G. Howell, *Labour Legislation, Labour Movements and Labour Leaders*, Vol. 1, London, 1905, p. 177.
5. R. Martin, *TUC: The Growth of a Pressure Group 1868–1976*, Oxford, 1980, p. 57.
6. B. and S. Webb, *Industrial Democracy*, 1911 edition, pp. 275–8.
7. Ibid., p. 277.
8. G. D. H. Cole and W. Mellor, 'The Greater Unionism, 1913', in B. C. Roberts, *The Trades Union Congress*, p. 262.
9. B. and S. Webb, *The History of Trade Unionism*, 1913 edition, pp. 468–72.
10. Martin, *TUC: The Growth of a Pressure Group*, pp. 162–3.
11. J. Holford, *Union Education in Britain: A TUC Activity*, Nottingham, 1994.
12. TUC, *Trade Unionism*, 1966, p. 66.
13. Ibid., p. 69.
14. Taylor, *The Fifth Estate*, pp. 37–8.
15. Ibid., p. 38.
16. W. Citrine, *Men and Work*, London, 1964, p. 228.
17. A. Carew et al. (eds), *The International Federation of Free Trade Unions*, Amsterdam, 2000.
18. M. Nicholson, *The TUC Overseas*, London, 1986.
19. R. Taylor, *The Future of The Trade Unions*, London, 1994, p. 162.
20. H. Clegg, *A History of British Trade Unions since 1889*, Volume 2, *1911–1933*, London, 1985, p. 309.
21. A. Bullock, *Life and Times of Ernest Bevin*, Volume I, London, 1960, p. 147.
22. Ibid., p. 148.
23. C. Crouch, 'The Snakes and Ladders of Twenty-First Century Trade Unionism', *Oxford Review of Economic Policy*, Vol. 16, No. 1, 2000, p. 80.

Chapter 1

I am grateful to the LSE library for access to the Citrine Papers. The best account of Citrine's life before 1939 remains his autobiography – *Men and Work* (London, 1964). But also see A. Bullock, *Life and Times of Ernest Bevin*, Volume I, *Trade Union Leader, 1881–1940* (London, 1960).

1. TUC Congress Report 1946, p. 269.
2. 'The Implications of Industrial Peace', 18 February 1927, Citrine Papers 1/1.
3. M. Foot, *Aneurin Bevan*, Vol. 1, London, 1965, p. 178.
4. W. Citrine, *ABC of Chairmanship*, reprint London 1970.
5. Citrine, *Men and Work*, London, 1964, pp. 267–8.
6. J. Lloyd, *Light and Liberty*, London, 1990.
7. Citrine, *Men and Work*, p. 67.
8. Ibid.
9. V. Allen, 'The Reorganisation of the Trades Union Congress 1918–1927', in his book, *The Sociology of Industrial Relations*, London, 1971.
10. B. C. Roberts, *The Trades Union Congress 1868–1921*, London, 1958, p. 346.
11. Citrine, *Men and Work*, p. 79.
12. TUC Congress Report 1925, pp. 226–37.
13. Citrine, *Men and Work*, p. 227.
14. W. Citrine, Memorandum, July 1925, Citrine Papers 1/2, pp. 26–8.
15. Ibid., pp. 31–2.
16. W. Citrine, 'Lessons from the Mining Dispute', *Labour* magazine, September 1925.
17. W. Citrine, November 1925, Citrine Papers 1/2.
18. H. Tracey, 'The Outlook for Labour', *Labour* magazine, December 1925.
19. W. Citrine, 'Essential Services During Trade Disputes', 16 February 1926, Citrine Papers 1/1.
20. W. Citrine, 'The Problem of Trade Union Leadership', *Labour* magazine, March 1926.
21. Citrine, *Men and Work*, p. 150.
22. W. Citrine, 'Mining Crisis and the National Strike', Volume 1, Citrine Papers 1/7, pp. 91–125.
23. For a full account of the TUC during the General Strike, see G. A. Phillips, *The General Strike: The Politics of Industrial Conflict*, London, 1976; and M. Morris, *The General Strike*, London, 1973.
24. Citrine, 'Mining Crisis and the National Strike', Volume 2, Citrine Papers 1/8, p. 232.
25. W. Citrine, Citrine diaries, 11 May 1926, Citrine Papers 1/8, p. 312.
26. Ibid., 11 May 1926, 1/8, p. 323.
27. Ibid., pp. 336–9.
28. Ibid., p. 351.
29. Ibid., p. 389.
30. Ibid., 1/7, p. 321.
31. Ibid., 1/8, pp. 390–1.
32. Ibid., p. 404.
33. Citrine, *Men and Work*, pp. 216–17.
34. Ibid., p. 228.

35. Ibid., pp. 223–4.
36. TUC Congress Report 1926, p. 497.
37. Citrine, *Men and Work*, p. 228.
38. A. Bullock, *Life and Times of Ernest Bevin*, Vol. 1, London, 1960, p. 590.
39. H. Clegg, *A History of British Trade Unions*, Vol. 2, *1911–1933*, Oxford, 1985, pp. 422–3.
40. TUC Defence Bulletin No. 2, May 1927, TUC Library.
41. Ibid., No. 4, July 1927, TUC Library.
42. TUC, *Democracy or Disruption?*, London, 1928.
43. *Manchester Guardian*, 30 November 1927. Also see Citrine's perceptive pamphlets, *The Future of Trade Unionism* and *Trade Unionism in Modern Industry*, both published by the TUC in 1929.
44. TUC Congress Report 1927, p. 67.
45. Ibid.,1928, p. 211.
46. Ibid., p. 219.
47. Ibid., pp. 209–10.
48. Ibid., p. 209.
49. W. Citrine, Citrine Papers 1/1, p. 63.
50. Ibid., p. 413.
51. Ibid., p. 334.
52. TUC Congress Report 1930, p. 366.
53. Clegg, *A History of British Trade Unions*, Vol. 3, p. 417.
54. W. Milne-Bailey, Memorandum, 1927, TUC Archives.
55. W. Citrine, 'Democracy or Disruption?', *Labour* magazine, December 1927 and January–March 1928. Also see R. Martin, *Communism and the British Trade Unions 1924–1933*, Oxford, 1969.
56. TUC Congress Report 1927, pp. 323–4.
57. Ibid., 1929, pp. 168–82.
58. Ibid., p. 347.
59. D. F. Calhoun, *The United Front: The TUC and The Russians 1923–1928*, Cambridge, 1976.
60. TUC Congress Report 1927, pp. 324–31.
61. Calhoun, *The United Front*, p. 381.
62. Citrine, *Men and Work*, p. 281.
63. TUC Congress Report 1930, pp. 215–16.
64. Ibid., p. 261.
65. Clegg, *A History of British Trade Unions*, Vol. 2, p. 502.
66. TUC Congress Report 1930, p. 69.
67. Ibid., 1931, p. 63.
68. D. Marquand, *Ramsay MacDonald*, London, 1977, p. 618.
69. Ibid., p. 621.
70. TUC Congress Report 1931, pp. 512–20.
71. H. Dalton, *Call Back Yesterday, Memoirs 1887–1931*, London, 1953, p. 274.
72. TUC Congress Report 1931.
73. Ibid., pp. 459–64.
74. TUC Congress Report 1932, p. 194.
75. H. Pelling, *A Short History of the Labour Party*, London, 1996 edition, p. 65.
76. T. Jones, *A Diary with Letters 1931–1950*, Oxford, 1954, p. 68.
77. TUC Congress Report 1933, p. 262.

78. Oslo Speech, May 1938, Bulletin of the IFTU, p. 2, TUC Library.
79. *Coal, The Labour Plan*, TUC, 1936, p. 3.
80. TUC Congress Report 1935, p. 349.
81. Ibid., 1937, pp. 406–7.
82. IFTU Report 1936, p. 406, TUC Library.
83. Bulletin of the IFTU, May 1938, p. 3.
84. Zurich speech, July 1939, IFTU. TUC Archives.
85. B. Webb, *Diaries*, 21 September 1931, London, p. 45.
86. Ibid., 10 October 1931, p. 291.
87. W. Milne-Bailey, *Trade Unions and the State*, London, 1934.
88. TUC Congress Report 1935, p. 426.
89. Citrine, *Men and Work*, p. 317.
90. Ibid., p. 367.
91. TUC Congress Report 1936, pp. 292–3.
92. *Seventy Years of Trade Unionism*, London, TUC, 1938, pp. 21–32.
93. *What the TUC has Done*, May 1939, TUC.
94. R. Lowe, *Adjusting to Democracy*, Oxford, 1986, p. 247.
95. TUC Congress Report 1937, p. 70.
96. Ibid., 1939, pp. 286–93.

Chapter 2

The second volume of Alan Bullock's masterly *The Life and Times of Ernest Bevin* (London, 1968) on his years as Minister of Labour and National Service is indispensable for an appreciation of his key role in the Second World War. But it was written before the opening of the public archives for 1940–45 and further research is badly needed to assess Bevin's achievement as the Churchill of the proletariat in the Workers War. However, Peter Weiler's short but incisive *Ernest Bevin* (Manchester, 1993) does use some of the wartime Ministry of Labour and National Service material. Also see *Bevin* by Trevor Evans (London, 1946) and *Ernest Bevin: Portrait of a Great Englishman* by Francis Williams (London, 1952). Bevin's own *The Balance Sheet of The Future* (New York, 1941) is a collection of his speeches in the early period of the war designed to make a popular appeal to the American labour movement.

A short account of the TUC's activities during the war can be found in Walter Citrine's autobiographical *Two Careers* (London, 1967). But also see Herbert Tracey, *Trade Unions Fight – For What?* (London, 1940). Books on trade unions and the war include James Hinton, *Shop Floor Citizens: Engineering Democracy in 1940s Britain* (Aldershot, 1994); Richard Croucher, *Engineers at War 1939–1945* (London, 1982); and Stephen Brooke, *Labour's War* (Oxford, 1992). The most enlightening short account of domestic wartime politics can be found in Sam Beer's *Modern British Politics* (London, 1945). However, the accessible sources for an appreciation of the TUC effort can be found in the printed quarterly reports produced by Citrine himself – *The TUC in Wartime* – that began in the autumn of 1939, as well as the voluminous annual Congress reports.

The nature of the TUC–government relationship during the Second World War is discussed in K. Middlemas, *Power, Competition and the State*, Volume 1, *Britain in Search of Balance 1940–1961* (Basingstoke, 1986), and in K. Middlemas, *Politics in Industrial Society: The Experience of the British System since 1911* (London, 1979). The wider implications of the wartime social settlement can be found in P. Addison's still indispensable *The Road to 1945* (London, 1975).

1. E. Bevin, 22 June 1945, BBC election broadcast, Bevin file, TUC Library.
2. W. Citrine, *British Trade Unions*, London, 1942, p. 48.
3. C. Attlee to Bevin, 26 May 1945, Bevin Papers.
4. Hansard Parliamentary Debates, Vol. 410, 2 May 1945, c 1405.
5. TUC Congress Report 1945, p. 263.
6. But see R. Croucher, *Engineers at War 1939–1954*, London, 1982; and J. Hinton, *Shopfloor Citizens: Engineering Democracy in 1940s Britain*, London, 1994.
7. S. Beer, *Modern British Politics*, London, 1945; and M. Gowing and K. Hancock, *The British War Economy*, London, 1949, p. 541.
8. D. Marquand, *The Progressive Dilemma*, London, 1900, p. 77.
9. A. J. P. Taylor, *Lord Beaverbrook*, London, 1982, p. 457.
10. Ibid., p. 517.
11. Minutes of the meeting with Chamberlain, 4 October 1939, TUC Archives.
12. Ibid., 12 October 1939.
13. TUC Congress Report, 1940, p. 169.
14. Quoted in S. Brooke, *Labour's War*, Oxford, 1900, p. 45.
15. Quoted in P. Weiler, *Ernest Bevin*, Manchester, 1993, p. 101.
16. A. Bullock, *Life and Times of Ernest Bevin*, vol. 1, London, 1960, p. 404.
17. TUC Congress Report 1940, p. 169.
18. Minutes of the National Council of Labour, 12 May 1940, Labour Party Archives.
19. Minutes of the National Joint Advisory Council, 22 May 1940, TUC Archives.
20. TUC Special Congress Report, 25 May 1940, p. 18.
21. BBC World Service broadcast, 25 May 1940, Bevin file, TUC Library.
22. Bullock, *Life and Times of Ernest Bevin*, vol. 2, London, 1967, p. 42.
23. TUC Special Congress Report, 25 May 1940, p. 10.
24. Ibid., p. 23.
25. TUC Congress Report 1940, p. 233.
26. J. Price, *Labour in the War*, London, 1940, p. 173.
27. TUC Congress Report 1940, p. 230.
28. Circular to the TUC, 8 June 1940, TUC Library.
29. TUC Congress Report 1940, p. 176.
30. Ibid., p. 178.
31. J. Jones, 'Ernest Bevin: Revolutionary By Consent', *Employment Gazette*, March 1981.
32. Bevin, Memorandum, Ministry of Information, 30 May 1940.
33. TUC Congress Report 1940, p. 325.
34. Minutes of meeting on 2 July 1941, TUC Archives.
35. E. Bevin, Notes, December 1941, Bevin Papers; also see N. Fishman's article on Order 1305 in *Historical Studies in Industrial Relations*, Autumn 1999.
36. TUC Congress Report 1941, pp. 364–5.
37. W. Citrine, 'Wage Regulation in Wartime', 18 December 1941, Citrine Papers.
38. TUC Congress Report 1942, p. 172.
39. TUC, *TUC In Wartime*, December 1941, p. 1.

40. TUC, *TUC in Wartime*, January 1942.
41. W. Citrine, *British Trade Unions*, London, 1942, p. 48.
42. TUC Congress Report, 1943.
43. TUC, *TUC in Wartime*, January 1943.
44. TUC Congress Report 1943, p. 146.
45. Ibid., 1941, p. 114.
46. Ibid., 1942.
47. W. Beveridge, *Power and Influence*, London, 1953, pp. 300–2.
48. TUC Congress Report 1943, p. 236.
49. TUC Memorandum on Education After the War, 1942, p. 2.
50. TUC Congress Report 1943, pp. 62–3.
51. Ibid., 1943, p. 67.
52. Ibid., 1944, pp. 251–2.
53. Ibid., 1943, p. 252.
54. Ibid., p. 252–3.
55. TUC Interim Report on Post-War Reconstruction, 1944, p. 30.
56. Ibid., pp. 31–2.
57. Ibid., p. 29.
58. Bullock, *Life and Times of Ernest Bevin*, vol. 2, pp. 319–20.
59. TUC, 1944, p. 41.
60. TUC Congress Report, 1944, 'Trade Union Structure and Closer Unity', pp. 349–84.
61. TUC, 'Call To The Workers', July 1945, TUC Archives.
62. TUC Congress Report, 1946, pp. 267–72.

Chapter 3

Two books were of immense value in writing this chapter. Vic Allen's *Trade Union Leadership* (London, 1955), on Deakin, and Geoffrey Goodman's *The Awkward Warrior* (London, 1979), on Cousins, were indispensable. I am extremely grateful to Bill Morris, Ray Collins and Regan Scott at the Transport and General Workers Union for giving me access to the union's archives in London. The verbatim records of the union's biennial delegate conferences are kept locked away in a safe at headquarters. They are the only copies available and provide a fascinating picture of both Deakin and Cousins in action as they dominated those conferences from start to finish. Useful insights on Deakin can also be found in a sympathetic portrait in the *Dictionary of Labour Biography*, Volume 2, edited by Joyce Bellamy and John Saville. There is a short biography on Cousins written by Margaret Stewart, just after his retirement in 1969, which is also of interest.

Other works worth consulting include J. Tomlinson, 'The Labour Government and the Trade Unions', in N. Tiratsoo (ed.) *The Attlee Years* (London, 1991); J Hinton, *Shopfloor Citizens* (London, 1994); K. Middlemas, *Power, Competition and the State*, Vol. 1, *1940–1961* (London, 1987); and H. Pelling, *The Labour Governments 1945–1951* (London 1984).

1. *TGWU Record*, January 1947.
2. Biennial Delegate Conference Verbatim Report, 1949, TGWU Archives.
3. *TGWU Record*, June 1957.

4. The history of the trade union's origins can be found in K. Coates and T. Topham, *The Making of The Labour Movement: The Formation of the TGWU 1870–1922* (Nottingham, 1994), and A. Bullock, *The Life and Times of Ernest Bevin*, Vol. 1, *Trade Union Leader 1881–1940* (London, 1960), pp. 180–220.
5. Bullock, *Life and Times of Ernest Bevin*, Vol. 1, p. 205.
6. J. Jones, *Union Man*, London, 1986, p. 132.
7. G. Goodman, *The Awkward Warrior, Frank Cousins: His Life and Times*, London, 1979, p. 100.
8. M. Foot, *Aneurin Bevan*, Vol. 2, *1945–1960*, London, 1973, p. 353.
9. H. Clegg, *A History of British Trade Unions since 1889*, Vol. 3, *1934–1951*, Oxford, 1994, pp. 363–4.
10. P. Williams, *Hugh Gaitskell*, London, 1979, pp. 335–6.
11. V. L. Allen, *Trade Unions and the Government*, London, 1960, p. 288.
12. V. L. Allen, *Trade Union Leadership*, London, 1957, p. 150.
13. N. Chester, *The Nationalisation of British Industry 1945–1951*, London, 1975, p. 79.
14. K. Morgan, *Labour in Power 1945–1951*, Oxford, 1984, p. 81.
15. A. Deakin, Quarterly Report to GEC, June 1945, TGWU Archives.
16. Ibid., December 1945.
17. 'The Nation's Fight for Economic Survival', *TGWU Record*, November 1945.
18. 'Full Ahead in The Great Drive for Exports', *TGWU Record*, September 1945.
19. A. Deakin, Quarterly Report to GEC, March 1946, TGWU Archives.
20. Labour Party Conference Report 1946, pp. 135–6.
21. A. Deakin, Quarterly Report to GEC, December 1946, TGWU Archives.
22. Ibid., March 1947.
23. 'The Need for Increased Productivity', *TGWU Record*, December 1948.
24. J. Phillips, 'Labour and the Cold War: The TGWU and the Politics of AntiCommunism 1945–1955', *Labour History Review*, Vol. 64, No. 1, Spring 1999. Also see J. Phillips, *The Great Alliance*, London, 1996; P. Weiler, *British Labour and The Cold War*, Stanford, 1988; N. Fishman, *The British Communist Party and The Trade Unions*, London, 1995.
25. K. G. J. C. Knowles, *Strikes*, Oxford, 1952, p. 39.
26. J. Goldstein, *The Government of British Trade Unions*, London, 1952, p. 271.
27. 'The Election: An Analysis and Lessons for The Future', *TGWU Record*, March 1950.
28. Biennial Delegate Conference Verbatim Report, 1947, TGWU Archives.
29. Labour Party Conference Report, 1947, p. 144.
30. Ibid., p. 156.
31. *TGWU Record*, November 1947.
32. Ibid., January 1948.
33. A. Deakin, Quarterly Report to GEC, March 1948, TGWU Archives.
34. Labour Party Conference Report, 1948, p. 142.
35. Ibid., p. 143.
36. A. Deakin, Quarterly Report to GEC, August 1948.
37. Ibid., December 1948.
38. Labour Party Conference Report, 1949, p. 142.
39. Biennial Delegate Conference Verbatim Report, 1949, TGWU Archives.
40. *TGWU Record*, November 1949.
41. Trades Union Congress Report, 1950.

42. A. Cairncross, *Years of Economic Recovery, British Economic Policy 1945–1951*, London, 1987, pp. 405–6.
43. K. Morgan, *Labour in Power 1945–1951*, Oxford, 1984, p. 378.
44. P. Hennessy, *Never Again, Britain 1945–1951*, London, 1992, p. 382.
45. A. Deakin, Quarterly Report to GEC, August 1950, TGWU Archives.
46. Ibid., November 1950.
47. Ibid., March 1951.
48. Ibid., June 1951.
49. Labour Party Conference Report, 1951, p. 92.
50. Ibid., 1952, pp. 125–7.
51. Ibid., p. 78.
52. P. Williams, *Hugh Gaitskell*, pp. 304–8.
53. Biennial Delegate Conference Verbatim Report, 1953, TGWU Archives.
54. *TGWU Record*, April, 1954.
55. Ibid., November 1954.
56. A. Deakin, Quarterly Report to GEC, June 1952, TGWU Archives.
57. Trades Union Congress Report, 1952, p. 508.
58. *TGWU Record*, August 1954.
59. Goodman, *The Awkward Warrior*, pp. 80–1.
60. M. Harrison, *Trade Unions and the Labour Party since 1945*, London, 1960, p. 135.
61. D. Buckle, *Hostilities Only*, Oxford, 1999, p. 66.
62. *TGWU Record*, January 1956.
63. Trades Union Congress Report, 1956, pp. 398–400.
64. Biennial Delegate Conference Verbatim Report, 1957, TGWU Archives.
65. Labour Party Conference Report, 1959, p. 131.
66. Goodman, *The Awkward Warrior*, pp. 215–18.
67. Labour Party Conference Report, 1960, p. 129.
68. Trades Union Congress Report, 1958, p. 434.
69. *TGWU Record*, October 1963.
70. Ibid., August 1964.
71. Goodman, *The Awkward Warrior*, p. 372.
72. Biennial Delegate Conference Verbatim Report, 1959, TGWU Archives.
73. Trades Union Congress Report, 1959, p. 460.
74. Labour Party Conference Report, 1956, p. 82.
75. T. Benn, *Years of Hope 1940–1962*, London, 1994, p. 346.
76. A. Flanders, *Trade Unions and Politics in Management and Unions*, London, 1970, pp. 34–6.
77. J. McKelvey, 'Trade Union Wage Policy in Post-War Britain', *Industrial and Labor Relations Review* 6, 1952, p. 19. Also see B. Roberts, *National Wages Policy in War and Peace*, London, 1958.
78. This debate is touched on in D. Marquand's brilliant *Unprincipled Society*, 1988, as well as by A. Fox in his perceptive *History and Heritage: The Social Origins of the British Industrial Relations System*, London, 1985.

Chapter 4

The author would like to thank Vilja Woodcock, the daughter of George Woodcock, for access to her father's papers. Most are to be eventually deposited at the Modern Records Centre at Warwick University.

1. Woodcock Papers (hereafter WP), G. Woodcock draft article, 12 December 1960.
2. WP, G. Woodcock, interview with Tony Lane, April 1972.
3. A. Benn, *Out of the Wilderness 1963–1967*, 1987, p. 486.
4. G. Brown, *In My Way*, 1970, p. 155.
5. R. H. S. Crossman, *Diaries of a Cabinet Minister*, Volume 3, 1977, p. 915.
6. B. Castle, *Fighting All The Way*, London, 1994, p. 420.
7. R. Maudling, *Memoirs*, 1978, p. 187.
8. WP, Interview with H. Webb, April, 1970.
9. J. Cole, *As It Seemed To Me*, 1995, pp. 54–7.
10. P. Jenkins, *Battle of Downing Street*, 1970, p. 76.
11. WP, Interview with B. Mycock, 8 October 1968.
12. WP, G. Woodcock, 'The Function of the TUC', 3 November 1950.
13. WP, G. Woodcock, 'Trade Unions in the 1970s', transcript of BBC Broadcast, 22 May 1968, pp. 4–5.
14. WP, G. Woodcock, *Trade Unions and Government*, Leicester, 1968, p. 6.
15. Ibid., p. 10.
16. WP, G. Woodcock, Broadcast, BBC Caribbean Service, 6 February 1959.
17. Ibid., 13 February 1959.
18. Ibid.
19. WP, G. Woodcock, Memorandum, 7 November 1964.
20. WP, Interview with B. Mycocks, 8 October 1968.
21. WP, G. Woodcock, Broadcast, BBC Carribean Service, 13 February 1959.
22. G. Woodcock, 'Trade Unions and Public Opinion', *Listener*, 23 July 1959, p. 119.
23. TUC Report, 1962, p. 244.
24. H. Chevins, 'British Unions on the Move', *Free Labour World*, February 1963.
25. WP, 'What Are We Here For?', Undated Memorandum, c. 1963.
26. WP, 'Trade Union Structure and Purposes', Notes for TUC Finance and General Purposes Committee, 10 December 1962.
27. Ibid.
28. WP, 'Trade Union Structure', Memorandum by G. Woodcock, 10 May 1963.
29. WP, Minutes of TUC Finance and General Purposes Committee, 10 May 1963.
30. Published in R. Taylor, *The Fifth Estate*, London, 1978, p. 42.
31. TUC Report, 1964, p. 261.
32. WP, 'Main achievements', 4 August 1967.
33. From BBC Interview, published as 'The Time of my Life', *Listener*, 10 September 1970, pp. 338–40.
34. Modern Records Centre, University of Warwick, Minutes of the Donovan Commission, 18 January 1966, para. 7.
35. Ibid., para. 11.
36. Ibid., 6 September 1966, para. 5.
37. Ibid., 5 October 1966, para. 2.
38. 'Trade Unionism', TUC evidence to the Donovan Commission, November 1966, p. 31.
39. WP, G. Woodcock in conversation with R. Shackleton, 11 December 1971.
40. WP, Draft Consultative Document by TUC on Donovan, 7 October 1968.
41. B. Castle, *Diaries 1964–1970*, London, 1984, p. 574.

42. WP, Conversation with H. Webb, April 1970.
43. Castle, *Diaries*, p. 574.
44. Ibid., p. 582.
45. Quoted in Taylor, *Fifth Estate*, p. 87.
46. W. Citrine, *Men and Work*, London, 1964, p. 228.
47. Ibid., p. 230.
48. Quoted in Taylor, *Fifth Estate*, p. 90.
49. WP, Conversation with the Open University, June 1972.
50. TUC Report, 1962, p. 291.
51. WP, 'Economic Planning', Woodcock meeting with union research officers, 8 November 1963.
52. Ibid.
53. WP, 'Main achievements', 4 August 1967, pp. 3–4.
54. WP, Conversation with the Open University, June 1972.
55. TUC evidence to Donovan Commission, p. 56.
56. WP, G. Woodcock, interview with Tony Lane, April 1972.
57. WP, G. Woodcock, conversation with R. Shackleton, 11 December 1971.
58. TUC Report, 1963, p. 392.
59. J. Callaghan, *Time and Change*, London, 1987, p. 5.
60. WP, 'Main achievements', 4 August 1967.
61. TUC Report, 1968, p. 550.
62. TUC Congress of Executives, 17 January 1968, pp. 96–105.
63. 'The Time of My Life', *Listener*, 10 September 1970, p. 338.
64. Quoted in Taylor, *Fifth Estate*, p. 104.
65. WP, G. Woodcock, lecture to Institute of Personnel Management, 1968.
66. WP, TUC Memorandum, August 1967.

Chapter 5

1. V. Feather, *Essence of Trade Unionism*, London, 1963, p. 10.
2. B. Castle, *Diaries 1964–1970*, London, 1984, Also see B. Castle, *Fighting All The Way*, London, 1993, pp. 34–5 and p. 407.
3. V. Feather in conversation with E. Silver, TUC Library.
4. Ibid.
5. J. Jones, *Union Man*, London, 1986, p. 215.
6. Castle, *Diaries*, p. 595.
7. Ibid., p. 421.
8. V. Feather in conversation with E. Silver, TUC Library.
9. Cabinet Minutes, 11 April 1969, PREM 13/2726 Public Record Office (PRO).
10. Ibid., 12 May 1969.
11. Ibid.
12. Ibid.
13. H. Wilson, Memorandum, 1 June 1969, PREM 13/2726 PRO.
14. K. Barnes to D. Allen, 3 June 1969, PREM 13/2727 PRO.
15. Feather to Wilson, 4 June 1969, PREM 13/2727 PRO.
16. Wilson to Castle, 6 June 1969, PREM 13/2727 PRO.
17. Ibid., 7 June 1969.
18. Wilson to the Management Committee, 8 June 1969, PREM 13/2727 PRO.

19. Wilson/TUC General Council Meeting, 9 June 1969, PREM 13/2727.
20. Wilson to the Management Committee, 9 June 1969, PREM 13/2728 PRO.
21. Cabinet Minutes, 17 June 1969, PREM 13/2728.
22. TUC/Wilson meeting, 18 June 1969, PREM 13/2728.
23. Wilson Cabinet Meeting, 18 June 1969, PREM 13/2728.
24. Castle, *Diaries*, pp. 424–5.
25. Jones, *Union Man*, p. 206.
26. H. Wilson, *The Labour Government 1964–1970*, London, 1971.
27. TUC Congress Report, 1969, p. 559.
28. E. Heath, *The Course of My Life*, London, 1998, p. 200.
29. Ibid., p. 329.
30. Ibid., p. 335.
31. Ibid., p. 345.
32. Ibid., p. 351.
33. B. Sewell, *British Economic Policy 1970–1974*, London, 1975, p. 33.
34. TUC Special Congress Report, 1971, p. 4.
35. TUC General Council Minutes, September 1971, TUC Archives.
36. TUC Congress Report, 1971, p. 427.
37. TUC Finance and General Purposes Committee, March 1972, TUC Archives.
38. Ibid., April 1972.
39. TUC General Council Minutes, April 1972, TUC Archives.
40. Ibid., May 1972.
41. Jones, *Union Man*, p. 259.
42. TUC General Council Minutes, April 1972, TUC Archives.
43. TUC General Council Documents, October 1972, TUC Archives.
44. Heath, *The Course of My Life*, p. 512.
45. TUC Finance and General Purposes Committee, 9 January 1974, TUC Archives.

Chapter 6

1. TGWU Biennial Conference Report, July 1977.
2. J. Jones, *New Statesman*, 16 April 1975.
3. *Observer*, 2 September 1975.
4. J. Barnett, *Inside the Treasury*, London, 1900, p. 49.
5. D. Healey, *The Time of My Life*, London, 1989, p. 376.
6. J. Jones, *Union Man*, London, 1986.
7. R. Croucher, *Engineers at War*, London, 1982, pp. 82–3, and J. Hinton, 'Coventry Communism: A Study of Factory Politics in the Second World War', History Workshop No. 10, 1980.
8. Jones, *Union Man*, p. 107.
9. Ibid., p. 110.
10. TGWU Biennial Conference Report, 1969.
11. Institute of Personnel Development Conference, 1969.
12. J. Jones, 'In Defence of Shop Stewards', *Spectator*, 3 April 1971.
13. B. Castle, *Diaries 1964–1970*, London, 1984, p. 23.
14. Ibid., p. 717.
15. Ibid., p. 652.

16. Report to the TGWU Executive Council, June 1969, TGWU Archives.
17. Labour Party Conference Report, 1970, p. 176.
18. Ibid., 1971. p. 169.
19. Jones, *Union Man*, p. 282.
20. Castle, *Diaries*, p. 10.
21. Ibid., p. 18.
22. T. Benn, *Against the Tide: Diaries 1973–1976*, London, 1989, p. 46.
23. Ibid., p. 62.
24. Jones, *Union Man*, p. 46.
25. Castle, *Diaries*, p. 418.
26. *Observer*, 5 September 1975.
27. *Financial Times*, 11 March 1974.
28. TUC Guidelines, 1974.
29. Castle, *Diaries*, p. 119.
30. TUC General Council Minutes, June 1974, TUC Archives.
31. *Observer*, 5 September 1975.
32. TUC Congress Report, 1974, p. 396.
33. Ibid., p. 378.
34. *Financial Times*, 1 October 1974.
35. Ibid., 3 October 1974.
36. Ibid., 18 October 1974.
37. TUC General Council Minutes, November 1974, TUC Archives.
38. TUC, *Collective Bargaining and the Social Contract*, London, 1974.
39. Castle, *Diaries*, pp. 283–4.
40. TUC General Council Minutes, April 1975, TUC Archives.
41. Castle, *Diaries*, p. 431.
42. TUC General Council Minutes, May 1975, TUC Archives.
43. Ibid., June 1975.
44. *Observer*, 2 September 1984.
45. TGWU Biennial Conference Verbatim Report, 1975.
46. TUC General Council Minutes, July 1975.
47. Castle, *Diaries*, p. 471.
48. Ibid., p. 478.
49. TUC General Council Minutes, December 1975, TUC Archives.
50. Ibid., January 1976.
51. Castle, *Diaries*, p. 658.
52. TUC General Council Minutes, February 1976, TUC Archives.
53. Ibid., April 1976.
54. Jones, *Union Man*, p. 307.
55. TUC General Council Minutes, June 1976, TUC Archives.
56. J. Jones, *A New Civilisation*, London, December 1975, TUC Library.
57. *TGWU Record*, January 1977.
58. Report to TGWU Executive Council, January 1977, TGWU Archives.
59. *Observer*, 6 July 1977.
60. TGWU Biennial Conference Verbatim Report, 1977, TGWU Archives.
61. Healey, *The Time of My Life*, p. 399.
62. J. Callaghan, *Time and Change*, London, 1987, p. 469.
63. Report to TGWU Executive Council, September 1977, TGWU Archives.
64. R. Taylor, *The Fifth Estate*, London, 1978, p. 212.

65. *Observer*, 2 September 1984.
66. In W. McCarthy (ed.), *Legal Interventions in Industrial Relations: Gains and Losses*, Oxford, 1992, p. 213.
67. W. Brown (ed.), *Changing Contours of Industrial Relations*, Oxford, 1981, p. 66.

Chapter 7

1. *Observer*, 2 September 1984.
2. TUC Congress Report, September 1992, p. 225.
3. R. Taylor, *The Fifth Estate*, London, 1978, p. 46.
4. L. Murray File, TUC Library, University of North London.
5. L. Murray, 'Trade Unions and the State', 1970 lecture, TUC Archives.
6. J. Callaghan, *Time and Change*, London, 1987, p. 407.
7. TUC Congress Report 1978, pp. 290–1.
8. *Observer*, 2 September 1984.
9. Callaghan, *Time and Change*, p. 422.
10. Minutes of Callaghan/TUC meeting, July 1978, TUC Archives.
11. *Observer*, 2 September 1984.
12. TUC Congress Report 1978, p. 543.
13. TUC, *TUC Guidance to Negotiators*, November 1978.
14. TUC General Council Minutes, November 1978, TUC Archives.
15. Ibid., December 1978.
16. TUC General Council meeting with Callaghan, 5 February 1979, TUC Archives.
17. TUC General Council Minutes, February 1979, TUC Archives.
18. *Observer*, 2 September 1984.
19. TUC General Council Minutes, July 1979, TUC Archives.
20. *Observer*, 2 September 1984.
21. L. Murray, 'The Democratic Bargain', Granada Lecture 1980.
22. TUC Congress Report 1983, p. 464.
23. *Observer*, 2 September 1984.
24. TUC General Council Minutes, March 1984, TUC Archives.
25. Ibid., May 1984.
26. *Observer*, 2 September 1984.
27. N. Tebbit, *Upwardly Mobile*, London, 1988, p. 193.
28. TUC Congress Report 1988, pp. 568–70.
29. R. Taylor, *The Future of the Trade Unions*, London, 1994, p. 164.

Chapter 8

1. R. Taylor, *The Future of the Trade Unions*, London, 1994, p. xi.
2. TUC Congress Report 1996, p. 60.
3. W. McCarthy (ed.), *Legal Interventions in Industrial Relations: Gains and Losses*, Oxford, 1992, p. 217.
4. Unions 21 Conference speech, 4 March 2000.
5. TUC Congress Report 1997, p. 61.
6. *Financial Times*, 10 September 1997.

7. TUC Congress Report 1995, pp. 109–13.
8. TUC, 'Partners for Progress', April 1999.
9. TUC 'Fairness at Work' conference, June 1998.
10. J. Monks, *The Future of Trade Unionism*, Manchester, 1999.
11. Unions 21 Conference speech, 4 March 2000.

Index

Compiled by Auriol Griffith-Jones